A FESTIVAL
OF
VIOLENCE

A FESTIVAL
OF
VIOLENCE

An Analysis of Southern Lynchings,
1882–1930

Stewart E. Tolnay
and E. M. Beck

University of Illinois Press
Urbana and Chicago

Winner of the 1992 President's Book Award of the Social Science History Association

Publication of this book was supported by grants from the Social Science History Association and the Research Foundation of the University of Georgia.

This book is printed on acid-free paper.

Library of Congress Cataloging-in-Publication Data

Tolnay, Stewart Emory.
    A festival of violence : an analysis of southern lynchings, 1882-1930 / Stewart E. Tolnay and E. M. Beck.
        p.   cm.
    Includes bibliographical references (p.   ) and index.
    ISBN 0-252-02127-4 (acid-free paper). — ISBN 0-252-06413-5 (pbk. : acid-free paper).
        1. Lynching—Southern States—History. 2. Afro-Americans—Crimes against—History. 3. Southern States—Race relations—History. I. Beck, E. M., 1945-   . II. Title.
    HV6464.T65   1995
    364.1'34—dc20   94-7396
                                                                             CIP

This book is dedicated to the memory
of Andy Burke, Lizzie Lowe, Henry Hamilton,
and the more than 2,800 other black and white citizens
who died in the hands of southern lynch mobs
between 1882 and 1930.

Contents

Preface

Through several years of research we have identified 2,805 victims of lynch mobs killed between 1882 and 1930 in ten southern states. Although mobs murdered almost 300 white men and women, the vast majority—almost 2,500—of lynch victims were African-American. Of these black victims, 94 percent died in the hands of white lynch mobs.[1] The scale of this carnage means that, on the average, a black man, woman, or child was murdered nearly once a week, every week, between 1882 and 1930 by a hate-driven white mob.

As staggering as the lynching toll was, it vastly understates the total volume of violence aimed toward African-American citizens of the South. Our lynching inventory does not count casualties of the urban race riots that erupted during those years, nor does it embrace victims of racially motivated murders by a single killer or pairs of assassins. Neither does it include the all too frequent beatings, whippings, verbal humiliations, threats, harangues, and other countless indignities suffered by the South's black population during this era. Yet even though mob violence only taps a modest portion of the overall quantity of violence directed toward southern blacks, it represents a dramatic and profoundly important public manifestation of social control of its citizenry of color and offers an opportunity to investigate the social, economic, and political dynamics that produced a period so ripe with racial violence.

Much recent work on lynchings has relied primarily on one of two strategies of investigation, either the case study method or the comparative method.[2] Classic examples of the case study approach to lynching can be found in McGovern's *Anatomy of a Lynching* (1982),

Smead's *Blood Justice* (1986), Dinnerstein's *The Leo Frank Case* (1968), and Downey and Hyser's *No Crooked Death* (1991).[3] Each is an in-depth exploration of the lynching of a single victim. McGovern is concerned with the lynching of Claude Neal in Florida; Smead examines the 1959 lynching of Charles Mack Parker in Mississippi; Dinnerstein considers the events surrounding the 1915 lynching of Leo Frank, a Georgian; and Downey and Hyser investigate the 1911 lynching of Zachariah Walker in Coatesville, Pennsylvania. A strength of this case study approach is the rich detail it furnishes about individual events, which can provide valuable insights into the behavior and motivation of a lynch mob, mob organization, and the particular circumstances surrounding a specific episode of racial violence. On the other hand, because the case study is tightly bound to a single event, generalizations to the broader record of lynchings must be drawn with great caution; furthermore, there are important issues and questions that the case study method cannot answer.

An alternative to the case study approach is the comparative method. In this strategy the object is to compile information about as many lynchings as possible, then search for underlying patterns in the data for clues that may reveal the forces driving mob violence. These patterns could be trends in the frequency of lynching over time or variation in the frequency of lynching across geographical areas. By relating such trends and variation in lynchings to corresponding trends and variation in other social and economic conditions, it is possible to assess the degree of support for competing explanations of the distribution of lynching behavior. A strength of this comparative approach is its ability to yield conclusions that transcend the single case and may be extrapolated to lynchings in general. But, it sacrifices the rich detail that the case study approach provides. Much of our previous research on lynching applies the comparative method, as does the work done by John Shelton Reed, Jay Corzine, and his colleagues, Fitzhugh Brundage, Susan Olzak, James Inverarity, Charles Phillips, Sarah Soule, and George Wright.[4]

In this book we largely adopt the comparative method. Our primary objective is to examine temporal and geographical patterns in the lynchings of African-Americans in the South, with an eye toward assessing support for various theoretical approaches to the phenomenon. We want to know why lynching was rampant during some periods and relatively rare during others. Why did some regions of the South experience frequent mob violence toward blacks while other, adjacent areas were relatively free of lynching? Was there a political dimension to racial violence? Did the South's dependence on cotton production and farm tenancy play a role as well? Was lynching a simple matter of "popular justice" being carried out in the face of an inadequate and underdeveloped legal system?

To address such questions, we have exploited information about thousands of lynchings that occurred in the South between 1882 and 1930. At the same time, however, we interject more specific detail about individual incidents to provide a balanced perspective on the broader patterns that emerge from our analyses. Nonetheless, we realize that we are straddling a substantial chasm that separates the more "narrative" tradition of historical research from the more "empirical" orientation of sociologists and economists. Being quantitative social scientists by training, we cannot abandon the habits of decades of combined experience; therefore, throughout this book we place heavier emphasis on description and interpretation of data. We hope that not too much of the human tragedy of lynching is lost amid the statistical analysis.

The book is organized around eight chapters, providing historical background, the conceptual foundations of the research, and analyses of macro-social factors affecting patterns of lynching activity. In chapter 1 we present an overview of the dynamics of race relations in the South during the Reconstruction period, paying particular attention to the role of violence as a means of social control over the indigenous black population as well as violence toward sympathetic whites. Chapter 2 is devoted to a description of the geographical and temporal contours of racial violence during the lynching era. In chapter 3 we sketch the profile of a basic theoretical model, focusing on the roles of social threat and competition for scarce resources as essential elements in understanding mob violence. One of the most common explanations of lynching was the notion of popular justice, which we address in chapter 4. In that chapter we attempt to test the adequacy of this interpretation, and find it lacking. Chapter 5 addresses the economic dimension of lynching by exploring the connection between mob violence and the price of cotton, as well as the relationship between lynching and other aspects of the "Cotton Culture." The political dimension is considered in chapter 6, where we ask whether there is any evidence of a linkage between mob violence and patterns of southern political participation. In chapter 7 we examine the relationship between violence toward blacks and patterns of black migration and suggest that the Great Migration may have had a role in initiating the demise of lynching. Finally, in chapter 8 we summarize our work and reach some conclusions about the causes and effects of the wave of antiblack violence that surged through the South during the lynching era.

Acknowledgments

Because this project has a long history, we have incurred an impressive number of debts to individuals, organizations, and institutions. We would like to acknowledge those debts in an effort to share the credit for the work we have produced. Unfortunately, we have been unable to think of an equally acceptable way to share the blame for whatever errors or shortcomings may remain in that work. However, we are pretty sure that they are not our fault.

We are deeply grateful to the Sociology Program of the National Science Foundation and the Research Foundation of the University of Georgia for their financial support. A project like this would be nearly impossible without such support. Certainly, without their support we would not have been able to make life so miserable for so many graduate research assistants for such a long time.

The collection, cleaning, and preparation of data required for this project took a depressingly long time to complete. We appreciate the diligence with which our graduate assistants, Cindy Holiny, Linda Kelley, and Joseph Park, scoured old issues of southern newspapers to confirm the lynchings in our inventory. The interlibrary loan office at the University of Georgia was extremely patient during our endless requests for microfilmed copies of those newspapers. Despite their heroic efforts, it was still necessary for our graduate assistants to make repeated trips to university libraries throughout the Southeast. We thank the staffs at the University of Florida, University of Tennessee, University of Kentucky, and Tuskegee University for their cooperation. Others who were generous of their time and effort during our attempt to gather relevant data include Daniel T. Williams, the archivist at Tuskegee University; Watt Espy; and Neil Fligstein. Whoever had the foresight to construct the *Historical, Demographic, Economic and Social Data* file for the Inter-university Consortium for Political and Social Research also deserves thanks. Patty Glynn's crackerjack programming skills were critical in our effort to prepare our complex and versatile database for analysis.

Once our data were clean enough to analyze, and we had attempted to make order out of the chaos of raw data, we imposed on a number of people to react to our written work. Some actually read complete working drafts of this book, including Fitzhugh Brundage, Larry

Criffin, William F. Holmes, Al Liska, Steve Messner, Tony Oberschall, and Susan Olzak. Allen Ballard, Martha Myers, and Larry Raffalovich read selected parts. We are especially indebted to Stanley Engerman for his thoughtful comments on two successive drafts of the entire manuscript. We willingly share with our colleagues whatever credit this book warrants, while absolving them of responsibility for any criticism it deserves.

Once the University of Illinois Press decided to publish our book, we benefited from the kindness, generosity, and talent of a new group of individuals and organizations. Let us begin by acknowledging the pecuniary assistance we have received. We were fortunate enough to receive the 1992 President's Book Award from the Social Science History Association for this book. As part of our prize, the association subsidized a portion of the production expenses for publication of our book. In addition, the Research Foundation of the University of Georgia provided a generous sum to the press for production expenses. Richard Martin, executive editor at the University of Illinois Press, has been extremely supportive of our project from the very beginning while also maintaining a good humor. Mary Giles, our copy editor, made a gallant effort to make the book more readable, in many cases saving us from sloppy and unclear writing. For the artwork, we acknowledge the cooperation of the *Chicago Defender, Crisis Magazine* (NAACP), the *New York Post,* and the Prints and Photographs Division of the Library of Congress. For permission to reprint selected passages from previously published work, we are grateful to the *American Sociological Review,* the *International Review of Social History,* and the State University of New York Press.

Acknowledgment of a few personal debts is also in order. Our friend and colleague Jim Massey collaborated on much of the early work from this project and played an important role in establishing the foundation for this research. Finally, we are especially indebted to Ginger Davis-Beck and Patty Glynn for the moral support and encouragement they provided throughout the project.

NOTES

1. See Table C-1 in Appendix C for the cross-classification of lynch victims by race, gender, and presumed composition of lynch mob.

2. An additional body of literature—more common during the lynching era—might be classified as "advocacy." The writing of Raper (1933), White (1929 [1969]), Ames (1942), Wells-Barnett (1892 [1969]), and even Cutler (1905) falls into this category. This work is essential for under-

standing the full scope and consequences of southern lynching, but the authors' active concern with ending such mob violence made for a different focus than would an inquiry into the socioeconomic forces driving the phenomenon. *The Tragedy of Lynching* by Raper, an active opponent of lynching, comes closest to a social scientific examination of lynching and its causes.

3. See also Frey and Thompson-Frey (1988).

4. See, for example, Brundage (1993); Corzine et al. (1983); Inverarity (1976); Olzak (1990); Phillips (1987); Reed (1972); Soule (1992); and Wright (1990).

A FESTIVAL
OF
VIOLENCE

1

A Legacy of Racial Violence

On the evening of Friday, March 20, 1981, racial tensions in Mobile, Alabama, were strained following the second trial of Josephus Anderson, an African-American charged with the murder of a white Birmingham police officer. Anderson's first trial ended with a deadlocked jury, and at 10 P.M., local television news reported that the second jury was also unable to reach a verdict. Both juries had been comprised of blacks and whites.

Shortly after ten, Beulah Mae Donald's youngest son Michael, nineteen, walked to a nearby gas station for cigarettes. At the same time, James "Tiger" Knowles and Henry Francis Hays, members of Klavern 900 of the United Klans of America, were cruising through Donald's mostly black neighborhood. They stopped their car to ask Michael Donald for directions to a local nightclub. As he approached the automobile, Knowles threatened him with a handgun and forced him into the car. The Klansmen then spirited the badly frightened and pleading young man to a secluded spot in the piney woods near Mobile Bay, where they placed a noose around his neck, beat him senseless, and slit his throat three times. The men returned to Mobile after unceremoniously dumping the body into the trunk of their car. Arriving back at Henry Hays's house, the two Klansmen hung Michael Donald's lifeless body from a tree nearby, where it remained until Saturday morning. Later Friday evening, two other members of Klavern 900 celebrated the murder by burning a cross on the lawn of the Mobile County courthouse.[1] But why had Tiger Knowles and Henry Hays murdered young Michael Donald? He was a technical student and a part-time worker for the Mobile *Press Register,* and there appeared to be little reason why anyone would want to harm him. He was not accused of any criminal offense, nor had he breached any code of racial etiquette.

Hays and Knowles were incensed that Josephus Anderson's trial for the murder of the white policeman had ended in a hung jury. For them, this meant that a black man could kill a white man with impunity so long as there were blacks on the jury. To avenge this perceived injustice, the Klansmen decided to kill a black man in retribution, and they chose Michael Donald at random. He was killed as a reprisal against the black community and to confirm the power of the Ku Klux Klan in south Alabama. Michael Donald's only "crime" was that of being a male African-American who had the misfortune to be alone in the wrong place at the wrong time.

Michael Donald was neither the most recent victim of racism nor, perhaps, the most publicized, but his death is significant because it is representative of the racial violence that has been long associated with the South. Visions of African-American men, women, and children being whipped by night-riding terrorists or murdered by loosely constituted lynch mobs are indelibly imprinted in southern history. This legacy of racism and violence had its origin in bloody encounters between resident Native Americans and the first explorers and settlers. It was then refined and institutionalized through more than two centuries of chattel slavery and persisted well into the late twentieth century.[2] In the 117 years between the Thirteenth Amendment (1865), which abolished slavery, and the killing of Michael Donald, southern blacks were commonly the target of racial violence.

Our interest in the gruesome history of racial violence during the "lynching era" was sparked by an interesting volume prepared by the NAACP in 1919. In *Thirty Years of Lynching in the United States, 1889–1918* the NAACP published a list of lynch victims, including information describing the date and location of the lynching, as well as the purported reason for the mob's action. Page after page of names attested to the truly incredible level of slaughter that had occurred during these three decades. Yet, aside from a few noble attempts by contemporaries to explain and interpret the "tragedy of lynching," and a small number of more recent efforts by social scientists to ferret out the primary "causes" of lynching, relatively little was known about the underlying forces that drove southern society to such extreme and violent behavior.[3]

Had we accepted the reasons for lynchings uncritically, as reported by the lynchers in the NAACP's list of victims, then we might have concluded that criminally inclined people were killed for breaking the law—primarily for committing such serious offenses as murder and rape. That conclusion would have yielded a rather easy, uncomplicated answer to the question about underlying causes. Had we accepted that explanation, this book would have been much different—if it had been written at all. In that "other" book we would have devoted most of our effort to explaining why southern blacks were prone to engaging in behavior so offensive that it triggered the white community's wrath. However, even relatively little knowledge of southern history, and of race relations during the lynching era, is sufficient to make one suspicious of that too obvious explanation for mob behavior.

This book, then, is largely the result of our suspicion of the obvious. In the following chapters, we attempt to translate our suspicions into reliable evidence that can further illuminate why a frenzy of lynching occurred between 1880 and 1930. Certain a priori assumptions motivated and shaped our investigation. For instance, we believe that it is too easy to argue that lynching was just an alternative method for punishing law violators. Although we do not deny that some lynch victims had committed crimes, sometimes heinous crimes, such behavior alone does not provide a sufficient explanation for lynching. Every lynch mob also could have chosen to turn its victim over to the legal authorities. Why did they lynch instead? The answer must be sought in the complex and sometimes confusing relationship between southern whites and blacks during the period.

We suspect that whites lynched African-Americans when they felt threatened in some way—economically, politically, or socially. Further complicating the situation was the peculiar southern caste system that helped shape the white community's expectations of its position in the social hierarchy with regard to that of blacks. It would be naive to claim that whites commiserated over their poor fortune and then decided to organize a mob to go out and lynch a black. Rather, our assumption is that competitive relations between the races, and the caste system, were capable of poisoning the social environment within which the two races coexisted. Within that environment whites were then predisposed to react violently to even the slightest provocation—or to invent provocative acts where none existed. Our foremost challenge in the ensuing chapters is to identify the dimensions of racial threat and search for evidence that they did indeed contribute to black lynchings.

The postbellum historical record chronicles the frequent assault and murder of freedmen, yet not until the early 1880s was there an attempt to catalog incidents of some types of racial violence systematically.[4] Although it is difficult to compare the extent of racial violence in the

Reconstruction period with racial violence after 1880, it is clear that an imposing wave of mob violence against blacks built in the 1880s, crested in the 1890s, receded during War World I, resurged in the early 1920s, and finally dwindled during the 1930s. It is also equally clear that mob violence against blacks was not uniform throughout the South, but exhibited marked regional variation (chapter 2). Before exploring the social, economic, and political forces shaping that avalanche of post-Reconstruction violence—the era of lynching—it is necessary to consider the dynamics of racial conflict in the South immediately following the cessation of Civil War hostilities.

Racial Violence after Appomattox

In the wake of the Civil War, the dynamics of race relations were unsettled because the Thirteenth Amendment ended legal slavery and much of the absolute control whites had over southern blacks.[5] This was of immediate importance because by the end of the war southern states experienced a critical shortage of labor. Many in the white male labor pool were casualties of war. Newly freed slaves often left plantation service in search of family or better working conditions. Of those freedmen who did remain on plantations, many refused to labor as arduously as they had before the war. In response to these alarming conditions, southern statehouses passed a series of measures, known as the "Black Codes," that were aimed at regaining control over the black labor force. In South Carolina, for example, it was illegal for freedmen to have any occupation other than as farmers or servants unless they paid a tax ranging from $10 to $100.[6] According to Louisiana's 1865 Labor Contract Act, "All persons [that is to say, freedmen] employed as laborers in agricultural pursuits shall be required, during the first ten days of the month of January of each year, to make contracts for labor for the then ensuing year." And according to section 9 of the statute, "The laborer shall work ten hours during the day in summer, and nine hours during the day in winter."[7] Along with laws regulating the supply of black labor, statutes were enacted to reduce any opportunity for armed rebellion among freedmen. Under one section of Mississippi's penal codes, it was against the law for any freedman "to keep or carry fire-arms of any kind, or any ammunition, dirk or bowie knife."[8] It was also illegal for any white person to sell or give away firearms, knives, ammunition, or liquor to freedmen.

Even though the effectiveness of such Black Codes was never tested fully, their goal of reestablishing the antebellum status quo was transparent.[9] In reaction to these developments, Congress passed sweeping civil rights legislation in March 1866, only to have it vetoed by President Andrew Johnson two weeks later. Early in April, Congress over-rode the presidential veto, and the Civil Rights Act of 1866 became law. Under this statute, African-Americans became citizens of the United States and had the legal right to enjoy all the entitlements accorded white citizens.[10] To be sure, this was disturbing news for the old Confederacy.

Thus, for the first time freedmen were abandoning the plantation, reaching for land, acquiring literacy, and entering the political process. African-American liberation threatened to topple the class structure of southern society and the racial caste system on which it was fabricated, and this challenge to the established social order could not go unanswered. If southern whites were to continue to enjoy an economy in which blacks labored to create wealth for the privileged, it would be necessary to devise some alternative mechanism to again harness African-American labor. One such tool was violent repression.[11]

The use of force to master the South's black population was by no means new, yet the amount of violence after Appomattox may have been unprecedented.[12] From April 29 to May 4, 1866, Memphis, Tennessee, witnessed race rioting that concluded with the death of forty-six blacks and two whites, many more wounded or injured, some black women raped, and black churches, schools, and homes burned. Later in July, New Orleans also weathered major rioting, with thirty-four blacks killed and scores wounded.[13] These riots signaled the beginning of a decade of racial tumult, with significant antiblack rioting in Camilla, Georgia (1868), Laurens, South Carolina (1870), Eutaw, Alabama (1870), Meridian, Mississippi (1871), Vicksburg, Mississippi (1874), Eufaula, Alabama (1874), Clinton, Mississippi (1875), and Hamburg and Ellenton, South Carolina (1876).[14]

Possibly the worst racial violence during Reconstruction occurred on Easter Sunday, April 13, 1873, in Colfax, Grant Parish, Louisiana. After days of heightened racial tension, Grant Parish sheriff Christopher Nash assembled a force exceeding a hundred white men from adjoining parishes to attack a large number of blacks who had erected defensive fortifications in the town of Colfax. After several hours of swapping bullets, Sheriff Nash's men routed the militants from their defenses, with nearly 150 blacks seeking safety in the Grant Parish courthouse. The entrapped men sought to surrender to Nash but were fired upon as they tried to leave the building. Soon the courthouse was set aflame; some men were shot as they bolted from the blaze, while others raced into the woods. Nash's men scoured the countryside for escaping black militants; those caught were arrested and held, only to be murdered by their guards later that night. By Monday morning, April 14, more than two hundred African-Americans lay slain in Grant Parish. Afterward one white observed, "A nigger in that parish puts his hat under his arm now when he talks to a white man. They are just the most respectful things you ever saw. But before the fight, oh, Lord! there was no living with them."[15] Such ruthless suppression of Colfax's black citizenry established the brutal lengths to which whites would go to ensure racial domination of southern society. Racial violence was not limited, however, to large-scale urban confrontations between roaming gangs of whites and retiring blacks; bands of organized terrorists also appeared.

Soon after the Army of Northern Virginia capitulated at Appomattox Court House and Federal troops occupied the former Confederacy, the South witnessed the birth and rapid expansion of white terrorist groups.[16] Whether the organization called itself the Ku Klux Klan, the White Brotherhood, the Pale Faces, the Invisible Empire, the Constitutional Union Guard, or the Knights of the White Camellia, all were dedicated to mastering the African-American population through psychological and physical intimidation. In a very real sense, these postwar leagues were the cultural progeny of antebellum slave "patrollers" or "regulators" in the South.[17] As Foner observes, "The Klan was a military force serving the interests of the Democratic party, the planter class, and all those who desired restoration of white supremacy."[18] During Reconstruction it was common for anyone challenging those interests to be harassed, flogged, or murdered.

By 1871, the violence reached such levels that Congress appointed a joint committee to investigate reported violations of the Fourteenth Amendment. During the summer of 1871 the seven senators and fourteen representatives of the Joint Select Committee listened to testimony describing conditions within the former Confederacy.[19] In particular, the committee was interested in the clandestine ventures of the Ku Klux and its brethren leagues. At hearings in Washington and in several southern states, witnesses repeatedly testified that during the late 1860s a surge of terrorism was directed against politically active blacks, black civil servants, blacks who were economically successful, and blacks who refused to kowtow to white supremacists. Liberal whites, white Republicans, and white school teachers and preachers who taught blacks were also frequent casualties of masked violence, and members of the hated Union League were often singled out for especially harsh mistreatment. The league had started in the North during the Civil War as a pro-Lincoln organization,

Figure 1-1. Thomas Nast's 1874 *Harper's Weekly* cartoon.

and it spread south soon after hostilities ended.[20] In the South it was supported by those who opposed the Confederacy and by many African-Americans and Republicans.

In every southern state there was an assault on any activity that contested the privileges of whites or threatened to hinder white domination of the black population, including wresting the reins of political power from blacks, northern carpetbaggers, and sympathetic white southerners, known as "scalawags."[21] In 1850, Andrew Cathcart, a fifty-six-year-old South Carolina slave, bought his freedom for $330, and by 1871 he had accumulated ninety-eight acres of York County farmland. Andrew Cathcart's upward mobility was extraordinary by any standard, and his good fortune did not go unnoticed. Testifying before the Joint Select Committee, Cathcart told of the night of March 11, 1871, when fifteen to twenty masked night riders roamed York County roads.[22] They had called at the home of one of his neighbors, Charlie Bryant, where the Klansmen pistol-whipped and assaulted Bryant's wife. From Bryant's they traipsed to Andrew Cathcart's home, where he was roused, whipped, beaten with a gun butt, and had his life threatened repeatedly. Before moving on, the company of men tried to burn an outbuilding used as a school for black children and the home of one of Cathcart's daughters. Apparently, Cathcart drew the fury of the Klan because he was a thriving, landowning freedman who dared to vote Republican and support African-American education, and his children had successfully escaped to freedom during slavery. Cathcart was fortunate to have escaped with his life, for many did not survive Klan visitations.

The 1871 court testimony of Shaffer Bowens, a white former resident of York County, South Carolina, exemplifies the ruthlessness of organized terrorists. Bowens told the court that he was initiated into the Ku Klux Klan in December 1867. When asked about the aims and methods of the Klan, he stated, "My understanding was, to advance the conservative party and put down the radical party. . . . By killing, and whipping, and crowding out men from the ballot-boxes."[23] On Bowen's first raid, a dozen Klansmen assembled at a small bridge over Buffalo Creek in York County, then galloped to the home of a man named Roundtree, a black thought to support the "radical" (Republican) party. On the command of KKK leader Ned Turner, the night riders opened fire on the house, driving Roundtree into his loft. From this vantage he shot and slightly wounded one of the Klansmen, Elijah Ross Sepaugh. A few moments later Roundtree climbed onto his roof, jumped, and ran away. The Klansmen opened fire, forcing Roundtree to the ground. Moments later Henry Sepaugh, Elijah's brother, approached the downed Roundtree, drew his bowie knife, and slit the black man's throat. Roundtree soon died.

While York County, South Carolina was certainly one of the cradles of Klan activity, organized terrorists were also busy in Alabama and Georgia. One night in December 1868, nine horsemen in white gowns descended on the home of William Blair, a black day laborer, and his sister, Eliza Jane, near the village of Vienna on the Tennessee River in Madison County, Alabama. Two of the men broke into the Blair home, clouted him with a pistol, and hauled him outside to be beaten by the remaining Klansmen. Presently, he was dragged from the house to a more secluded spot over a hill. What happened next is best described in Eliza Jane Blair's own words before the Joint Select Committee: "About an hour afterward, I heard a noise, and my sister went out of the house to see what caused it; she came back, carrying in her arms my brother, William Blair; I saw his clothes were covered with blood, and I examined and found his back, arms, and legs were all cut open, first one way and then across; the bottom of his feet were cut open, his thighs, and calves of his legs were split open, and deep gashes cut across them again."[24] The Klansmen had tortured deep crosses into William Blair's flesh. Later he died of the mutilating wounds.

But not only were proactive African-Americans targeted, carpetbaggers from the North and native scalawags were often victimized as well. In January 1871, the Klansmen of York County, South Carolina, were active again. Fifteen to twenty night riders broke into three groups to visit the homes of Red John Moss and two other black families.[25] Two of the bands found empty houses and returned to the third, now near John Moss's house. As the Klansmen regrouped, they noticed three black men fleeing over a hill in the direction of the cabin of a white woman by the name of Skates. The Klansmen soon surrounded her house, broke down her door, and began to search for the missing men. One of the Klansmen pried up a floor board to discover John Wright and Jake Wright hiding below, while another pried a second plank uncovering Red John Moss. The three men were taken outside and whipped by the gang before they managed to break free and escape. The Klansmen next returned to the woman's house to punish her for concealing John Moss and the Wrights. A batch of tar and lime was prepared, she was forced to the ground, and one of the Klansmen was ordered to pour the mixture into her vagina and then use a "paddle" to spread it over her body. After suffering this humiliation, she was ordered to leave the county within three days.

Organized terrorists did not shirk from attacking the well known and highly visible. Following the war, the Alabama state board of education was faced with reopening the state university at Tuscaloosa, including appointing a new president and faculty. In 1868 the Republican-dominated state board elected to place the university in the hands of A. S. Lakin, a Methodist Episcopal cleric and recent immigrant from Ohio. Being viewed as a carpetbagger, Lakin was not a popular choice for the position; for some, he represented unwarranted and incendiary northern intrusion into state affairs. When Lakin and N. B. Cloud, the state superintendent of education and an Alabama native, arrived in Tuscaloosa they were met by public belligerence and a care-taker president—a Professor Wyman—who would not surrender the keys to the university.[26] Fearing for his life, Lakin left town immediately, and narrowly missed being captured later that evening by a band of armed Klansmen. To make the message unmistakable, the September 1, 1868, edition of the Tuscaloosa *Independent Monitor* printed an obvious threat against the lives of Lakin and Cloud. Commenting on Wyman's refusal to relinquish control of the university, the *Independent Monitor* clucked: "We think Professor Wyman did exactly right in pursuing this bold course; for he has thus saved the university from the everlasting stigma of having once been polluted by the obnoxious presence of a nigger-worshiping faculty, and of black and white spotted alumni."[27] The blatant race-baiting of the *Independent Monitor* editorial typifies the hostility directed at those who might alter the distribution of power in the South, even those in such an indirect position as the president of a state university, and the explicit endorsement of violence by the newspaper legitimated the use of terrorism to ensure this white supremacy.

After weeks of testimony from scores of witnesses ranging from Eliza Jane Blair and the Reverend A. S. Lakin to Ku Klux Klan Grand Wizard Nathan Bedford Forrest, the Joint Select Committee's majority report concluded that most terrorist violence was politically inspired. Its targets were generally people who voted Republican or "radical" or African-Americans in positions of authority and respect, such as educators, public office holders and seekers, militia officers, or civil servants. The purpose of the violence was to dislodge African-Americans and sympathetic whites from positions of influence, to eliminate hated Yankee interference in southern life, and to restore Democratic one-party white rule to the South.

Even before the Joint Select Committee had been appointed, reports of extensive violence against blacks in the South motivated legislative reaction in Washington. On May 31, 1870, Congress passed the first Enforcement Act, which was aimed at ending bribery or intimidation of voters, and prohibited groups of persons from conspiring to deprive any one of their rights of citizenship under the Fourteenth and Fifteenth amendments.[28] A second Enforcement Act passed the next year strengthened federal supervision over the electoral process. Neither law, however, had much effect on reducing racial violence in the South. Later that year, Congress once again drafted legislation designed to protect citizens from terroristic control. On April 20, President Ulysses S. Grant signed the Ku Klux Klan Act, making it a federal crime to conspire to deny persons equal protection under the law. It also awarded the president the power to use federal troops to enforce the act, including the right for the temporary suspension of the writ of habeas corpus.

From accounts from the South Carolina uplands, it appeared that much of the state was firmly in the control of the Ku Klux Klan, especially York County.[29] At Governor Robert Kingston Scott's request, in the spring of 1871 President Grant sent elements of the Seventh Cavalry Regiment under the command of Major Lewis W. Merrill to York County to suppress terrorism. He faced a demanding situation. Not only did terrorists enjoy broad support within the white community, but the state's criminal justice system also seemed to be in the hands of the Klan or its sympathizers. Merrill reported to Washington that night riders were responsible for three to four hundred whippings and murders in York County alone, and yet the civil authorities refused to prosecute.[30]

Race troubles in York County provided an opportunity to exercise the Ku Klux Klan Act, and on October 16, President Grant suspended the writ of habeas corpus. Soon afterward, the army began arresting and indicting suspected terrorists. Although the arrests flooded the court system beyond capacity, they adversely affected Klan activity, with some Klansmen turning state's evidence while others fled the state altogether. Yet despite this initial success in South Carolina, national interest in the Confederacy waned. Federal attempts to enforce the Fourteenth and Fifteenth amendments weakened and by the end of 1874 were effectively nonexistent. Shifting social, political, and economic conditions were marking the death of radical Reconstruction and the end of federal efforts to protect the lives and civil rights of freedmen.

The devastating business panic of 1873 had created a new set of problems for federal and state governments, and tackling the fiscal crisis became a greater priority than protecting the rights of freedmen and southern Reconstruction. Public attention was increasingly focused more on economic issues and labor strife than on Dixie's racial problems. The seriousness of this economic dislocation is indicated by the significant increase in business failures during the period. In 1871, only sixty-four out of ten thousand enterprises failed, but by 1878 the figure had more than doubled, and 158 out of ten thousand failed (Figure 1-2).[31] To put this in proper perspective, that rate of failure was not matched until the height of the Great Depression of the 1930s, when the rate rocketed to 154 per ten thousand in 1932. The business bust of the mid-1870s plunged the nation into an economic crises that demanded immediate attention.

During such changing times, many diehard radical reconstructionists faded from national prominence, and the Republican conservative wing began to assert leadership in party politics. In reaction to worsening economic fortunes, the long-reigning Republican party lost control of the House in the election of 1876. Although the Forty-Third Congress struggled to pass sweeping legislation that prohibited segregation in public accommodations and barred discrimination in schools, the 1875 Civil Rights Act was never enforced meaningfully, and in 1883 the Supreme Court ruled the act unconstitutional. With shifting public opinion and President Grant's trouble-ridden second administration's retreat from Reconstruction, southern states were free again to manage their own affairs, including the continued subjugation of their African-American population. This "redemption" accelerated after the elections of 1876, and it was

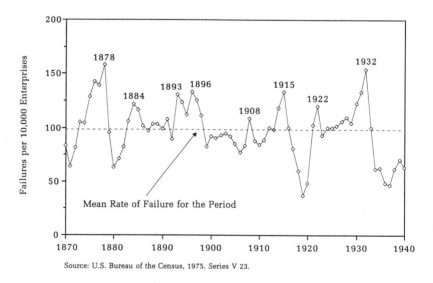

Source: U.S. Bureau of the Census, 1975. Series V 23.

Figure 1-2. Rate of Business Failures in the United States, 1870–1940.

not too long before the last remnants of federal intrusion were retired from Dixie.[32]

Not only were the executive branch and Congress withdrawing from the ideals of Reconstruction, but the courts were also active in restraining reconstructionist policies. In a test of the Fourteenth Amendment in 1873, the Supreme Court ruled in a 5-4 decision on the New Orleans Slaughterhouse Cases that the Fourteenth Amendment concerned only rights conferred by the federal government and that the amendment did not apply to rights given by individual states.[33] This implied a distinction between federal and state citizenship and that federal citizenship guaranteed only a few, narrowly defined rights, such as the right to run for federal office. In effect, the Slaughterhouse decision meant that the states—not the federal government—had the primary responsibility for ensuring civil rights of its citizens.

A second critical ruling came three years later in the case of *U.S. v. Cruikshank*. In this 1876 decision the Supreme Court reversed the convictions of three persons charged with conspiring to deny blacks of their civil rights during the April 1873 bloodbath in Colfax, Grant Parish, Louisiana. In the *Cruikshank* decision, the Court directed that under the Fourteenth Amendment the federal government could intervene only to ban *states* from violating the civil rights of freedmen. The separate states, and the local courts, were responsible for prosecuting individuals who breached African-Americans' civil rights. In Foner's words, "The [*Cruikshank*] decision rendered national prosecution of crimes committed against blacks virtually impossible, and gave a green light to acts of terror where local officials either could not or would not enforce the law."[34] These legal setbacks to the incipient civil rights movement set the stage for what was to follow—the continuation of violence in the form of the lynching of African-Americans by southern white mobs.

Conclusions

During the nineteenth century, wealth in the South was founded on a plantation economy fueled by world demand for cotton and stoked by a captive African-American labor force. By 1865 the traditional keystone of this plantation society was undermined by the abolition of slavery. Although antebellum slavery was embedded in, indeed necessitated, violent coercion, after the Civil War a virtual "reign of terror" was led by such organized white supremacist groups as the Ku Klux Klan, and the siege did not weaken until the mid-1870s. The purpose of this terrorism was to restore the antebellum structure of social relations, embracing democratic one-party male rule and a caste system in which every white stood above all blacks. Targets for violence included politically active or successful African-Americans, northern carpetbaggers, and southern scalawags.

Armed with the judicial weaponry of the Fourteenth and Fifteenth amendments and the Ku Klux Klan Act, the federal government made some effort at interdicting state-sanctioned terrorism, yet the policies fell significantly short of being an all-out assault on discrimination. As the country became increasingly preoccupied with disturbing economic conditions and labor militancy, attention was redirected from Dixie and its dilemmas toward the nation-state and its domestic problems. The federal government and its judiciary abandoned southern blacks and their civil rights, leaving matters in the hands of recently "redeemed" southern assemblies and local courts.

Following redemption and the revival of one-party white rule, the face of racial violence continued to evolve. The familiar imagery of organized, night-riding terrorists was succeeded, at least in part, by the passionate violence of lynch-mob "justice." Images of bold black politicians and imprudent civil servants faded, as did the antebellum invention of the contented, childlike plantation sambo. These stereotypes were being replaced with that of the threatening black "beast"— a coarse caricature ripe with animalistic violence. Through the mythology of racial retrogression, African-American males were widely portrayed as sexually driven "brutes" with a special affinity for white women, and many whites were convinced that these atavistic threats could be controlled only through extralegal sanctioning.[35] Accordingly, by the end of 1877, occupying federal troops had been withdrawn, civil rights legislation nullified, and southern statehouses "redeemed." As a result, racial violence persisted in the South and entered a new stage in the next decade, that of the rule of the lethal lynch mob.

NOTES

1. For more details on the Michael Donald murder and the subsequent trials, see reports by Judge (1987) and Kornbluth (1987).

2. See Jordan (1974) and Frederickson (1988, 189–205) for concise histories of American racism, and Takaki (1979) for a discussion of the relationships between racial stereotypes and the development of the United States.

3. See Cutler (1905), Raper (1933), White (1929 [1969]), Young (1928–29), Corzine et al. (1983), Inverarity (1976), and Reed (1972).

4. In 1882, the Chicago *Tribune* began to compile reports of lynchings

and to publish an annual inventory of both lynchings and legal executions. These summary data have become the basis for many of the existing inventories of lynching in the United States. See Appendix A for a discussion of the sources of lynching data.

5. This section draws heavily on Foner (1988), Nolen (1967), Rable (1984), Shapiro (1988), Trelease (1971), Wade (1987), Williamson (1984), and the various reports of the U.S. Congress, Joint Select Committee (1872).

6. Foner (1988, 200).

7. Commager (1963, 455–56).

8. Commager (1963, 454–55).

9. By late 1866, most southern states had eliminated those provisions of the Black Codes that pertained exclusively to African-Americans (Foner 1988).

10. Questions about the constitutionality of the Civil Rights Act prompted Congress to incorporate many of the act's provisions into the Fourteenth Amendment. This amendment to the Constitution was offered to state legislatures in the summer of 1866, and was finally ratified on July 28, 1868. Its most important features included extending citizenship to freedmen; limiting states from dispossessing "any person of life, liberty, or property, without due process of law"; or denying "any person . . . the equal protection of the laws."

11. In addition to violence, most southern states passed a web of legislation designed to hold black labor to the land. Enticement and emigrant-agent statutes, vagrancy laws, false-pretense acts, fence laws, and convict labor all sought to strengthen black involuntary servitude (Cohen 1976, 1991; Jaynes 1986; Mandle 1978, 1992; Novak 1978).

12. See Aptheker (1943), Eaton (1942), and Fry (1975) for discussions of racial and mob violence in the South before the Civil War, and Mohr (1986) for a revealing description of racial violence during the Civil War. Mellon's (1988) compilation of freedmen narratives provides telling scenes of both physical and psychological violence against slaves. Also worthwhile is Wyatt-Brown's (1986) description of racial violence within the more general cultural context of southern violence. For a discussion of antebellum racial violence in the North, see Slaughter (1991).

13. See Waller (1984) for an account of the Memphis riot, and Reynolds (1964) for a description of the New Orleans riot.

14. For descriptions of other incidents during Reconstruction, see Vandal's (1991) account of antiblack violence in Caddo Parish, Louisiana, and Crouch's (1984) description of postwar racial violence in Texas. Also see Carpenter's (1962) overview.

15. As cited by Nolen (1967, 45).

16. Terrorism in the post-Civil War South could be viewed as a logical extension of the older tradition of vigilantism in America. See Brown (1969) for a brief history of American vigilantism, and Culberson (1990) for a more theoretically grounded view of historical vigilantism. Cutler (1905) also presents valuable background on lynching and vigilantism before the Civil War.

17. Fry (1975).

18. Foner (1988, 425).

19. U.S. Congress, Joint Select Committee (1872a).

20. Fitzgerald (1989).

21. The assault spread to Kentucky even though that state had not joined the Confederacy and had remained loyal to the Union (Wright 1990).

22. U.S. Congress, Joint Select Committee (1872b, 1591–97).

23. U.S. Congress, Joint Select Committee (1872b, 1863).

24. U.S. Congress, Joint Select Committee (1872c, 149).

25. U.S. Congress, Joint Select Committee (1872b, 1864–65).

26. U.S. Congress, Joint Select Committee (1872c, 112).

27. U.S. Congress, Joint Select Committee (1872c, 114).

28. The Fifteenth Amendment (1870) forbids both the states and the federal government from denying the right to vote on the basis of "race, color, previous condition of servitude."

29. For a more detailed account and analysis of Klan violence in the South Carolina up-country, see Stagg (1974). Burton's (1978) analysis of the roles of economics and politics in shaping racial conflict within Edgefield County, South Carolina, also provides valuable detail on the social dynamics within one conflict-prone community.

30. U.S. Congress, Joint Select Committee (1872a, 40).

31. These data are from the U.S. Bureau of the Census (1975), series 5:23, 912–13. Business failures refer only to commercial and industrial failures, excluding banks and railroads.

32. Redemption did not go unchallenged; see Hyman (1990) for a vivid account.

33. See Foner (1988, 529–31) for more detail on the Slaughterhouse Cases.

34. Foner (1988, 531).

35. Williamson (1984, 111–39).

2

A Portrait of the Lynching Era, 1880–1930

The lynching era encompasses roughly the five decades between the end of Reconstruction and the beginning of the Great Depression. During these years we estimate that there were 2,018 separate incidents of lynching in which at least 2,462 African-American men, women, and children met their deaths in the grasp of southern mobs, comprised mostly of whites.[1] Although lynchings and mob killings occurred before 1880, notably during early Reconstruction when blacks were enfranchised, radical racism and mob violence peaked during the 1890s in a surge of terrorism that did not dissipate until well into the twentieth century. Because of the numbers of persons killed, the method of execution, the extralegal nature of lynching, and the popular support given to mob violence, it is important to consider the role of lynching in the post-Reconstruction South. Clearly, it was more than an infrequent interruption of the region's otherwise tranquil racial relations. Rather, it was a routine and systematic effort to subjugate the African-American minority.

If asked, many nineteenth-century white southerners would have claimed that lynching was the only effective means for protecting against unpredictable black aggression. After Reconstruction, and coinciding with the rise of Social Darwinism and the doctrine of "Scientific Racism," many whites believed that there was an increasing wave of black crime against the white community—that blacks were out of control, especially those who, recently born, had not known the "domesticating" influences of slavery.[2] Many whites found little to separate law-abiding from law-breaking blacks. In 1876, John T. Brown, the principal keeper of the Georgia Penitentiary, expressed what appears to have been a common sentiment: "The only difference existing between colored convicts and the colored people at large consists in the fact that the former have been caught in the commission of a crime, tried and convicted, while the latter have not. The entire race is destitute of character."[3]

Faced with what many whites perceived as increasing black-on-white crime, some thought that the formal system of criminal justice was too weak, slow, and uncertain to mete out fitting punishment.[4] In the absence of an effective system, the community had to assume extralegal responsibility to punish offenders. Yet even if the criminal justice system had operated more efficiently, it was often voiced that courts and prisons were "too good" for black murderers, rapists, and arsonists, and the only equitable resolution was "popular justice," administered with the pistol, rope, or faggot.[5] For example, following the alleged assault of a white female by a black man a few weeks before the election of 1906, an Atlanta *Journal* editorial of August 1, boldly asserted: "He [the black man] grows more bumptious on the street. More impudent in his dealings with white men; and then, when he cannot achieve social equality as he wishes, with the instinct of the barbarian to destroy what he cannot attain to, he lies in wait, as that dastardly brute did yesterday near this city, and assaults the fair young girlhood of the south."[6]

Although falling short of demanding a lynching, such public rhetoric went a long way toward vindicating mob violence and likely was a catalyst for the bloody Atlanta race riots that erupted following the elections of 1906.[7] The Georgia populist Tom Watson rejoiced in popular justice as a means for countering the black threat: "In the South, we have to lynch him [the Negro] occasionally, and flog him, now and then, to keep him from blaspheming the Almighty, by his conduct, on account of his smell and his color. . . . *Lynch law is a good sign: it shows that a sense of justice yet lives among the people."*[8]

While the popular justice apology was often voiced, especially to northern critics of southern mob violence, it is overly simplistic. It ignores the fact that no evidence suggests that southern courts were hesitant or unwilling to dispense lethal punishment. Indeed, they administered the death sentence to African-Americans in prodigious numbers.[9] We believe that to understand post-Reconstruction racial violence we must go beyond the bravado of popular justice and consider broader issues of economic and social life.[10] In addition to the punishment of specific criminal offenders, lynching in the American South had three entwined functions: first, to maintain social control over the black population through terrorism; second, to suppress or eliminate black competitors for economic, political, or social rewards; and third, to stabilize the white class structure and preserve the privileged status of the white aristocracy.

State-Sanctioned Terrorism

The purported justification of lynching was to rid the white community of rogues accused of violating criminal laws and racial codes of etiquette, but lynching may have had as much to do with creating a climate of terror as it did with the punishment of a specific offender. The terrorism of night riders and lynch mobs was a weapon for maintaining some degree of control over the African-American labor force. Groups of both kinds remained common throughout the South until the widespread passage of Jim Crow legislation, which—with the blessing of the Supreme Court—formalized and codified a system of state-enforced de jure segregation and racial domination. As James Cutler asserts in the conclusion to his well-known study, "Lynching has been resorted to by the whites not merely to wreak vengeance, but to terrorize and restrain this lawless element in the negro population. Among Southern people the conviction is general that terror is the only restraining influence that can be brought to bear upon vicious negroes. The negroes fear nothing so much as force, and should they once get the notion that there is a reasonable hope of escape from punishment, the whites in many parts of the South would be at their mercy."[11]

Although the majority of victims of lynchings stood accused of murder, rape, theft, or other felonies, a significant number of blacks were killed for what would seem to be trivial violations of the moral order. This was not happenstance. Lethal mob violence for seemingly minor infractions of the caste codes of behavior was more fundamental for maintaining terroristic social control than punishment for what would seem to be more serious violations of the criminal codes. When it came to overt aggression, the rules governing racial conduct were clearly drawn and understood: A black accused of killing a white man, sexually assaulting a white woman, or destroying white-owned property faced a strong chance of being murdered by a lynch mob. Even if the accused escaped lynching, white judges and juries frequently invoked the death penalty in such cases. But many African-American men met their death at the hands of a white lynch mob for acts far less serious than rape or arson.

It was not, in fact, at all clear what behavior would lead to mob violence, and it was this uncertainty that would have created terror within the black community. Blacks never knew when whites would

Figure 2-1. "O say, can you see by the Dawn's early light, / What so proudly we hailed at the Twilight's last gleaming!" From *The Crisis*, February 1915, 197.

interpret the most innocent or trivial of behavior—an impertinent glance, ill-advised stare, or surly word—as insolent or threatening and worthy of brutal retribution. This meant that many African-Americans lived at the discretion of the white community and its whims. The killings of Columbus Lewis, Kitt Bookard, a young woman from Holmes County, Mississippi, and William Hardeman are examples of the ruthlessness of mob violence, even for what would appear to be paltry transgressions.

Columbus Lewis of Lincoln Parish, Louisiana, paid the ultimate price for insolence. On April 23, 1898, after quarreling with a white man, Lewis was driven from his home by a mob of twelve whites. They gunned him down with shotguns, leaving him for dead. After a local white physician refused to treat his wounds, Lewis bled to death.[12] A similar fate awaited Kitt Bookard of Berkeley County, South Carolina. Bookard became embroiled in argument with a young white man in the midsummer of 1904. The particulars of the disagreement are unknown, but apparently an angry Bookard cursed the youth and threatened to paddle him. After the boy reported the incident, Bookard was taken to jail in Eutawville, only to be forcibly carried away by a mob that broke into the jail house somewhat later. On July 15, Bookard's broken and mutilated body was found floating in the Santee River, his hands bound with rope and an iron weight lashed to his body.[13] In September 1923, a black youth from Pickens, Holmes County, Mississippi, borrowed 50 cents from a white man. When he repaid the loan, the white man demanded 10 cents interest, which the boy did not have. He and his father fled, thinking that nothing would be done to the boy's mother and sister, who remained behind. Later a mob of nine white men attacked the boy's home and riddled his sister with bullets, killing her as she tried to run.[14] And finally, on the day after Christmas 1923, William Hardeman, a forty-nine-year-old black preacher, was murdered at his home in Elliott Station, Mississippi. According to the Memphis *Commercial Appeal,* Hardeman had incensed the community by making sarcastic remarks to Mrs. S. M. Neal, a white resident of Elliott.[15] Between nine and ten o'clock that evening, a gang of white men drove to Hardeman's house and killed him with a blast from a shotgun.

As Columbus Lewis, William Hardeman, and the others discovered, the fact that the punishment could be so harsh and unforgiving for even trifling offenses is bitter confirmation of the power that whites held. Yet there is still another important dimension to this type of terrorism: Mob violence not only meant death, but also possibly torture.

Figure 2.2. "Christmas in Georgia, A.D. 1916." From *The Crisis*, December 1916, 78–79.

Although most lynchings were straightforward, albeit illegal, executions with little ceremony or celebration, many went far beyond a mere taking of a human life. At times lynchings acquired a macabre, carnival-like aspect, with the victim being tortured and mutilated for the amusement of onlookers. On April 23, 1899, a substantial mob from Coweta County, Georgia, lynched Sam Holt for the alleged murder of Alfred Cranford, Holt's white employer. According to the New York *Tribune* of April 24,

> Sam Hose [Holt] . . . was burned at the stake in a public road, one and a half miles from here [Newnan, Georgia]. Before the torch was applied to the pyre, the Negro was deprived of his ears, fingers and other portions of his body with surprising fortitude. Before the body was cool, it was cut into pieces, the bones were crushed into small bits and even the tree upon which the wretch met his fate was torn up and disposed of as souvenirs. The Negro's heart was cut into several pieces, as was also his liver. Those unable to obtain ghastly relics directly, paid more fortunate possessors extravagant sums for them. Small pieces of bone went for 25 cents and a bit of liver, crisply cooked, for 10 cents.[16]

The ritualistic killing of Sam Holt sent two messages to the black community: first, aggression toward whites would not be tolerated and violators would be put to death; second, some kinds of deaths are truly more horrible and frightening than others. Clearly, these messages were not idle boasts.

But how could "decent" citizens participate in such savage rituals? It is important to understand that years of racist propaganda had, in the minds of many whites, lessened blacks to simplistic and often animalistic, stereotypes.[17] These debasing images further depersonalized and dehumanized the victim, reducing him or her to a hated object devoid of worth. By defining the victim as a loathsome threat, the lynch mob's actions were psychologically comforting and reassuring because it was defending its community from black brutality. The "good" citizens of Coweta County, Georgia, tortured, mutilated, and finally murdered Sam Holt because he had been distilled to a subhuman stereotype lacking in human value. To be reduced to such low status that other human beings—whites—were unrestrained in their punishment would have created terror within the black community. It is also important to recognize that not only were the mutilation and killing of Sam Holt significant, but also the gruesome details of his ordeal, which were widely published for the benefit of both races. Such vivid publicity was, in part, a weapon for the further psychological torment of the entire African-American community.

Elimination of Competition

Because of the crop-lien system and a failing market for cotton, it was common for local merchants to join the landed gentry through foreclosure, then hire black tenants and sharecroppers to cultivate the cotton fields.[18] This reduced, or threatened to reduce, the number of smaller yeoman white farmers, and replaced white tenants with more easily controlled black tenants.[19] These actions were detrimental to the economic interests of both landowning and landless whites and did not go unchallenged. Marginal white landholders found their status jeopardized as owners, and landless whites found the potential for locating good positions as tenants on prime agricultural land threatened.

Early in the 1890s, poor white dirt farmers living in the piney woods of southern Mississippi actively engaged in "whitecapping" to intimidate black laborers and tenants of absentee landowning merchants. In Mississippi, William F. Holmes notes, "Whitecapping specifically meant the attempt to force a person to abandon his home or property; it meant driving Negroes off land they owned or rented."[20] A few days before Christmas 1903, Eli Hilson of Lincoln County, Mississippi, discovered too late the significance of whitecapping. As the Memphis *Commercial Appeal* described the details,

> Eli Hilson, a negro living eight miles from Brookhaven, was assassinated yesterday while on the way home from town alone in his buggy. Last winter Hilson, who lived on a farm of his own and was prosperous, was warned by the whitecaps to leave, which warning he disregarded. About three or four weeks ago his home was visited in the night by whitecaps and several volleys fired into it. He still disregarded the warning, and remained on his place. Hilson is the second negro murdered by whitecaps in that portion of Lincoln County within the last month, and the other negroes are greatly alarmed over the situation.[21]

Clearly, the white community did not view Eli Hilson's pluck and prosperity favorably. It is ironic indeed that the very qualities so highly touted in American folklore—including southern folklore—were the same qualities that got Hilson killed. He was murdered because he did not limit his aspirations to laboring for whites, and this independence was unacceptable. Possibly even more significant than Eli Hilson himself was the fear that other Lincoln County blacks might see him as a role model and follow in his footsteps, acquiring land, banking assets, and trying to break away from white domination. The prospect of large numbers of blacks becoming more independent was intolerable to most white Mississippians, as it would have been to most whites throughout the South. The former Mississippi governor James K. Vardaman summed up the feelings of many whites: "If it is necessary every Negro in the state will be lynched; it will be done to maintain white supremacy."[22]

Yet the issue was not only one of struggle over the control of land, labor, and jobs, but also one of social ranking. Blacks working fields for absentee landlords had more latitude for independent action and freedom than did those cropping under the watchful eye of the white overseer.[23] And in some regions of the South, African-Americans began to acquire small plots of land and enter the agrarian yeomanry. This elevation of status and economic advancement undermined the status of marginal whites. For many poor whites, seeing blacks do well was an intolerable, even perverse, inversion of the social structure and threatened their economic interests as well as their social esteem. As a result, "Every prosperous negro who *shows his prosperity in a way to be seen by the whites* is a focus for hatred on the part of the 'lower' whites."[24]

Racial Solidarity and White Class Structure

When newspapers reported that a lynch mob included many prominent and respected members of the white community, they not only legitimated mob violence, but also left the clear message of racial solidarity—of all whites united against the common foe. In 1914, Thomas P. Bailey, a southern observer, noted that whites shared a fifteen-point manifesto of caste racism:

1. "Blood will tell."
2. The white race must dominate.
3. The Teutonic peoples stand for race purity.
4. The negro is inferior and will remain so.
5. "This is white man's country."
6. No social equality.
7. No political equality.
8. In matters of civil rights and legal adjustments give the white

man, as opposed to the colored man, the benefit of the doubt; and under no circumstances interfere with the prestige of the white race.

9. In educational policy let the negro have the crumbs that fall from the white man's table.
10. Let there be such industrial education of the negro as will best fit him to serve the white man.
11. Only Southerners understand the negro question.
12. Let the South settle the negro question.
13. The status of peasantry is all the negro may hope for, if the races are to live together in peace.
14. Let the lowest white man count for more than the highest negro.
15. The above statements indicate the leanings of Providence.[25]

Although no public opinion polls were taken, it is likely that there would have been broad agreement within the white community on these points. The relationship between caste solidarity and mob violence was complex. To advertise that support for lynching cut across class lines would have produced a heightened sense of singularity of purpose among whites, thus directing attention away from potentially divisive class conflicts. The knowledge that a consolidated caste agreed upon the necessity, and even desirability, of lynching would—in itself—have helped create a normative environment conducive to mob violence.

The October 10, 1911, lynching of Willis Jackson at Honea Path, Anderson County, South Carolina, for allegedly attacking a white child is the quintessential example of class solidarity in action. A mob lead by Joshua W. Ashley, a member of the South Carolina State Legislature, and Victor B. Cheshire, editor of a local newspaper, the *Intelligencer,* captured Jackson, who was hanged "to a tree by his feet and was riddled with bullets." Later the *Intelligencer* reported that one of its staff (Cheshire) had been at the lynching, and that he "went out to see the *fun* with not the least objection to being a party to help lynch the brute."[26] As was typically the case, the coroner's jury concluded that Jackson met his death "at the hands of parties unknown." Although the mob leaders were well known, Governor Cole Blease refused to intervene and bring the lynchers to court. In fact, rather than use his office to protect Willis Jackson, Blease said he would rather "have resigned the office and come to Honeapath and led the mob."[27] The *Intelligencer*'s glorification of mob rule and the reaction of Governor Blease reinforced race solidarity by providing a common ground on which all whites, from the poorest white tenant to the governor, could make a stand against a shared and threatening enemy, the black "brute."

This commonality of interest was important because to maintain a stable white class structure it was necessary to construct a vigorous racial caste system. Reinforcing the caste boundary and affirming white racial superiority diminished the odds that an alienated white lower class might unite with blacks to challenge the privileged position of influential whites, a point not lost on the black intelligencia. A. Philip Randolph, the African-American essayist and co-editor of *The Messenger,* urged his readers in 1918 to abandon caste interests in favor of the interests of their social class: "If the employers can keep the white and black dogs, on account of race prejudice, fighting over a bone; the yellow capitalist dog will get away with the bone—the bone, to which we refer, is profits."[28] To be sure, the white lower class was caught in the tug between caste and class interests, but in the final analysis the appeal of caste solidarity outweighed those forces attempting to wed the class interests of impoverished whites and blacks. For decades to come, racism would be the glue that bound white society together, and lynching was the public affirmation of that fraternal bond, as a black man from Chicago discovered in 1919.

In the heat of July 1919, whites and blacks battled for a week on Chicago's South Side. Although bloody urban race riots were not unheard of, the Chicago riot was unusual in that blacks actively defended themselves from white violence—they fought back. A few weeks later, an unknown black man traveling by train through Georgia on August fifth boasted to his fellow travelers that he was from Chicago,and that the blacks of Georgia should do what the blacks of Chicago had just done.[29] He was taken from the passenger train by a mob of enraged whites and hanged from a small tree near Cochran for his incendiary comments. A few weeks later, on the night of August 27, 1919, a group of fifteen to twenty white Georgians dragged Eli Cooper from his home near Cadwell, Laurens County, and carried him to Petway's Church in neighboring Dodge County, where he was shot, the church set on fire, and his body pitched into the flames.[30] Cooper's "crime" was talking with his friends and neighbors about rebelling against white racial supremacy. As the two cases suggest, visibly opposing the prevailing social order was no trifling offense. When African-Americans seemed insolent, rebellious, or too "uppity," death was often their reward.

Opposition to Lynching

Although without doubt some individual members of the white community condemned lynching, it is equally clear that a majority supported outlaw mob violence.[31] The first signs of large-scale opposition to lynchings among whites became visible only after African-Americans had been deprived of political sovereignty, only after legislation formalizing racial oppression had been enacted, only after the black exodus from the South began to frighten those who depended on African-American labor, and only after it was felt that racial violence was discouraging northern capital from moving south.

One of the first widely known antilynching activists was Ida B. Wells, the black coeditor of the newspaper *Free Speech and Headlight.* In a series of editorials and speeches beginning in 1889, she spoke passionately against mob violence. Although her writings may have had little effect on southern whites, they attracted considerable national and international attention to the plight of African-Americans in the South. In the wake of the 1908 race riot in Springfield, Illinois, elements that supported blacks united to form the National Association for the Advancement of Colored People (NAACP).

From early in its history, the NAACP began to keep tallies of lynchings in the United States, publicize cases of racial injustice and mob rule in its newspaper, *The Crisis,* and lobby for antilynching legislation at the federal level. Later, as a reaction to post-World War I racial conflict, the Commission on Inter–racial Cooperation (CIC) was created, with Will Alexander as its director. The biracial commission sought to moderate white attitudes toward African-Americans, including white acceptance of racial violence as a southern norm. In 1930 Jessie Daniel Ames, the CIC's director of women's work, created a separate organization aimed directly at the problem of lynchings: the Association of Southern Women for the Prevention of Lynching.[32] From 1930 though 1942, the organization of white women combated the racial and sexual stereotypes that nurtured racial violence.

Lynching was a public celebration of whites' contemptuous disregard for black lives, and all too commonly African-Americans were beyond the protective umbrella of law, stranded far outside the due process guaranteed by the Fourteenth Amendment. The de facto legitimacy of mob rule was championed by many southern newspapers, often pardoned by southern churches, and implicitly upheld by southern courts. By failing to punish, or even indict, known members of terrorist gangs, the criminal justice system did little to ensure and protect the civil liberties of black citizens.[33] This state-sanctioned terrorism sent a message to the African-American community that was as unambiguous as it was frightening.

Patterns of African-American Lynchings in the South

The five decades between Reconstruction and the Great Depression witnessed many important events in national and southern life that had an important bearing on the course of race relations in the South: Southern whites "redeemed" their society and reversed many of the changes implemented during Reconstruction; disenfranchisement of black voters became the rule; Jim Crow legislation provided a legal basis for the secondary status of southern blacks; southern workers flirted with radical change during the Populist Era; the nation partic-ipated in its first war in Europe; economic recessions came and went with some regularity; and blacks participated in a "Great Migration" that saw many leave the countryside to relocate in southern cities or northern states.

Given the dramatic and sometimes turbulent events of the period, it would be surprising to find that lynchings occurred at a constant pace throughout the era. Indeed, that definitely was not the case (Fig-ures 2-3a, 2-3b). We have graphed the annual trend in the number of lynching victims without regard to race of victim or composition of the lynch mob, the trend in the number of black victims, and the trend in the number of black victims of white mobs (Figure 2-3a).[34] These trends reveal the same general pattern and clearly show that the fre-quency with which black lynching occurred in southern states fluc-tuated substantially from 1882 to 1930. In Figure 2-3b, we compare the trend in the number of black victims of white mobs (the same trend as displayed in Figure 2-3a) with the trend in the number of incidents of white mobs lynching at least one black victim. This comparison shows that the same pattern of lynching activity holds, regardless of whether one concentrates on the number of victims or on the num-ber of incidents.

The lynching record suggests two broad patterns over the period. Between 1882 and the late 1890s, the annual number of black victims grew alarmingly—exceeding ninety in 1892 and 1893. From the ze-nith reached during the "bloody '90s," the number of blacks killed by lynch mobs began a protracted decline over the next three decades, reaching a nadir of fewer than ten victims annually in 1928 and 1929. However, two noteworthy reversals interrupted the generally down-ward trend after the turn of the twentieth century. First, the last few years of the first decade of the century saw a sharp upturn in the num-

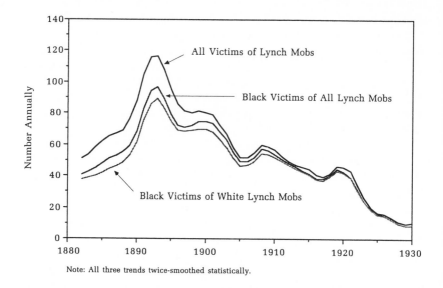

Note: All three trends twice-smoothed statistically.

Figure 2-3a. Trends in Victims of Lynch Mobs, 1882–1930.

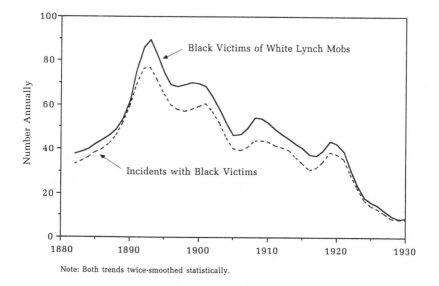

Note: Both trends twice-smoothed statistically.

Figure 2-3b. Trends in Black Lynch Victims of White Mobs and Incidents of Black Lynchings by White Mobs, 1882–1930.

ber of blacks lynched. In 1908, lynchings peaked at sixty-seven victims, a level not to be matched again during the following twenty-two
years. A second reversal occurred during the few years following
World War I, a period also characterized by a resurgence of Klan activity in the South and a rise in nativism in the country as a whole.
Consistent with the generally declining level of lynching throughout
the twentieth century, however, neither reversal reached the same
levels of violence as that of the 1890s, and each subsequent upturn
in lynchings topped off at lower absolute levels.

As for the pattern of lynching incidents (Figure 2-3b), the trend
closely parallels that of lynching victims. Although most (86 percent)
incidents involved only a single African-American victim, some involved as many as eight (Table 2-1).[35] It is important to note that the
ratio of victims per lynching incident was not constant throughout
these years. In the 1890s, 598 incidents claimed the lives of 744 blacks,
for an average of 1.24 victims per incident. During the 1920s, however, the average diminished to 1.12 victims per incident. The decline
indicates that group lynchings became increasingly rare during the
twentieth century, although three of the five most vicious incidents
on record occurred after 1900 (Table 2-1).

The simple curve describing the trends of blacks lynched (Figures
2-3a, 2-3b) is, in its own right, an enigma. Although it provides a basic description of the path of black lynchings over five decades, the
temporal pattern itself raises the fundamental question of whether it
is possible to explain the course of lynching activity over the five
decades as a response to changing social, economic, or political conditions in the South. There is no shortage of potential explanations
for all, or part, of the temporal history of black lynchings, but there is
a dearth of supporting empirical evidence.

Table 2-1. The Five Worst Incidents of Lynchings with Black Victims

Date	Location	No. of Victims
December 12, 1889	Barnwell Co., South Carolina	8
October 3, 1908	Fulton Co., Kentucky	8
June 29, 1905	Oconee Co., Georgia	7[a]
August 31, 1894	Shelby Co., Tennessee	6
May 21, 1911	Columbia Co., Florida	6

a. One white was also killed by the lynch mob, for a total of eight victims in this
incident.

Some have suggested that swings in the value of the southern cotton crop can help explain the temporal variation in the intensity of lynching. According to this argument, during lean economic times, with the nominal price of cotton lurking below 10 cents a pound, whites lashed out at nearby blacks either out of sheer frustration over economic hardship or more instrumental motives.[36] In contrast, when the price paid to farmers for their cotton soared to new heights of more than 25 cents a pound, the economic pressure slackened, and whites were less inclined to victimize blacks. Others have attributed the sharp jump in lynchings during the 1890s to more psychological processes, such as the rise of "radical racism."[37] As the mentality of southern whites shifted to view African-American males as threatening beasts rather than faithful, obsequious sambos, lynching became a common method for maintaining social order as well as reinforcing the strict separation of the races.

Still others have suggested that the decline in lynching after the turn of the twentieth century can be attributed partially to the disenfranchisement of African-American voters.[38] After being politically neutralized, southern blacks were less threatening to whites and therefore were less likely to be the targets of lethal violence. Finally, the virtual collapse of lynching during the 1920s has been linked to the Great Migration.[39] According to this scenario, black migration not only reduced the level of black-white economic competition, but also threatened the supply of cheap labor to which southern planters and employers had become accustomed.

Two sets of facts are indisputable: The lynching of African-Americans varied in intensity during the five decades under consideration, and the social, economic, and political climate of the South changed in several important respects during the same period. The question of exactly how, and even whether, these two sets of facts are connected more than coincidentally rests at the heart of efforts by social scientists to understand and explain the violence of the era. Connecting these two, in a causal sense, remains a challenge we will take up in subsequent chapters.

Seasonal Variation

The long-term annual variation in lynching that has been described is only one kind of temporal pattern that might provide clues to the underlying causes of lynching behavior. Another potentially informative pattern concerns variation in the intensity of lynching throughout the year. If there were no seasonal variation in the frequency of mob violence, then we should expect about one-twelfth of all lynchings to occur during each month. On the other hand, if lynchings were more common during certain seasons, then we should find a substantially greater proportion of lynchings during those months.

The horizontal line in Figure 2-4, the monthly distribution of black lynchings within all ten states aggregated over the five decades under consideration, represents the "expected" number of lynchings—assuming that they were distributed evenly throughout the year. Deviations above the horizontal line indicate a larger than expected number of lynchings in the month; deviations below the line represent fewer lynchings in that month than expected.

It is clear that there was a definite "season" for mob activity. More lynchings occurred from May through September than we would expect from an even monthly distribution of lynchings throughout the year. Lynchings were especially concentrated during the hot summer months of June, July, and August. In each of these months, the observed number of black lynchings was at least 20 percent greater than would be expected were there no seasonality to mob violence.

On the other hand, mob violence dampened considerably during the winter. January and February in particular claimed fewer lynch victims than we would expect were lynchings to occur at a constant pace throughout the year: 16 percent fewer than expected during Jan-

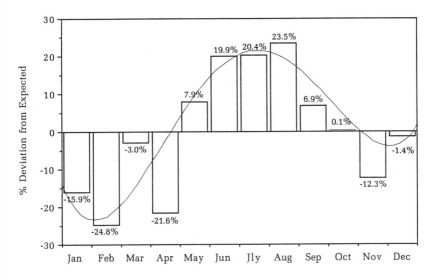

Figure 2-4. Black Lynchings by Month for the Period 1882–1930.

uary and 25 percent fewer during February. April and November were also deficit months, whereas March, October, and December deviated only slightly from the expected level.

As with the annual trend in lynching, the seasonal patterns are both informative and enigmatic. Although the data definitely reveal a concentration of mob violence in certain months and relative infrequency in others, they also pique our curiosity about the underlying causes of the seasonal variation. Why should there have been substantially more lynchings during the summer and many fewer during the winter? Other observers have also noted the irregular distribution of lynchings and proposed possible interpretations. Some have suggested that lynchings followed the same general seasonal pattern as all violent crimes.[40] For example, homicides are known to occur more frequently during some months of the year than during others.[41] According to this view, lynchings, like homicides, increase when more frequent interaction among groups and individuals presents greater opportunity for conflict and interpersonal violence. Such interaction is greater during the summer. Others have drawn a parallel between lynching and the other forms of recreation and entertainment that southern whites enjoyed. Thus, lynchings, like the circus and church revivals, were more concentrated in the summer. A final possibility rests on the assumption that lynchings were a form of labor control and so tied to the cyclical demand for labor in the agricultural South.[42] Therefore, we would expect to find relatively more lynchings occurring when black labor was in greatest demand.

Whether it is how lynchings were distributed across the forty-nine years of this period of study or how they were distributed seasonally, the temporal variation in mob violence is clear. This variation is grist for the social scientist's explanatory mill, and a systematic consideration of explorations for these general descriptive temporal patterns is reserved for later chapters.

Patterns across States

The American South is a heterogeneous region; southern states vary considerably in climate, terrain, economy, and history. Taken together, these differences produce substantial subregional variation in the contexts within which people live and work. This is quite evident across states as well as within them. For example, traveling south in Georgia from the Georgia-Tennessee state line, one begins in the southern Appalachian Mountains of northern Georgia, a region that never participated actively in the cotton economy of the Deep South and traditionally has been the home to a small African-American population. In some north Georgia counties, residents held only weak allegiance to the Confederacy, indicative of profound differences between the region and other parts of the South.

Leaving the north Georgia mountains, one comes next to the piedmont region, where the landscape still bears the scars of the intensive cotton cultivation that drove its economy for decades. Given the central role of slaves and later freedmen in the cotton economy, it is not surprising that the piedmont has a much larger black population than the northern region. The piedmont is part of the Black Belt that cuts across several of the Deep South states. Moving farther south, the Georgia piedmont yields to the sandy soil of the coastal plain, which shares much in common with the Florida panhandle. Historically less dependent on cotton, the agricultural economy of south Georgia has traditionally been more diversified than the piedmont, and its African-American population somewhat smaller.

Similar variation could be described both within and across other southern states. The ten states included in this study represent the entire southeast region of the United States as well part of the south central region. Although all except Kentucky were members of the Confederacy, the states are by no means homogeneous. They differ considerably in many important respects, including racial composition, economic organization, political history, agricultural specialization, religious composition, and cultural heritage. It is this heterogeneity that makes it unlikely that the ten states compiled identical lynching records during the five decades under study.

Although any categorization risks lumping unlike states together or distinguishing among similar states, it is possible to think of the states as representing two general subregions: the Deep South (Alabama, Georgia, Louisiana, Mississippi, and South Carolina) and the Border South (Arkansas, Florida, Kentucky, North Carolina, and Tennessee). Some have maintained that the Deep South and the Border South had somewhat different cultures that may have influenced the propensity of their citizenry to lynch.[43] In general, the Deep South was more dependent on King Cotton, more dominated by a plantation system, and home to a considerably larger black population. The dichotomy is more a matter of convenience for descriptive purposes at this point, however, and should not be overdrawn. In fact, it might be quite difficult to demonstrate that there were greater differences between, rather than within, the two subregions.

An initial idea of the general distribution of lynchings throughout the South can be gained from Figure 2-5, in which each victim lynched between 1882 and 1930 is represented by a single dot. Although the

Figure 2-5. Map of Black Victims of White Lynch Mobs in the South,
1882–1930.

geographic pattern is not perfect, it appears that lynchings were concentrated in a swath running through Georgia, Alabama, Mississippi,
and Louisiana—the region often referred to as the "Black Belt." The
Mississippi River delta experienced an especially heavy concentration of lynchings, as did the piedmont region of Georgia. Outside of
that "lynching band," another area of intensive mob activity is found
in the southern part of Georgia and the northern sections of Florida,
especially in the panhandle region. To gain a better idea of the intensity of lynching within individual states one must examine the sheer
numbers of African-American victims of lynching claimed within each
(Table 2-2).

The cross-state comparisons based on absolute numbers of black
lynch victims are somewhat corrupted by the great variability in the
size of African-American populations across states. Other things being equal, we might expect to find that larger absolute numbers of

Table 2-2. Black Victims of White Lynch
Mobs by State, 1882–1930

State	No. of Victims
Deep South	
Mississippi	462
Georgia	423
Louisiana	283
Alabama	262
South Carolina	143
Border South	
Florida	212
Tennessee	174
Arkansas	162
Kentucky	118
North Carolina	75

blacks were lynched in states with larger black populations. That is, the interstate variation in lynching evident in Table 2-2 might reflect only concomitant interstate variation in racial composition. One way to remove this potential confounding is to standardize each state's lynching record for the size of its black population (Table 2-3). The figures in the table cannot be interpreted as lynching rates because the sizes of the states' black populations are computed as an average of the population reported in the decennial censuses between 1880 and 1930. Rather, the figures complement the figures for the absolute number of lynching victims by providing a somewhat preferable indicator of the hazard of lynching that the African-American community faced.

The picture of cross-state variation in black lynchings changes dramatically when size of the black population is taken into consideration. Most noticeably, the relatively neat Deep South-Border South dichotomy of lynching observed in Table 2-2 breaks down completely. The Deep South states no longer stand out for having claimed more black lynch victims than the Border South. In fact, blacks living in Florida actually bore the highest "per capita hazard" of being victimized by mob violence (Table 2-3). Furthermore, the standardized lynching values for the border states of Arkansas, Kentucky, and Tennessee now exceed, or at least rival, those for Deep South states such

Table 2-3. Black Victims of Lynchings per
100,000 Blacks by State, 1882–1930

State	No. of Victims per 100,000
Deep South	
Mississippi	52.8
Georgia	41.8
Louisiana	43.7
Alabama	32.4
South Carolina	18.8
Border South	
Florida	79.8
Tennessee	38.4
Arkansas	42.6
Kentucky	45.7
North Carolina	11.0

as Alabama, Georgia, and Louisiana. Compared to other southern states, blacks in North Carolina and South Carolina faced relatively little risk of being lynched.

Although altered in character, the evidence presented in Tables 2-2 and 2-3 continues to document the considerable variation in lynching that existed across the southern states. Whether in terms of absolute numbers of victims or victims per exposed population, it is clear that some areas of the South were more likely to experience mob violence than were other areas. The contrast between Tables 2-2 and 2-3 also illustrates the need to consider the size of the population at risk when comparing spatial patterns in lynching. It is important to note, however, that both tables also strongly suggest the operation of underlying forces that produced the divergent lynching histories they describe.

Although the state-level patterns described thus far provide a general idea of how lynchings were distributed, they overlook the fact that southern states were also characterized by considerable internal diversity. If the spatial distribution of lynchings is used to discern the underlying causes of the phenomenon, then it is probably necessary to focus on smaller spatial units. In chapter 3 we will argue that the intensity of lynching was responsive to prevailing social, economic, and political conditions. Specifically, southern whites were more likely to resort to lynching wherever they felt threatened by the African-American population, either socially, economically, or politically. Perceptions of threat were probably most salient at a local level, the community or county, rather than on the state or national level. Thus, the county is probably a better unit of analysis than the state for examination of the spatial patterns in lynching in relation to corresponding spatial patterns in threats to the white population.

Intrastate Variation: The Case of Mississippi

In this book, a good deal of consideration of the spatial distribution of blacks lynched will focus on events at the county level throughout all ten southern states. On the conceptual level, counties historically have been important units for governmental administration, including law enforcement and criminal justice, within the South. People, especially in the rural South, tended to identify closely with their county of origin or residence. Similar observations led Charles S. Johnson to claim, "Although every county may have some variation within its borders, the type of underlying economy that dominates tends to enforce itself throughout the county and to be reflected in the characteristics of social organization. In many cases in the South in particular, the county appears to be a community in itself and to reflect a natural history of development."[44] Thus, by focusing on counties the degree of "within-group" variation in social context is reduced while a considerable degree of "between-group" variation is maintained. The question becomes one of whether black lynchings varied systematically according to that between-group variation in social context.

There are also pragmatic reasons for using counties as the basic spatial units of analysis. First, a reasonably good collection of contemporary historical, county-level data exists that can be used to describe and measure a variety of characteristics of the social context. Second, it is possible to situate the majority of lynchings within specific counties. Yet in most cases it is impossible to assign lynchings to areal units smaller than counties. Thus, counties represent the smallest spatial unit with which it is possible to study the geographic distribution of southern lynchings on a wide scale. In this chapter, however, it is unnecessary to illustrate the crude county-level patterns for all states in the South. Rather, the state of Mississippi will constutute an example of the character and degree of variation in lynchings across counties (Figure 2-6).

A considerable variability in the number of black lynch victims is evident across the counties of Mississippi. In some, like Choctaw and

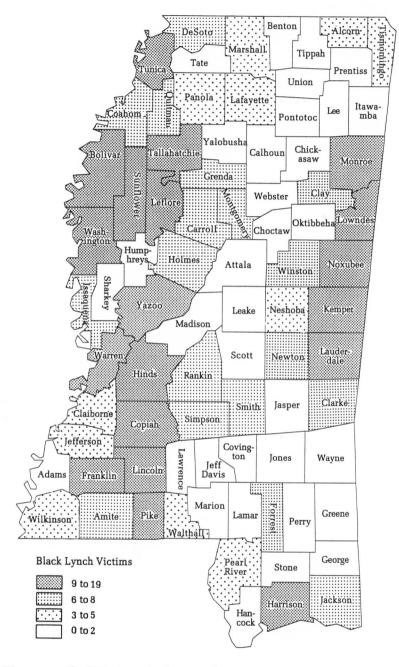

Figure 2-6. Black Victims of White Lynch Mobs in Mississippi, 1882–1930.

Scott, no African-Americans were lynched during the era. Other counties, however, claimed large numbers of victims. For instance, nineteen blacks died at the hands of white lynch mobs in Yazoo County, seventeen in Hinds County, and another fourteen were killed in Lowndes and Harrison counties.

A few generalizations can be made about the distribution of black lynchings throughout Mississippi. Two areas of heavy activity are noticeable along the eastern and western borders of the state. Several counties bordering the Mississippi River to the west registered relatively large numbers of black lynch victims. In addition to Yazoo County, Washington County lynched thirteen blacks, and twelve died in Sunflower County. On the other side of the state, equally bloody histories of lynching are evident along the Mississippi-Alabama state line. In addition to the fourteen victims in Lowndes County, thirteen blacks were lynched in Monroe County, and twelve in Lauderdale County. At the other extreme, the northeast corner of the state was an area of relatively light activity, with several counties (e.g., Tippah, Benton, Prentiss, and Union) claiming only one victim each. In no county in that region were more than five blacks lynched. Was this unequal distribution of black lynchings a quirk resulting purely from chance? Or, is it possible to link the spatial variation in lynchings with aspects of the social, economic, or cultural environment that prevailed within local areas of the state? That question will drive the remainder of this book.

The last lynching incident of the nineteenth century in Yazoo County occurred on March 18, 1899.[45] There had been seven previous lynching victims in the county, and there would be nine more before 1930. In the days preceding March 18, there had been a racial confrontation on The Midnight, a plantation near Silver City. During that encounter, shots were exchanged between blacks and whites, but no one was injured. Following the incident, three "ring leaders" of the black insurrection were arrested: Minor Wilson, C. C. Reed, and Willis Boyd. As so often happened, however, the wheels of formal justice were not allowed to grind this case to its natural completion. While being transported to Silver City, Wilson, Reed, and Boyd were taken from law officers by a mob of determined whites. The three men were shot to death, then their bodies were weighted down and thrown into the Yazoo River.

At the time of the lynching, the social and economic environment in Yazoo County had many characteristics typically associated with lynch-prone areas. First, the county's population was largely African-American—77 percent black compared with 53 percent for the state

THE CHALLENGE

Figure 2-7. "Mississippi sends a message to Congress." From *The Crisis*, June 1937, 176.

as a whole. Second, a sharp class division existed among whites. Although about half of all farms occupied by whites were operated by tenants (compared with 33 percent in the entire state), roughly 20 percent of all farms owned by whites had more than five hundred acres (compared with 12 percent in the state as a whole). Third, relative to other counties in the state, opportunities for additional farm expansion were relatively limited in Yazoo County. Fifty-six percent of all farmland was already improved by the turn of the century in contrast to 41 percent for all counties in the state. Finally, the agricultural economy of Yazoo County was heavily dominated by cotton. Forty-eight percent of all improved farmland was planted in cotton, whereas the average for all Mississippi counties was 35 percent.

Thus African-Americans represented a large numerical majority in Yazoo County, and many rural whites were of marginal status and faced limited economic opportunity. Nearly half of all white farmers were mired in tenancy, and the relative wealth of a small group of farm owners who were white likely aggravated the economic deprivation felt by the large group of others who were landless. The frustrated economic fortunes of a significant number of whites, combined with substantial competition from the county's subordinate blacks, may have fostered an atmosphere of racial hostility and created the potential for the kind of mob activity that claimed the lives of Minor Wilson, C. C. Reed, and Willis Boyd on March 18, 1899, as well as the other sixteen African-Americans who died at the hands of lynch mobs between 1882 and 1930.

Unlike Yazoo County, Tippah County was comparatively tranquil. Located in the northeastern corner of Mississippi and bordering Tennessee, Tippah County claimed only a single black lynch victim between 1882 and 1930. In early August of 1898, a black male allegedly entered the house of a white family, intending to assault a young woman. Surprised by members of the family and pursued by more than a hundred white men, the intruder fled northward in the direction of the Mississippi-Tennessee border. After a protracted manhunt that included bloodhounds, Richard Thurmond was captured in Middleton, Tennessee, and placed on a train for transportation back to Mississippi. As he was being escorted to the Ripley jail in Tippah County, Thurmond was seized by a mob of "determined men" and hung from a telephone pole, where, according to the Memphis *Commercial Appeal,* "His cold, stiff body [was] an object lesson to the worthless bucks that lounge around there, and serves to remind them that in this country it means death to enter the home of the white man with criminal intent."[46] Thurmond was the first, and last, African-American to be lynched in Tippah County.

At the time of the incident, the social and economic atmosphere in Tippah County was as different from Yazoo County's as was its lynching history. Only 22 percent of the county's population was black. Sixty percent of the white farmers owned their land, and only 4 percent of white farm owners held estates larger than five hundred acres. In addition, there was substantially more undeveloped farmland in Tippah County (70 percent) than in Yazoo County, and the grip of King Cotton was much weaker, with only 27 percent of all improved farmland planted in cotton. When compared with the situation in lynch-prone Yazoo County, Tippah County whites, as a group, probably perceived less threat from the much smaller black population. Moreover, they had less reason to feel disgruntled about their economic plight and good reason to be sanguine about their prospects for upward mobility. Given these contrasts, it is not surprising that whites in Yazoo County lynched nineteen blacks to Tippah County's single victim.

If the distinction between counties with high and low lynching totals was always as clear as that between Yazoo and Tippah counties, then social setting could explain a high percentage of the spatial variation in lynching. Although we wish this were the case, these cases were selected for purely illustrative reasons. Further, it is possible to identify other cases that do not as neatly fit the simple framework developed using these examples. For example, in Harrison County in the southeast corner of Mississippi, among the most lynch-prone counties in the state, fourteen victims were recorded between 1882 and 1930. Yet, far from the situation in Yazoo County, 30 percent of Harrison County's population was black. Nor did whites in Harrison County face a particularly desperate economic situation or a serious class division. Only 6 percent were tenants, and only 4 percent of the farm owners who were white owned more than five hundred acres. Furthermore, less than 1 percent of improved land in Harrison County was planted in cotton, and only about 10 percent of all farmland was improved.[47]

Whether Harrison County represents a deviant case from an otherwise powerful explanatory framework or illustrates the need for additional explanatory factors in the framework cannot be determined from this kind of case-by-case consideration. When our purpose shifts from illustrating the spatial variation in lynching to explaining that variation, we must expand our focus to include a broader geographic landscape and turn to the more powerful tools of multivariate statistical analysis.

Proneness for Lynching

The preceding discussion demonstrated that the number of black victims of white mobs varied across the South, with Mississippi and Georgia having the dubious distinction of recording more antiblack violence than any other southern state. A slightly different aspect of the lynching picture is that of the proneness, or consistency, of regions to have lynching incidents (Table 2-4). Fully one-third (34.4 percent) of the counties experienced no blacks lynched between 1882 and 1929, and another fifth (22.7 percent) had incidents in only one of the five periods. Taken together, this indicates that black lynchings were relatively rare in more than 50 percent of the counties in the South during the era. On the other hand, only 4.1 percent of the counties recorded the lynching of blacks in all five decades, and another 8.6 percent had lynchings during four of the five periods. Thus, our data suggest that only slightly less than 13 percent (12.7 percent) of the counties could be characterized as being extremely prone to antiblack mob violence. But where were these lynch-prone counties?

Figure 2-8 maps the counties most prone to lynching African-Americans; that is, those counties that recorded black victims of white lynch mobs in at least four of the five decades between 1880 and 1930. Not entirely surprisingly, the counties most prone to antiblack violence

Table 2-4. Proneness of Counties for
White Mobs to Lynch Blacks

At Least One Black Victim	Percent
All five decades[a]	4.1
Four of five decades	8.6
Three of five decades	13.7
Two of five decades	16.5
One of five decades	22.7
No lynching incidents	34.4
Total	100.0
Number of counties	883

a. 1882–89, 1890–99, 1900–1909, 1910–19, 1920–29.

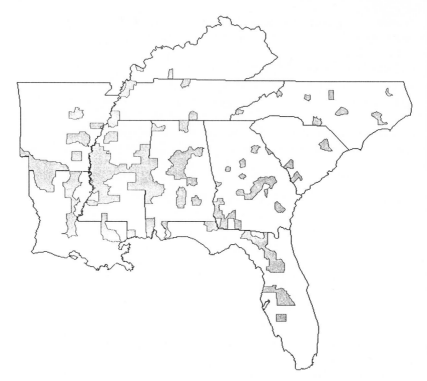

Figure 2-8. Counties Most Prone to Lynching Activity, 1882–1930.

were those located in the central portion of Alabama, central and southwest Georgia, northern Florida, along the Mississippi-Alabama border, in the Mississippi River delta region, and in southwestern Arkansas and northwestern Louisiana. Clearly, there is something special about these regions of the South, issues we will explore in subsequent chapters.

Lynch Mob Allegations

Regardless of the location or time period, lynch mobs typically claimed to have acceptable reasons for their violence. Victims were almost always accused of having violated either a criminal statute or some norm of the racial caste code. In popular racist mythology, African-American males were viewed as savage beasts with almost uncontrollable sexual tastes for white women, and the only thing standing between these "brutes" and the flower of southern gentility was the threat of lynch mob justice. Apologists for mob violence used this defense as a justification of extralegal executions as well as an argument against antilynching legislation in Congress.

In Table 2-5 we have cataloged some of the allegations stated by mobs for the lynching of blacks.[48] These justifications represent a broad variety of criminal and noncriminal transgressions against the white community, ranging from rapes, murders, and assaults to insulting a white man, trying to vote, and being obnoxious. The listing clearly reveals that a broad spectrum of alleged behavior could lead to mob violence. To be sure, not all reasons were mentioned with the same

Table 2-5. The Reasons Given for Black Lynchings

Acting suspiciously	Gambling	Race hatred
Adultery	Grave robbing	Race troubles
Aiding murderer	Improper with white	Rape
Arguing with white	woman	Rape-murders
man	Incest	Resisting mob
Arson	Inciting to riot	Revenge
Assassination	Inciting trouble	Robbery
Attempted murder	Indolence	Running a bordello
Banditry	Inflammatory language	Sedition
Being disreputable	Informing	Slander
Being obnoxious	Injuring livestock	Spreading disease
Boasting about riot	Insulting white man	Stealing
Burglary	Insulting white woman	Suing white man
Child abuse	Insurrection	Swindling
Conjuring	Kidnapping	Terrorism
Courting white woman	Killing livestock	Testifying against
Criminal assault	Living with white	white man
Cutting levee	woman	Throwing stones
Defending rapist	Looting	Train wrecking
Demanding respect	Making threats	Trying to colonize
Disorderly conduct	Miscegenation	blacks
Eloping with white	Mistaken identity	Trying to vote
woman	Molestation	Unpopularity
Entered white wom-	Murder	Unruly remarks
an's room	Nonsexual assault	Using obscene lan-
Enticement	Peeping Tom	guage
Extortion	Pillage	Vagrancy
Fraud	Plotting to kill	Violated quarantine
Frightening white	Poisoning well	Voodooism
woman	Quarreling	Voting for wrong party

frequency. To consider the relative frequency of the justifications, we have grouped the reasons listed in Table 2-5 into categories of allegations for each of the 2,314 black lynchings by white mobs in the South between 1882 and 1930 (Table 2-6). Lynching of those charged of murder and nonsexual assaults were the most frequent (47.1 percent); the second most commonly (33.6 percent) lynched were those African-Americans accused of some sexual norm violation (rape, incest, miscegenation, or improper conduct with a woman). Taken together, simple murders, rape-murders, sexual and nonsexual assaults, and related incidents accounted for more than 82 percent of the African-American victims between 1882 and 1930. Contrary to what we have reported earlier, there appears to be little regional variation in the reasons given for mob violence, and in each category there is only a

Table 2-6. Justifications for Lynching of Southern Blacks by White Mobs

Alleged Offense	South (%)	Deep South[a] (%)	Border South[b] (%)
Sexual norm violation			
Sexual assault	29.2	28.7	30.2
Miscegenation	0.6	0.8	0.3
Other	3.8	3.5	4.3
Subtotal	33.6	33.0	34.8
Rape and murder	1.9	1.3	3.1
Murder and assaults			
Murder	37.3	38.7	34.3
Nonsexual assaults	9.8	9.0	11.5
Subtotal	47.1	47.7	45.8
Theft and robbery	4.0	4.6	2.8
Arson	4.3	4.6	3.5
Incendiarism	1.5	1.5	1.6
Race prejudice	1.7	1.3	2.6
Miscellaneous	2.8	2.9	2.7
Unknown reason	3.2	3.2	3.1
Total	100.1	100.1	100.0
Number of black victims	2,314	1,573	741

a. Alabama, Georgia, Louisiana, Mississippi, and South Carolina.
b. Arkansas, Florida, Kentucky, North Carolina, and Tennessee.

minor difference between the percentages for the Deep South and the Border South. The rhetoric rationalizing mob violence was shared throughout the South.

There could be temporal differences, however, for lynching blacks. Some justifications were more common during particular times. To explore this possibility we tabulated by five-year periods the reasons given for lynching. An examination of these data showed that there was a marked change in the kinds of rationalizations employed before 1900 and those expressed after 1900, in particular the relative likelihood of a black victim being accused of rape or murder shifted over the period (Table 2-7).[49]

The summary data in Table 2-7 show only limited differences between the Deep South and the Border South in either period, thus we will ignore these minimal regional differences and concentrate on the South as a whole. In the South between 1882 and 1899, 38.1 percent of black lynch victims were accused of rape or rape-murder; 34.9 percent were charged with murder. The similarity between these two percentages shows that the murder justification and the rape justification for lynchings in this earlier period were about equally frequent,

Table 2-7. Percentages of Black Victims Lynched for Rape or Murder, by Period and Region

Period and Region	Percent Accused of		Murder/Rape Ratio
	Rape[a]	Murder	
1882–99			
Deep South[b]	36.8	36.2	0.984
Border South[c]	40.6	32.4	0.796
Whole South	38.1	34.9	0.916
1900–1930			
Deep South	23.9	40.9	1.711
Border South	26.7	36.0	1.348
Whole South	24.8	39.3	1.585
1882–1930			
Deep South	30.0	38.7	1.290
Border South	33.3	34.3	1.030
Whole South	31.1	37.3	1.199

a. Percent black victims lynched by white mobs for rape or rape-murders.
b. Alabama, Georgia, Louisiana, Mississippi, and South Carolina.
c. Arkansas, Florida, Kentucky, North Carolina, and Tennessee.

with the rape allegation being very slightly more common. This is shown in the ratio of murder-to-rape lynchings being slightly less than unity, 0.916.

After the turn of the century, the situation changed markedly. The percent of lynch victims accused of rape, or rape-murder, declined sharply from 38.1 percent to 24.8 percent, while the percent accused of murder rose only slightly from 34.9 percent to 39.3 percent. As a result of these two trends, after 1900 the likelihood that a black victim would have been charged with murder was about 1.585 times more probable than being accused of rape or rape-murder.

In sum, the data reported in Tables 2-6 and 2-7 demonstrate, contrary to what some apologists for lynching alleged at the time, that over the entire forty-nine-year lynching era, murder—not rape—was the most common rationalization for lynching African-Americans. This became increasingly the case in the first three decades of this century, when a far greater percentage of black victims were accused of murder than were charged with rape, especially in the Deep South. This evidence supports the claims of opponents of lynching that sexual assaults were not the most common justification for white mob violence. The evidence also raises the possibility that the defense of southern white womanhood was little more than a thin smoke screen to justify violence toward the African-American community.[50]

Conclusions

Mob violence against African-Americans served four functions within southern society during the lynching era: (1) to eradicate specific persons accused of crimes against the white community; (2) as a mechanism of state-sanctioned terrorism designed to maintain a degree of leverage over the African-American population; (3) to eliminate or neutralize African-American competitors for social, economic, or political rewards; and (4) as a symbolic manifestation of the unity of white supremacy. Although only the first was the manifest function of lynching, the three latent functions are critical for understanding why the practice was so pervasive in the fifty years before the Great Depression.

Clearly, southern lynchings were not distributed randomly. Rather, they tended to mass together during particular periods and within certain locations. The existence of such variation is reassuring because it presents an opportunity to explain why it exists. Several explanations are possible: the overall economic well-being of southern whites, opportunities for whites to improve their economic fortunes, the degree of inequality within the white population, and the threat of competition from the black population. But a careful and thorough consideration of those potential explanations requires going beyond the basic descriptive information presented thus far. This chapter simply illustrates the raw material from which a compelling story of the southern lynching phenomenon must be fashioned.

NOTES

1. The South includes Alabama, Arkansas, Florida, Georgia, Kentucky, Louisiana, Mississippi, North Carolina, South Carolina, Tennessee. For our purposes, by lynching "victim" we mean the killing of a black person through extralegal mob action. A black lynching "incident" is a lynching with at least one black victim. Approximately 14 percent of the 2,018 black lynching incidents involved more than one victim (Table C-5 in Appendix C). Of the 2,462 black victims, only 3 percent (74) were female. In addition to the black victims of mob violence, at least 228 incidents also involved at least one white victim (288 white victims) and 55 involved victims of other races or people whose race is unknown. See Table C-1 in Appendix C for the distribution of lynching victims by race and gender.

Although we will consider the issue of white lynchings in a later chapter, between 1882 and 1889 the ratio of black lynch victims to white lynch victims was 4 to 1; during the next decade, 1890–99, the ratio increased to more than 6 to 1; and after 1900, the ratio of black victims to white victims soared to more than 17 to 1. Thus, over time, especially after the turn of the century, lynching in the South became increasingly and exclusively a matter of white mobs murdering African-Americans.

It is also significant that lynchings were strictly racially segregated. Of a total of 2,278 incidents between 1882 and 1930, only 13 involved both black and white victims, while 2,004 involved exclusively black victims, 214 had exclusively white victims, and victims of 47 incidents were either of other races or their race was unknown. See Table C-2 in Appendix C.

2. See Hoffman (1896), Shaler (1890), and Smith (1905).

3. Principal Keeper of the Penitentiary (1876).

4. Ayers (1984) offers a penetrating examination of criminal justice in the South during this historical period; see Walker (1980) for a history of popular justice in America.

5. Many transgressions of the racial etiquette were not violations of the formal criminal codes, thus not directly punishable by the established legal system. There was a perceived need, therefore, for popular justice

to sanction those who dared to violate the informal racial caste norms (Walker 1980).

    6. As cited by Woodward (1963, 379).

    7. Shapiro (1988, 96–103) and Williamson (1984, 215–23) contain discussions of the Atlanta race riot of 1906 and its causes.

    8. As cited by Woodward (1963, 432), emphasis added.

    9. See Beck et al. (1989), Tolnay et al. (1992), and Tolnay and Beck (1992b).

    10. This does not mean, however, that the popular justice argument was never applicable. Indeed, although relatively infrequent, there were cases of white mobs lynching white victims and of black mobs killing black victims. Explanations based on racial prejudice would seem to be inadequate for accounting for these lynchings. See chapter 4 for a discussion of intraracial mob violence.

    11. Cutler (1905, 273–74).

    12. New Orleans *Times-Democrat,* April 26, 1898, 9.

    13. Charleston, S.C., *News and Courier,* July 18, 1904, 2.

    14. Memphis *Commercial Appeal,* October 7, 1923, 3.

    15. Memphis *Commercial Appeal,* December 28, 1923, 8.

    16. As cited by the NAACP ([1919] 1969, 13). In other accounts the victim is named Sam Holt rather than Sam Hose.

    17. See Fredrickson (1988) and Takaki (1979) for a more complete discussion of racial stereotyping.

    18. For valuable insights into the causes and effects of the crop-lien system in the South, see Ayers (1992), Flynn (1983), Hahn (1983), Jaynes (1986), McMillen (1989), Mandle (1978), Mandle (1992), Ransom and Sutch (1977), Woodward (1951), and Wright (1986).

    19. Holmes (1973b, 139n14).

    20. Holmes (1969, 166).

    21. Memphis *Commercial Appeal,* December 22, 1903, 2. We have been unable to identify and confirm the second lynch victim mentioned in the article.

    22. As cited by McMillen (1989, 224).

    23. Jaynes (1986, 297).

    24. Bailey (1914, 30), emphasis in the original. Also see Doyle's (1937) description and analysis of the "etiquette" of interracial social interactions.

    25. Bailey (1914, 92–93), also in Woodward (1951, 355–56).

    26. *The Crisis,* December 1911, 56.

    27. *The Crisis,* December 1911, 57. Some of the local white clergy were incensed at the behavior of the Governor, Ashley, Cheshire, and the lynch mob participants and delivered sermons to that effect (61).

28. *The Messenger,* July 1918, 14.

29. Atlanta *Constitution,* August 6, 1919, 18.

30. Atlanta *Constitution,* August 29, 1919, 5.

31. For detailed accounts of the antilynching movement, see the work of Ferrell (1986), Hall (1979), and Zangrando (1980). The support was especially evident when the transgression involved a white woman. For any black man to act disrespectfully toward a white woman was not only offensive, but also an act of overt sedition that explicitly challenged the complete structure of caste relations in the South—clearly an act that demanded immediate retaliation. A significant number of black men were lynched for making "indecent proposals," "improper advances," or "insulting propositions" to white females. Hall (1979) has made a powerful argument that the oppression of black men, black women, and white women were all part of the same repressive social system. As for lynching, she concludes, "The ritual of lynching, then, served as a dramatization of hierarchical power relationships based both *on gender and on race"* (1979, 156, emphasis added).

32. See Hall (1979) and Miller (1978).

33. In fact, according to some reports the police were often passive bystanders and sometimes willing accomplices to the violence (Cash 1969, 309–11).

34. As will be explained in more detail later, our empirical data on victims of mob violence are limited to 1882 through 1930. We have no systematic information on lynchings for the five-year period between 1877 and 1881, or for the Reconstruction period from 1865 to 1877, even though there were certainly black lynchings before 1882, especially during the early period of Reconstruction as southern whites resisted the increasing voice of blacks in society and politics. The end of the period (1930) coincides roughly with the demise of widespread lynching in the South, although some incidents have occurred since 1930. See Appendixes A and B for a detailed discussion of the lynching data and its quality. The trend lines have been twice-smoothed statistically using three-year moving averages for greater visual clarity (see Table C-3 in Appendix C for the raw data). The raw trends were smoothed first by computing three-year moving averages (the raw number of victims in a given year was replaced by the average of the number of victims in the preceding year, the current year, and the subsequent year). The first smoothed series was then smoothed again by replicating this procedure. This two-step smoothing procedure allows the underlying trend to emerge by masking much of the interannual variation in the frequency of lynching.

35. We report two instances of incidents with eight black victims. One occurred on December 29, 1889, in Barnwell, South Carolina, when eight

black men were lynched for murder. The second instance involved the lynching of the David Walker family in Hickman, Kentucky, on October 3, 1908. Walker was accused of cursing a white woman. Later that night, a large mob set fire to his home, then shot the Walkers as they ran outside. Although we suspect that a total of eight were killed in this episode, Wright (1990) counts seven dead.

36. See Beck and Tolnay (1990).

37. Williamson (1984).

38. Wright (1990); we pursue this point in greater detail in chapter 6.

39. Tolnay and Beck (1990, 1992a).

40. Southern Commission on the Study of Lynching (1932).

41. Cheatwood (1988) and U.S. Bureau of Justice Statistics (1980).

42. Hahn (1983, 86–133); Hyman (1990).

43. Williamson (1984).

44. Johnson (1941, 3).

45. New Orleans *Daily Picayune,* March 24, 1899, 9.

46. Memphis *Commercial Appeal,* August 9, 1898, 2.

47. These characteristics of Harrison County are from the 1900 census, as were the data for Yazoo and Tippah counties.

48. It must be kept in mind, however, that there is no way to determine the veracity of these allegations. Rather than thinking of these mob assertions as truths of conduct, they are better viewed as rationalization of mob behavior.

49. The other reasons cited for lynching, such as theft, robbery, arson, incendiarism, and miscegenation, showed no distinct shift across time. Only the relative likelihood of being lynched for the offenses of rape, rape-murder, and murder showed significant temporal variation.

50. As shown in Table 2-7, only in the Border South for the 1882–99 period did the number of rape-based lynchings exceed in any significant way the number of murder-based lynchings, 40.6 percent accused of rape versus 32.4 percent accused of murder.

3

Social Threat, Competition, and Mob Violence

The legacy of lynching has been a disturbing and powerful attribute of southern society. When Tiger Knowles and Henry Hays brutally murdered Michael Donald in 1981 they were following a well-established tradition. The case of Michael Donald is disturbingly reminiscent of countless other killings of southern blacks. As in the past, the two white men sought to send a cold message to the local black community—that the Klan and its agenda was not dead. As in the past, they prominently displayed the victim's corpse to assure that the message would be received. The major difference between Alabama in 1981 and Alabama in 1881 is that when Knowles and Hays killed young Donald they were sorrily out of step with the mainstream southern race relations of their day. Had their great-great grandfathers attempted to send a similar message, white southern society would more likely have tolerated, if not enthusiastically embraced, their behavior.

The deep historical roots of lynching are relatively easy to document, and the distribution of lynchings over time and across the southern landscape is quite easily shown. In contrast, the underlying social, economic, and political forces responsible for lynching have proven much more difficult to isolate. This is not necessarily due to a lack of interest or effort. From the very earliest observations about the lynching era to the most recent sophisticated quantitative efforts to unearth the underlying causes of the phenomenon, many investigators have struggled with one overriding question: Why would otherwise law-abiding citizens take the law into their own hands and carry out summary executions? Despite an impressive accumulation of research devoted to that question, a definitive answer is still a very long way away. As Ayers observed in the mid-1980s, "The triggers of lynching, for all the attention devoted to it by contemporaries, sociologists, and historians, are still not known."[1]

Aggravating the search for the triggers of mob violence is the impressive diversity of the phenomenon itself. Mobs varied considerably in composition. Some were comprised primarily of poor whites down on their luck and with little prospect for reversing their economic fortunes. Other mobs included the most prominent members of the community. Mobs also varied in their behavior. Some were disciplined and systematic in their mission, carrying out the punishment with little ceremony or celebration. Other mobs engaged in drunken debauchery and prolonged the grisly ordeal by submitting the victim to unthinkable torture for the entertainment of spectators. Victims were similarly varied. Some of those lynched were prosperous and respected members of their communities. Others were drifters with no ties to the community or outcasts situated on society's fringes. The reasons given for lynchings were also diverse, ranging from minor offenses such as "being disrespectful to a white man" to such serious violations as murdering children and serving their remains to surviving family members for dinner.[2]

All lynchings do, however, share one commonality: The mob acted illegally, choosing to circumvent the formal system of criminal justice in order to carry out the lethal punishment personally. Aside from lynchings in the frontier regions of the American West, most mob violence occurred in areas with established law enforcement agencies and courts. Legally then, lynch mobs engaged in criminal behavior, no matter how heinous the alleged crime of the lynch victim may have been. In the majority of cases, the formal, established criminal justice system would have been vigorous in pursuing the arrest and trying and punishing the victim had the lynch mob not interceded. Indeed, in many cases mobs snatched victims from the hands of the authorities, sometimes with fatal consequences for law officers and mob members alike.

If additional social and psychic costs were associated with breaking the law, as lynch mobs did, then it must be assumed that powerful motivating forces drove the behavior of the mobs. Evidently, normally law-abiding citizens were willing to break the law in order to punish alleged offenders personally because by doing so they believed that they neutralized perceived threats to their well-being effectively and with nominal personal cost.

Toward a Threat Model of Black Lynchings

Throughout the era under consideration, southern whites thought themselves to be a population under siege.[3] Before the Civil War, the institution of slavery had controlled the large African-American population rigidly. The extraordinary authority vested in slave owners was buttressed by the political and legal machinery of the Old South. Emancipation brought revolutionary change to the South and presented significant challenges to white southerners (chapter 1). Whites saw nearly four million southern blacks suddenly transformed from personal property to potential competitors. The political and economic hegemony that whites had enjoyed was threatened. And, if successful, blacks threatened the superior status position that whites were used to taking for granted. Complicating these new conditions was a perception by whites of a burgeoning crime problem among freedmen. To counteract these potential threats, southern white society required measures that could be as effective as slavery had been in regulating the black population. Although the Black Codes were a legal failure, later Jim Crow legislation, disenfranchisement, judicial discrimination, debt peonage, and violent intimidation were included in the repertory of social control techniques. It is within this context that mob violence can be viewed as an instrument of social control over a "threatening" southern black population.

A threat interpretation of black lynching, however, transcends ubiquitous concerns for safety on the part of southern whites. In its broader formulation it emanates from the family of conflict theories of social control.[4] These theories begin with the premise that coexistent minority and majority groups differ significantly in the power and resources they command. The majority group enjoys greater access to power and resources and takes whatever steps necessary to perpetuate its advantage over the minority. When the perceived threat from the minority group increases, the intensity of the majority group's repression of the minority will also increase.

To be useful in an examination of southern lynchings, the conflict perspective must be able to identify relevant dimensions of majority privilege that the minority group threatens. Blalock has provided some valuable direction on this score by claiming that three dimensions of majority privilege can be jeopardized by a threatening minority group: economic, political, and status.[5] He stresses the economic and political dimensions and chooses not to deal with status threats from the minority group.

But how can we measure the degree to which a minority group is threatening, and how are we to know which type of threat motivates the majority group to discriminate? Its size in relation to the dominant group's population is a commonly used indicator of the threat that a minority group presents. Thus, conflict theories of social control predict a positive association between the minority's relative size and the repressive measures the majority uses to protect its privileged social position. Further, Blalock argues that political threats and economic competition should produce somewhat different relationships between minority concentration and discriminatory efforts by the majority group. In both cases, the minority group's population concentration should be related positively with the majority group's discriminatory efforts, as conflict theory argues. However, when majority-minority competition is primarily economic in nature, the relationship should become weaker as minority concentration increases. When competition is primarily political, Blalock expects the relationship to intensify at higher concentrations of minority population.[6]

Blalock's power threat and economic competition hypotheses provide valuable direction in the search for the underlying causes of discriminatory behavior by the majority. However, tests of the conflict orientation of social control that focus too heavily on the relative size of the minority population are in danger of overlooking the importance of heterogeneity within the majority group itself. Generally, the majority population will not be monolithic; rather, it will be stratified along class lines. The different classes may have divergent interests in the nature of majority-minority relations as well as in the specific repressive social control techniques used against the minority. Specifically, it is possible for a large minority population to be "threatening" to the interests of one class in the majority hierarchy but beneficial for another class. This is a distinct possibility within southern society during the late nineteenth and early twentieth centuries, when the white population was severely stratified along class lines.

Two variants of the conflict perspective recognize the possibility of divergent class interests in the use of violent persecution as social control. According to the more orthodox Marxist orientation, repression of the black minority was primarily in the interest of the white elite of merchants and planters, who benefited from the presence of a large, subservient, cheap labor force.[7] The character of southern social structure after Emancipation was strongly influenced by the white elite to assure that its political and economic interests were served. A web of legal and social arrangements effectively restricted the mobility of black laborers and severely limited their ability to redress grievances against white employers.[8] And when necessary to supplement these arrangements, the white elite used violent tactics such as lynching.[9] Moreover, according to the orthodox Marxist argument, a virulent racist atmosphere and the violence it spawned also served the interests of the white elite in another way. The intense antagonisms between blacks and poor whites precluded a coalition of laborers that might otherwise have risen in opposition to powerful whites and threatened their hegemony.

Bonacich's split labor market theory of racial antagonism paints a somewhat different picture while maintaining a conflict orientation.[10] According to Bonacich, the postwar South was comprised of three primary classes: (1) white planters and employers; (2) higher-priced white laborers; and (3) cheaper black laborers. The primary concern for white planters and employers was to hire workers as cheaply as possible to guarantee larger profits. The goal of white workers was to extract the highest wage possible. The presence of a bountiful supply of cheaper black laborers served the interests of the white elite but frustrated the efforts of white labor. As long as the supply of workers was adequate, white employers had little incentive to intimidate black laborers. On the other hand, the economic competition between white and black labor led white laborers to restrict economic competition from blacks. Although Bonacich does not stress racial violence by white laborers as a strategy for achieving their objectives, it is a logical implication of her theory.

A threat perspective of southern lynchings is obligated, then, to identify some dimensions of conflict between whites and African-Americans over their relative access to society's scarce resources. In short, whites attacked when they believed that blacks were threatening their privileged access to those resources. The precise nature of this conflict, however, and its manifestation in racial violence, must be considered within the context of southern social structure, which was doubly stratified by caste and class. As a result, the lines of social conflict ran in two, largely orthogonal, directions. The caste line tended to unite all whites against all blacks, and class divisions within the white community separated the economic interests of poor and well-to-do whites. For the white elite, the danger was ever-present that the caste line would evaporate, increasing the likelihood of a coalition between white and black labor. At the same time, however, lower-class whites also had a vested interest in the integrity of the caste line, which provided a basis for their claim of superiority—however slim—over African-Americans.

In examining the ways in which the black population threatened southern whites, it is useful to keep in mind the importance of the class issues identified by the orthodox Marxist and split labor market theories, as well as the importance of the caste system that divided the South racially. Whether it was fear of black criminals, or fear of black competitors, or fear of a black-white coalition of labor, it is quite evident that southern whites had ample opportunity to feel threatened. Whether those threats were justified is, of course, a separate issue.

The Popular Justice Model and Fear of Black Crime

Judging from the reporting of lynchings in southern newspapers, and from the frequent defenses of lynching advanced by southern politicians and editorialists, it was an unfortunate (although understandable) response from a white community besieged by a criminal black population. Whites saw neither property nor person as safe from the predatory black male, who was especially driven to violate the purity of southern white womanhood. At the same time, the dominance and popularity of theories of scientific racism legitimized the image of blacks as an inherently defective race, prone to violence and criminal activity. Thus, according to the popular conception of southern lynchings, whites lynched to defend themselves against victimization from black criminals. Whether such fears had a legitimate basis is difficult to determine because crime statistics for the era are notoriously incomplete and unreliable, except for scattered isolated locales.

Even some commentators who opposed mob violence and sought ways to remedy the problem expressed basic sympathy with the concern over black criminality. For instance, James Elbert Cutler, one of the first social scientists to grapple seriously with the problem, acknowledged the popular justice motive even while condemning mob violence:

> The law and its administration seem utterly unsuited to the function of dealing with negro criminals. A judicial system adapted to a highly civilized and cultural race is not equally applicable to a race of inferior civilization, and the failure to realize this fact and act upon it, by making special provision for the control of the negro population in the Southern States since slavery was abolished is a fundamental reason for the disrepute into which legal procedure has fallen as regards negroes accused of offenses against the whites.[11]

Cutler endorsed a suggestion by U.S. Supreme Court Justice David J. Brewer, who sat on the bench from 1889 to 1910. Brewer believed that the level of mob violence could be reduced by limiting defendants' right of appeal in criminal cases. Apparently, neither Cutler nor Brewer appreciated the irony of a solution that argues for a resolution to the objectionable practice of mob violence that would make the justice system itself function more like the mobs. In order to appease the populace by reducing its impatience with due process and sating its appetite for vengeance, U.S. courts should weaken the system's protection against abuse or mistakes and shuffle defendants quickly to the gallows.

There are two somewhat different dimensions to the popular justice model for black lynchings. First, we might attribute mob behavior to southern whites concerned about the certainty and severity of punishment for individual law violators. By taking the law into their own hands, these whites assured that criminals would be punished and that the severity of the punishment would be appropriate to the seriousness of the offense. They might perceive such action to be necessary if they lacked confidence in the ability of the formal justice system to accomplish these two objectives or if the "offenses" they wished to punish were violations of social, not legal, rules. In legal cases, whites could not necessarily rely on the formal justice system to satisfy their need for punishment. The first dimension of the popular justice model represents an instrumental function of mob violence, as an auxiliary to the established criminal justice system.

The second dimension is more expressive in nature than the first. By carrying out swift and severe punishment for unacceptable behavior, legally or socially, the white population was sending a clear message intended to etch into the minds of the black community that such behavior was unacceptable and had a cost. In some cases, mobs gave the message additional emphasis by subjecting victims to hideous forms of torture and mutilation, as in the brutal lynching of Sam Holt (chapter 2). To borrow the jargon of criminologists, the two dimensions of the popular justice model can be classified as the "specific" and "general" deterrence functions of mob violence, respectively.

It is difficult to be convinced of the need for mob violence to guarantee swift and severe punishment for true violations of the law, especially for capital crimes such as murder and rape. The southern criminal justice system did not treat black criminals leniently. Rather, they were exposed to the same discriminatory treatment in the courts as in the other spheres of southern society. For example, statistics on legal executions in the South clearly indicate that blacks were especially vulnerable to the death penalty.[12] Raper even refers to the state-sanctioned execution of blacks as "legal lynchings"—a sentiment echoed by Harry S. Truman's Committee on Civil Rights.[13] In the majority of cases, the formal justice system dealt harshly enough with African-Americans accused of crimes to satisfy the punitive interests of most whites. Sometimes mobs took lynch victims from police custody, however, often after conviction. Clearly, whites lynched even after the wheels of justice had begun to grind.

Despite the woeful prospects for blacks within the southern criminal justice system, in many cases mob violence was triggered by the prospect of acquittal or the handing down of a sentence perceived as too lenient. Ike Fitzgerald was an African-American accused of raping a young woman in early March of 1901.[14] He was arrested, jailed, and prosecuted for the crime in Tiptonville, Tennessee. After deliberating for some time, the jury in the case entered the courtroom at about 7:00 P.M. on March 17 and announced that they were unable to agree on a verdict. Caught by surprise at the jury's indecision, several observers stormed to the front of the courtroom, seized Fitzgerald, rushed him into the street, and hung him from a tree. Clearly, his possible innocence was not reason enough to prevent the mob from carrying out its own version of justice and doing what the formal justice system had failed to do.

In other cases it was the sentence, not the verdict, that offended white sensibilities. For example, on the afternoon of April 18, 1918, an all-white jury in Poplarville, Mississippi, had just pronounced Claud Singleton, who was black, guilty of murder.[15] Fully expecting the death penalty, the whites of Poplarville were shocked and disappointed when Singleton received a life sentence instead. That night, a mob of about a hundred men gathered, proceeded to the sheriff's house, and forced him to turn over the keys to the jail. Singleton was then taken from his cell, marched to a tree by the cemetery, and hung.

Not all "offensive" behaviors by southern blacks were true violations of the law, however. It was a society in which a clear caste line separated the races. As members of the subordinate caste, African-Americans were expected to follow relatively well-established rules of conduct. For instance, appropriate social contact between black males and white females was carefully defined and circumscribed. In addition, all blacks were expected to show deference to all whites—regardless of their social status—during all encounters. Any breach of the unwritten rules was a threat to the superior status of whites. Moreover, symbolic importance was often ascribed to violations of the rules. For example, excessively friendly behavior by a black man toward a white woman meant that sexual advances were sure to follow, and disrespectful behavior toward whites meant that blacks were "uppity" and attempting to challenge their inferior station. The formal justice system offered relatively little help to whites who sought to punish such transgressions, which were either beyond the reach of the formal legal system or led to formal punishment that was considered inadequate. Instead, whites were forced to rely on the imposition of informal sanctions, including mob violence.

The lynching record abounds with cases of African-Americans being lynched for what seem to be relatively trivial offenses but which, in fact, were serious challenges to the southern social order and white supremacy. Henry Scott was a porter on the Atlantic Coast railway line, one of the few nonagricultural occupational opportunities available to black males. During May 1920, his train made a swing through the South, including the state of Florida. Somewhere near Lakeland, a white passenger complained that Scott had insulted her.[16] When the train reached Lakeland, she informed the sheriff of the offense, and Scott was arrested. As the sheriff was transporting Scott from Lakeland to Bartow, the accused was seized by a mob and summarily executed. Even though, in this case, Scott was virtually certain to be punished within the formal legal system, it is unlikely that his punishment would have been severe enough to satisfy the white citizens who attached symbolic importance to his disrespectful behavior. He had not simply insulted a female passenger, he had challenged the social norms that forbade such behavior.

In other cases, infractions of the behavioral rules were punished without the formal justice system ever entering the picture. For example, in August 1888, Nash Griffin, a black man living in Ocheeshee, Florida, was accused of writing an insulting note to a young white woman.[17] After she showed the note to some white men, a mob visited Griffin and gave him a hundred lashes as punishment. They also ordered him to leave the county. When he failed to do so, a group of forty masked men caught Griffin and shot him to death.

In both types of situations, mob violence served the purpose of specific deterrence. In the first instance, whites resorted to popular justice in order to compensate for the perceived leniency of the formal justice system—either its failure to convict, or its failure to impose adequate punishment. In the second instance, the mob supplemented the formal justice system by assuming responsibility for punishing African-Americans for infractions of behavioral rules that were either beyond the reach of "the law" or for which the law was simply incapable—as opposed to unwilling—of meting out appropriate punishment.

At the same time, lethal mob violence was designed to achieve general deterrence by informing blacks that certain behaviors would be followed by swift and serious punishment. It is not difficult to imagine that Scott's and Griffin's cases had a strong impact on the general black population. No doubt, the lynchings of Ike Fitzgerald and Claud Singleton also informed local blacks that those accused of murder had a very short life expectancy, whether or not the formal justice system imposed the death penalty. Similarly, the lynchings of Henry Scott and Nash Griffin put local black residents on notice that violations of the caste-dictated rules of black-white social interaction would be punished severely, even if the formal justice system was incapable of handing out adequate punishment.

In many cases, the message was not so subtle, as four lynchings in South Carolina during 1882 indicate. In each case, the note pinned to the victim's body conveyed a clear threat to the African-American population that white society would act swiftly to protect the virtue of southern womanhood. All four victims were accused of raping white women, but, of course, their guilt or innocence was never legally determined. When the mob in Winnsboro lynched Caleb Campbell in June 1882, the note they attached to his body read, "Our mothers, wives and sisters shall be protected, even with our lives." A similar, although briefer, message—"our women shall be protected"—was attached to the body of John Johnson, "the Rock Hill Ravisher," who was lynched near Rock Hill, also in June 1882. An identical note was affixed to the body of Martin Beckett, who was lynched in Hampton County in July 1882. And, finally, after he was lynched in Williston in September 1882, Nathan Bonnet's broken corpse carried the warning that "our wives, mothers, sisters and daughters shall be respected."[18]

Such warnings were not reserved for alleged sexual assaults on white women, however. When the mob lynched Nathaniel Bowman, Iziah Rollins, George Beckham, and Charles Elliot in Tangipahoa Parish in Louisiana on September 21, 1900, its stated purpose was to "teach the worthless blacks in town a lesson."[19] The four victims had been accused of robbery and were being held in the Ponchatoula jail. The mob broke into the unguarded jail with axes, took the four men to an oak tree in a nearby park, and hung them. Significantly, the park in which the lynching occurred had been given over to local blacks for picnics and parties. Using a strategy that was common, the mob carried out its deed in the heart of the African-American community to convey the intended message more efficiently.

Again, in some cases lynch mobs subjected victims to extreme forms of cruelty in order to emphasize the potential consequences of certain kinds of unacceptable behavior, as well as with the virtually complete freedom of the white community to exact the type of justice it felt appropriate and necessary. This certainly was true of the systematic torture of Sam Holt before he was burned by a Georgia mob in 1899. It also was true in the case of an unnamed black man lynched for kidnapping and raping a white school teacher near Arcadia, Louisiana, in 1891.[20] When the mob finally caught him, it skinned him alive and cut his body into small pieces.

The popular justice model of lynching describes a white population that felt threatened by black behavior that violated southern norms. Whether that behavior was clearly criminal or merely unacceptable in light of the caste segmentation of southern society, the implications for the African-American population were often the same. When they felt it was necessary, whites would resort to extreme and illegal measures to assure that "appropriate" punishment was applied. Although the popular justice model does not necessarily condone such responses, it does imply that blacks sometimes triggered mob behavior by violating well-established behavioral rules, whether codified laws or the unwritten rules of the southern caste system. Thus, according to this model, southern blacks were at least guilty of provoking whites by knowingly threatening their security. There were other ways, however, in which southern blacks threatened whites while simply going about the business of trying to achieve a comfortable level of living. The competition model of lynchings articulates this component of the threat perspective.

A Competition Model of Southern Black Lynchings

Southern whites were fond of complimenting local blacks for "knowing their place" and not being uppity. In the southern context, "being uppity" meant considerably more than disrespectful or insolent behavior, as described in the lynchings of Henry Scott and Columbus Lewis. Rather, these compliments can be translated more broadly to mean that local blacks did not expect more from southern society than southern whites were willing to give. Insolent blacks were those who did not "know" their place, aspired to a larger piece of the southern pie, and bridled at the obstacles constructed by whites. Such African-Americans were part of the "Negro Problem" over which white society continually wrung its hands. They also represented a serious "threat" as they pursued greater access to political power, economic success, and enhanced social status. In many respects, African-Americans threatened whites simply by participating in southern life actively and pursuing a share of these scarce resources, making competition with whites inevitable. Although the three sources of competition (property, power, and status) can be treated separately, they are intricately intertwined dimensions of general well-being.

Lynching and Political Competition

During Reconstruction, the southern political scene was radically transformed by increased participation and representation on the part of African-Americans.[21] In some areas, emancipated slaves comprised an actual numerical majority of the population and, therefore, represented a significant challenge to political order. For the first time in southern history, blacks were elected to positions at all levels of government. Not only did this threaten to weaken the grip on southern politics traditionally enjoyed by the white elite, but it also insulted poor whites who had themselves been largely marginal to the southern political process. The notion of freedmen voting and holding public office was extremely offensive to virtually all southern whites. After all, blacks were widely perceived as members of an inferior race that was incapable of achieving the same high plane of civilization that whites had constructed in the South. Consequently, black participation in, not to mention domination of, the political process was thought to represent the death knell for southern society. Whites were also annoyed because the postbellum southern social order was, in part, the construction of northern carpetbaggers who were unfamiliar with the limitations of the subordinate caste. The extent to which this political transformation offended southern whites is clear from the testimony heard by the U.S. congressional joint committee that investigated Klan activity during the early 1870s. Violence directed at blacks during Reconstruction, that committee concluded, was largely politically motivated.

Southern whites eventually responded to this political threat by designing and implementing a variety of restrictive voting statutes that effectively disenfranchised the black population by the early 1900s. Until disenfranchised, however, black voters were occasionally the wild card of southern politics. Given the large numbers of blacks in some locales, white political parties were forced to vie for their votes if they wanted to prevail. Early in Reconstruction, it was the Republican party that competed most successfully for black voters to the detriment of the historically dominant Democratic party. Later, the Populist party engaged in a brief but potentially disruptive flirtation with African-American voters.[22] Although the Democratic party also curried favor with blacks, it stood to lose the most because blacks were often loathe to support the party that included some of the most virulent racist voices in the South.

Where the black vote could not be purchased or neutralized through fraud, whites sometimes resorted to violent intimidation. It is quite clear that murder and lynching were occasionally employed to reduce the political threat from the black population, even following Reconstruction. For example, political competition was a fundamental cause of the preelection riot in Wilmington, North Carolina, in 1898, as evidenced by the instructions of the soon-to-be mayor to white voters: "Go to the polls tomorrow and if you find the negro out voting, tell him to leave the polls, and if he refuses kill him; shoot him down in his tracks. We shall win tomorrow if we have to do it with guns."[23] And at times it was necessary for whites to use their guns and other weapons in order to neutralize the black political threat.

Sometimes creative explanations were constructed in order to justify lynchings that were actually politically motivated, as in the lynching of Jack Turner in Choctaw County, Alabama, during August 1882. The white press described Turner as "a turbulent and dangerous character, a regular firebrand in the community" and claimed that he was the ringleader of a plot to kill all of the white people in Choctaw County.[24] In actuality, it appears that Turner and his alleged "conspirators" were simply Republicans trying to unseat all of the white Democrats in Choctaw County. In other cases, the political motives for a lynching were not so obscure. For example, S. S. Mincey, a black Republican leader, was lynched in Montgomery County, Georgia.[25] On July 29, 1930, Mincey was kidnapped from his home by a mob of masked men who demanded that he give up all of his political posts. After refusing to cooperate, Mincey was severely beaten and died soon after. Even whites were not immune from mob violence with a political motive as long as there was concern over white political hegemony. For example, in July 1890, Marsh Cook, a white Republican, had just won political office by carrying the black vote in Jasper County, Mississippi. On July 25, he was found dead in the middle of the road, riddled with buckshot.[26] The only apparent reason for Cook's lynching was his political success based on the support of local black voters. When it was used, mob violence was an efficient weapon against the political success that African-Americans enjoyed in some southern locales.

But how likely is it that political competition was one of the most powerful social forces behind the broader bloody history of black lynchings, especially after the early years of Reconstruction? Is it possible to go beyond identification of a few lynchings that clearly had political motives to conclude that mob violence was a widespread mechanism for neutralizing the threat of black voters? In fact, there is some reason to believe that political competition between southern whites and blacks may have played only a relatively minor role in black lynchings after Reconstruction.

It is true that the large African-American population in southern states represented a potentially serious numerical threat. However, it is also the case that southern whites were quite effective at neutralizing black political participation quickly, even before the widespread adoption of restrictive voting statutes. For instance, Kousser has shown that black participation in presidential elections, even before disenfranchisement, was pitifully low. Such evidence led Williamson to conclude, "After Reconstruction black voting never threatened white supremacy in the South as a whole, nor was it ever an active threat in a given state for very long. The threat of black voting was spotty and it was sporadic. When it arose, white politicians dealt with it locally and relatively quickly." It is understandable then that Ayers minimizes the political dimension to black lynchings and observes, "Very few observers, whatever their race, region, or politics, pointed to political coercion as the direct cause of lynching."[27]

After Reconstruction, relatively few contemporary observers of the lynching era placed great emphasis on black political competition. In contrast, it has received more intensive scrutiny from modern researchers than has any other possible underlying cause of black lynchings. Most investigators have attempted to test Blalock's hypothesis that political competition between majority and minority groups should produce a positive association between minority population concentration and discrimination, with an increasingly strong relationship at higher percentages minority. Reed found support for Blalock's power threat hypothesis within Mississippi counties, and Corzine et al. presented more general support for the Deep South, especially before disenfranchisement. In both cases, lynching increased steadily in frequency with the percent of black population but rose sharply in counties where blacks comprised more than 80 percent of the population. However, work by Tolnay et al. subsequently cast serious doubt on the evidence offered by Reed and Corzine et al.[28]

After a variety of conceptual and methodological errors were corrected, neither Reed's nor Corzine et al.'s findings could be replicated. Using a somewhat different methodological approach to this issue, Olzak concluded that more lynchings occurred during years in which third parties (including the Populists) mounted political challenges to the dominant Democrats and Republicans. However, her analysis included lynchings and political contests throughout the entire country, not just in southern states. Soule also investigated the relationship between populism and mob violence but found no relationship between the level of Populist vote and black lynchings in Georgia.[29] Considering the inconclusive nature of prior tests, the political threat model must be considered a viable explanation of southern black lynchings, although still only weakly supported.

In sum, it is still premature to accept or reject a political threat model of black lynchings. At certain times, and in specific areas, African-Americans were able to exert political power that threatened the political hegemony of the southern white elite. In those instances, whites sometimes resorted to violence to intimidate black voters. We still do not know, however, whether those events were relatively isolated or were repeated frequently enough to represent a significant part of the lynching story. We also do not know whether unstated political motives were really behind lynchings for which other stated reasons were given, as in the case of Jack Turner.

Lynching and Economic Competition

The economic position of many rural whites deteriorated significantly during the 1890s and early in the twentieth century. A growing rural population put extreme pressure on southern land, and with alarming frequency white farmers were reduced to a landless status.[30] The image of the southern white yeoman farmer quickly gave way to an image of the southern white sharecropper crippled by the crop-lien system that forced the use of sales from crops to pay off debts leveraged by those same crops. For example, between 1900 and 1930 the number of white tenant farmers in the South increased by 61 percent, while the number of black tenants increased only 27 percent.[31] As a result, despite their membership in the dominating caste, more rural whites began to sink to the same disadvantaged economic position as blacks. For the first time, sizable numbers of southern white farmers found themselves in direct economic competition with southern black farmers. According to a U.S. Department of Labor report, "The small white farmer on the unproductive soils that constitute a large part of the uplands regards the Negro and his child as taking the place in the sun needed by the white farmer for his own children. There is barely enough to go around, even if the whole product of the soil is reserved for the whites."[32]

White landowners often added insult to economic injury by demonstrating a preference for black tenants, who were easier to control and had little legal protection under the discriminatory southern justice system, making white planters virtually immune to charges of fraudulent bookkeeping or physical intimidation. On the other hand, white laborers would have been offered somewhat greater legal protection against such extortionate practices.

To whites on the brink of economic oblivion, African-Americans scraping a living from the same exhausted soil were all too obvious competitors for an already shrunken economic pie. Black tenants farmed land that otherwise might have been tilled by whites. Black owners occupied farms that could have been purchased by whites after they mustered the necessary resources. And black laborers took jobs that might have gone to whites while working for wages below that expected by whites. It is not difficult to imagine how marginal rural whites could have felt economically threatened.

The declining economic fortunes of many rural whites, along with modest progress by some rural blacks, created a situation ripe for confrontation. As a response to economic stress and black competition, lynching could have served two different kinds of purposes for poor whites. First, it may have been a simple aggressive response to frustration as Hovland and Sears claimed.[33] That is, African-Americans served as a convenient, vulnerable target against which whites could vent the anger and frustration created by blocked economic ambitions. Second, lynching could have served a more instrumental purpose to improve the economic position of whites with regard to blacks.

Two contemporary observers of the lynching era believed that competition between white and black labor did result in black lynchings. Raper claimed that mob violence against blacks was sometimes part of "organized efforts of the whites to displace Negro laborers with unemployed whites," and White observed that "the majority of Southern whites in the rural South were and are sinking into an economic morass which makes them the prey of Klan organizers, anti-evolution mountebanks, mob hysteria, and every manner of charlatanry."[34]

There are numerous examples of lynchings that apparently had their roots in this competition. Especially common were those motivated by resentment of economically successful African-Americans. In some of these, no reason was given for the mob activity; in others, some alleged offense was concocted to justify the lynchings that were clearly economically motivated. In 1898 Frazier B. Baker was appointed the postmaster of Lake City, South Carolina, an overwhelmingly

white town. Baker's appointment to this desirable federal post ignit-
ed strong resentment among Lake City's white residents who, as the
Charleston *News and Courier* wrote, "were justly indignant at the
appointment of this negro as their postmaster." On the night of February 22, a mob of three or four hundred whites gathered in front of
Baker's home, which was in the same building as the post office. They
set fire to the building, then shot Frazier Baker dead as he tried to
escape. Baker's infant daughter was also shot dead in her mother's
arms as Mrs. Baker tried to flee the burning building. She and three
other Baker children were also shot and seriously wounded.

The press coverage of the Baker lynching is revealing in a number of respects. First, the report advanced the popular argument that
local whites were not involved in the violence. Second, it disap-
proved of the lynching while, at the same time, expressing clear
sympathy with the motives of the mob. Third, it provided important
clues about the economic status of most African-Americans in the
Lake City community:

> Lake City . . . people are noted for their sobriety, and it is con-
> sidered one of the most moral towns in Eastern South Carolina.
> Very few people seem to think that any of the citizens of Lake
> City had anything to do with this unfortunate affair or that they
> were in the mob at all. Lake City has always been known as a
> white man's town, not over a dozen negroes living in the place,
> and not one owning a foot of land in the corporate limits of the
> town, and this makes it all the more strange that a negro should
> have been appointed postmaster at Lake City.[35]

The paper did not speculate about why nonresidents of Lake City
should have been so concerned about the town's black postmaster. Nor
did it enumerate the mechanisms that had been used to keep Lake City
"a white man's town" and prohibit black ownership of land.

Dennis Cobb of Arcadia, Louisiana, was another successful black
who paid for his success with his life. On March 26, 1892, Cobb, a
"well-to-do and highly respected colored man," was abducted from
his house by a mob of white men who dragged him to a nearby forest.
There, with no apparent motive, they "placed the rope around his neck
and swung him to a limb. While dangling between earth and sky they
proceeded to fill his body with lead, one ball striking him in the neck
near the jugular vein, a load of buckshot tearing away the flesh of one
arm and still another lacerating his thigh and a bullet piercing his
abdomen."[36] Thinking he was dead, the mob left. However, before

Cobb was strangled by the rope or bled to death from his wounds, the tree limb broke, and he managed to crawl back to his house. There he soon succumbed to the wounds inflicted by the mob.

Thus far, the discussion of economic motives for black lynchings, and the illustrative cases, have emphasized competition between working-class whites and black laborers. Put crudely, poor whites lynched poor African-Americans because they represented a threat to economic well-being. This perspective identifies the white lower, or working, class as the primary instigators, and beneficiaries, of black lynching. Such an emphasis overlooks the possibility that the white elite also had economic motives for encouraging, or minimally not discouraging, mob violence. White planters and employers likely benefited from the presence of black workers, who were cheaper than white labor. Contrary to the perspective of white labor, therefore, black laborers represented an opportunity to make larger profits, not a threat to their economic security.

Yet the white aristocracy could benefit economically from mob violence against blacks in at least two ways. First, in some situations racial violence may have been an instrument that white planters and employers used to maintain control over African-American laborers. Given their great dependence on black labor, employers could not countenance laziness or, worse, resistance. Second, the white elite may have used racial violence to maintain a sharp cleavage between black and white labor. As long as workers remained rigidly divided by the caste line, white planters and employers could use the presence of black labor to maximize profits and hold down the wages of whites. A perennial threat to the white elite, however, was the potential for the caste line to weaken, resulting in the formation of the opposition coalition of white and black labor that was threatened during the early stages of the Populist Movement. Therefore, it was in the interest of the white elite to guarantee the integrity of the southern caste system, especially its ability to preclude the development of common interests between poor whites and blacks.

Some writers have emphasized the motives of the white elite (over those of poor whites) in their interpretations of black lynchings. For example, Bloom argues that racism and terror primarily served the interests of the southern white elite by driving a wedge between black and white workers. He writes, "For most of the second half of the nineteenth century, black and white labor were not primarily in competition with each other. They existed mainly in different geographical locations. . . . the upper class created the atmosphere that promoted attacks on blacks and often actually carried out lynching and other

Figure 3-1. From *The Messenger*, August 1919, 4.

forms of terror." Shapiro echoes this sentiment when he notes, "When those committed to racial subordination saw the possibility of blacks and whites coming together for common purposes, their response most often was to reach for the gun and rope."[37] A. Philip Randolph also argued that powerful whites benefited from racial hostility and violence that drove a wedge between poor whites and blacks.[38] Others focused less on the white elite's efforts to prevent a coalition of white and black labor and stressed instead the use of violence to maintain order and obedience.[39]

It is virtually impossible to discern from the alleged reasons reported for lynching those intended to drive a wedge between white and black laborers. In fact, to the extent that such lynchings occurred they probably were carried out under a pretext that inflamed the white citizenry in general. It is hardly plausible that the white elite sponsored and organized lynchings with the stated purpose of preventing a racial coalition of workers. On the other hand, some lynchings clearly were motivated by a concern to "control" black workers who, for one reason or another, were causing trouble. The lynching of Will Millans, a black coal miner in Brighton, Alabama, fits this description. Millans was one of the leaders of, and a vocal spokesman for, a coal miners' strike in Brighton during August 1908. According to the Atlanta *Constitution,* "Millans is known . . . to have been one of the most violent of agitating strikers, and he has made many speeches and has done much to imbue men to come out of the mines."[40] During the course of the strike, the mine was dynamited. Despite the widespread belief in Brighton that Millans had nothing to do with the dynamiting, he was lynched by a mob of whites that included at least two deputy sheriffs. The exact role of the mine owners in Millans's lynching, of course, remained unstated.

A different kind of threat to white employers probably accounts for the lynching of Joseph Hardy, a blind preacher, in Talbot County, Georgia. During June 1909, Hardy had been making speeches in Talbot County urging blacks not to work for whites. As the Atlanta *Constitution* explained, "The preacher is said to have urged negroes not to work for whites, and to have had sufficient influence to keep many of the negroes away from their regular employment on white men's farms."[41] Sometime between June 19 and 23, Hardy was taken from his house by a mob of white men. Several days later, his body was found in a creek. He had been severely whipped and apparently left to die from his wounds.

In addition to the lynchings like those of Millans and Hardy, several blacks were lynched for "breach of contract." What these lynchings all have in common, of course, is that they helped preserve the hierarchical arrangement that ordered relations between white employers and black workers. Whenever that arrangement was challenged, it threatened the economic hegemony of the white elite and increased the probability of mob violence to restore racial order.

Clearly, there is ample reason to believe that African-Americans may have been lynched because they represented an economic threat to white southerners. It is also very likely that poor whites and the white elite alike attempted to neutralize these threats by resorting to mob violence, although their specific motivations were quite different. Unlike the case of the political threat represented by southern blacks, however, economic explanations of lynching have not been as systematically explored. Two possible exceptions stand out. First, the relationship between cotton prices and lynching has received considerable attention since the 1930s.[42] Second, Corzine and his colleagues have examined the usefulness of split labor market theory for explaining areal variation in lynching.[43] Once again, therefore, we must consider the economic threat model to be a potentially useful candidate for explaining black lynchings, but a model that is, as yet, untested.

Lynching and Status Competition

The premier indicator of status within southern society during the late nineteenth and early twentieth centuries was one's race. Southern culture was transfixed with the notion of race supremacy, and virtually all other aspects of southern society must be considered with this in mind. In principle, all whites were superior to all African-Americans, and the rigidity of the caste line separating the races assured even the poorest of whites this one taste of superiority. As Flynn notes, "When white southerners discussed social and economic issues, there were southerners, and then there were blacks. There was society, and then there were blacks. There were people, and then there were blacks."[44] For many (probably most) white southerners, the sanctity of the caste line that perpetuated this ubiquitous distinction was critically important, for it guaranteed that at least somebody in southern society occupied a lower social position. And anything that threatened the integrity of the caste line was certain to be vigorously, and possibly violently, opposed.

One factor contributing to the white southerner's obsession with the caste boundary was the emergence during the latter part of the century of scientific theories and "evidence" that purported to prove the inferiority of the black race. Natural and physical scientists amassed evidence of racial differences in cranial capacity, anatomy, and behavioral characteristics in an attempt to document the innate inferiority of blacks and the superiority of whites.[45] The "scientific" evidence, coupled with later widespread use of standardized intelligence tests, established a seemingly legitimate basis for the longstanding conventional wisdom that viewed African-Americans (and virtually all non-white groups) as an inferior race.[46] This scientific racism metastasized to the popular media, where the white public greeted it enthusiastically.[47] Even illiterate and isolated whites would eventually be affected by the doctrine of scientific racism as it reinforced the southern folklore of racial supremacy and helped shape the southern mentality at all levels of society.

Scientific racism also raised the white southerner's consciousness of another potential threat from the black population—that inter-racial reproduction could contaminate the "superior" white gene pool. Racial amalgamation was suddenly viewed in a new light and became an even more terrifying prospect. It is small exaggeration to describe white preoccupation with miscegenation and racial amalgamation as a regional paranoia. Virtually every aspect of social life, when it concerned blacks, was ultimately considered in relation to its potential to promote sexual contact between the races. This concern is expressed very well by William Benjamin Smith, who warned in his racist diatribe *The Color Line: A Brief in Behalf of the Unborn* that "if we sit with Negroes at our tables, if we entertain them as our guests and social equals, if we disregard the colour line in all other relations, is it possible to maintain it fixedly in the sexual relation, in the marriage of our sons and daughters, in the propagation of our species?"[48] The caste boundary, therefore, offered protection against a variety of threats from the African-American population, all related in one way or another to the dogma of white supremacy that set the agenda for much of southern life.

Although there was near unanimity among whites that the caste line must be maintained at virtually any cost, there is reason to believe that this concern was particularly salient to lower-class whites. All classes could share in the fear that racial amalgamation would biologically contaminate the superior race, but the elevated status guaranteed to whites by the caste boundary was particularly critical for the lower class.

In the South, a large and growing constituency of poor whites occupied an economic niche very similar to that occupied by most blacks. This similarity created a dissonance for poor whites, who could see little difference between themselves and blacks in terms of basic standards of living although their caste membership told them that they were socially, morally, biologically, and intellectually superior. Without a clear economic claim to superiority, the caste division became even more important as a source of status differentiation. As Woodward summarizes, "As the Negroes invaded the new mining and industrial towns of the uplands in greater numbers, and the hill-country whites were driven into more frequent and closer association with them, and as the two races were brought into rivalry for subsistence wages in the cotton fields, mines, and wharves, the lower-class white man's demand for Jim Crow laws became more insistent. It took the ritual and Jim Crow to bolster the creed of white supremacy in the bosom of a white man working for a black man's wages."[49] Although Woodward's conclusion was directed at race relations in the southern up-country, we believe that it can be generalized to encompass much of the South.

Did whites lynch blacks to maintain a sharp caste boundary between the races in response to status threats from the black population? As discussed earlier in relation to the popular justice model of black lynchings, many African-Americans were lynched for relatively trivial reasons that indicate an effort to etch the caste boundary more indelibly. Lynchings for such offenses as "speaking disrespectfully to whites," "failure to give way on a sidewalk," or "acting like a white man" suggest such a purpose. Legal mechanisms for punishing caste violations were either not in place or were too anemic to satisfy the popular demand for acceptable behavior.

Lynchings to punish consenting sexual relations between blacks and whites also indicate a deep concern in maintaining the caste line and racial separation at all costs. In May 1929, Jim Mobley, seventy-two, was found in the company of a white woman in Hamilton County, Florida.[50] A small band of white men confronted Mobley and began abusing him for his transgression. Eventually, the mob severed his hands and threw him into the Suwannee River to drown. Mobley's punishment was a common price paid by black men who violated the rigid rule of the southern caste system that forbade their intimate contact with white women.

Even relations between white males and African-American women were sometimes subject to the same harsh punishment, especially if more than fleeting assignations were involved. Patrick Morris, who was white, was married to Charlotte Morris, a black, in Jefferson Parish, Louisiana. They had one child, Patrick Morris, Jr. On January 12, 1896, a mob of about twenty white men visited the Morrises at their house on the levee of the Mississippi River.[51] After shooting the couple, the mob placed them on their bed and used axes to hack their bodies to pieces. Finally, they burned the house to the ground. While the mob was going about its grisly business, Patrick, Jr., managed to escape by swimming across the river. Had he not escaped, however, there is little doubt that the mob's determination to enforce the caste-mandated separation of the races would have extended to him as well.

The hideous forms of torture and mutilation involved in many lynchings served as reminders that whites were free to exercise un-encumbered control over blacks.[52] Public exhibition of the victim's body (often after mutilation) was frequent and had the express pur-pose of reminding African-Americans of their subservient place in the southern social hierarchy—and the consequences for them if they forgot it. In some incidents the mob either attached signs to their vic-tim's bodies or clearly stated the message they intended to send, for example, to "teach the worthless blacks in town a lesson." These as-pects of the lynching record strongly suggest white responses to a black population that threatened their status advantage in southern society.

Once more, little effort has been expended to examine the impor-tance of caste maintenance as a motivation for black lynchings. Al-though not by specific design, Inverarity's research on the relationship between "boundary crises" and the use of lynching as "repressive justice" touches a theme closely related to the status version of the race-threat framework. According to Inverarity, the Populist Move-ment in Louisiana in the 1890s created social disruption that led to lynchings in an effort to help restore solidarity to the southern white community through the very visible punishment of a common ene-my, black Louisianians. However, Inverarity's work has not been ac-cepted without criticism, indicating the need for additional research.[53]

There is a large overlap between the kinds of status threats dis-cussed here and the political and economic threats described earlier. If blacks made political and economic gains in southern society, then they necessarily threatened the presumed status difference between the races. Thus, testing the status threat model of lynching is prob-lematic because it is difficult to separate the unique effects of status threats from those of economic and political threats. For instance, political and economic competition from the African-American pop-ulation are hypothesized to increase the use of lynching as social con-trol, but we would also expect the status of southern whites (especially lower-class whites) to be most seriously threatened where political and economic competition is keenest. There is also overlap between these status threats and the popular justice motivation for lynching. That is, when mobs lynched blacks to punish them for behavior that vio-lated caste but not legal rules, they were also attempting to preserve the status hierarchy of races. It was a serious norm violation for a black man to fail to yield the sidewalk to a white woman. For a white man to do the same was inconsiderate but certainly not a life-threatening folkway violation. For these reasons, we will not directly examine the status threat model in following chapters. However, where appropriate, we will note where status threats were likely to have played a role in explaining the temporal or spatial distribution of lynchings.

We do not believe that lynching was a behavior confined to the lower stratum of southern whites, nor to the white elite. Rather, we believe that the lynching era was the combined product of proletariat and bourgeois social, political, and economic interests. Consequently, it would be inadequate to pursue explanations for lynching that are based on the motives of a single class of southern whites. Poor whites were threatened by the economic and status competition they perceived from blacks. Powerful whites had reason to fear the political influence of large African-American populations as well as the potential coalition of white and black labor. Thus, racial prejudice, discrimination, and even violence could serve the purposes of all classes of whites. Indeed, the potentially universal "appeal" of lynching is probably an important reason for why the practice was tolerated for so long. There is no reason to believe, however, that the various class interests in racial violence were necessarily aligned. During a given period, or in a particular setting, lynching might be best understood by examining the motives of the white elite. In a different period or in another setting the interests of poor whites might best explain lynching behavior.

Alternative Social Control Measures

Any discussion of the use of mob violence to counteract perceived threats from the black population would be incomplete without mentioning the wide variety of other social control techniques that could have achieved the same objective. To the extent that those alternative methods of social control were effective, we would expect lynching to have been less common. In fact, it is possible that lethal sanctioning was a last resort to which southern whites turned when the other, less drastic, techniques proved ineffective. These alternative techniques included such practices as political disenfranchisement, economic discrimination, the widespread adoption of Jim Crow laws, and a discriminatory system of criminal justice.

We have already described briefly the effectiveness of disenfranchisement as a strategy for neutralizing political competition from the

black population. By 1910, virtually every southern state had instituted some type of restrictive voting statute that drastically reduced
the number of registered African-Americans and the number of African-American voters. Disenfranchisement was not a subtle process.
It was explicitly designed and implemented to eliminate black political influence. For instance, while campaigning in 1906 for the gov-
ernorship of Georgia, Hoke Smith asserted that "legislation can be
passed which will . . . not interfere with the right of any white man
to vote, and get rid of 95 percent of the Negro voters."[54] By 1908, such
legislation was passed in Georgia, including a literacy test, a property test, an understanding clause, and a grandfather clause.[55]

White southerners also instituted an impressive repertory of techniques to retard black economic progress and thereby reduce the economic threat. Mandle describes very well the social barriers that were
erected to reduce economic and geographic mobility among southern
blacks, including obstacles to land ownership, denial of credit for
investment, debt peonage, and constriction of employment opportunities outside of plantation agriculture.[56] In addition, educational
opportunities were deliberately restricted by inadequate investments
in facilities and teachers for blacks.[57] Even as late as 1930, it was the
rule for southern counties to fund black schools at about one-fifth to
one-tenth the level of white schools.[58] If lynchings really were the
result of economic competition between whites and blacks, then they
should have been less frequent where economic discrimination effectively neutralized the black economic threat.

Southern culture also included abundant reminders to the African-
American population of their inferior and subordinate social status.
The intricate web of Jim Crow restrictions officially reduced the black
population to second-class status by forcing the use of separate, and
inferior, facilities for transportation, accommodations, dining, and
entertainment.[59] If southern culture successfully relegated blacks to
their "place," then race-based status threats would have been mini-
mized. It is even possible that they may have significantly reduced the
salience of status threats that had roots in economic and political
competition.

A final set of alternative social control techniques that may have
mitigated the need for lynching can be found in the extremely discriminatory system of southern criminal justice. As some viewed matters,
legal executions of southern blacks were often little more than "legal
lynchings." If this is true, then legal executions may have served the
same social control function as lynchings, a response to perceived
threats from the black population. Indeed, an analysis by Tolnay et al.

provides preliminary evidence that this may have been the case.[60] Before disenfranchisement, for example, black executions in the Deep South were more common in counties where economic competition from blacks was more intense and in counties that had larger concentrations of blacks. After disenfranchisement, however, these relationships virtually disappeared. As yet, little evidence suggests that legal executions served as substitutes for lynching as social control of southern blacks.[61]

Clearly, southern whites exploited an impressive arsenal of social control techniques to reduce the intensity of competition from the "threatening" African-American population. Lynching was only one of these, albeit the most extreme. The relationships among these various techniques are undoubtedly extremely complex. They may have been complementary, or they may have reinforced each another. Efforts to examine empirically the validity of the threat perspective of southern black lynchings should consider the possibility that these alternative methods of social control obviated, or reduced, the need for lynching. Thus, where possible, they should be included in conceptual models that seek to explain black lynchings from a threat perspective.

Conclusions

Lynchings were more likely to occur where, and when, southern whites felt threatened in some way by their African-American neighbors. This perceived threat could arise from concerns for popular justice over offending black behavior or from the more subtle threats of black competition for greater access to economic, political, or status resources. Thus, efforts to explain variation in lynching over time and across space must emphasize the social conditions that aggravated these perceived threats among the white population. In addition, diversity within the white population must also be recognized. Sharp class cleavages in southern white society were likely to determine which threats were most salient to different groups and whether those threats resulted in mob violence. Finally, lynching was not the only mechanism that the white population used to reduce the level of perceived race threat. Alternative measures such as disenfranchisement, legal executions, and Jim Crow laws were also employed.

There are a number of ways in which these various social forces might be arranged in a conceptual model of lynchings. At this point, it is not our intent to propose a model that will serve as a reliable road map for each twist and turn we follow during subsequent chapters.

Consistent with the framework laid out in this chapter, Figure 3-2 depicts mob violence as an immediate function of the level of threat perceived by the white population in all of its dimensions. In addition, the conceptual model portrays the level and type of perceived threat as a product of (1) alternative sources of social control that may or may not reduce the level of threat through successful execution, and (2) the nature of the white class structure that determines which types of perceived threats are most likely to surface. Whether explicitly or implicitly, the processes sketched in this model will reoccur throughout the remainder of this book.

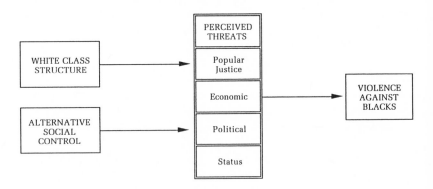

Figure 3-2. Conceptual Model of Threat Perspective of Black Lynchings.

NOTES

1. Ayers (1984, 238).

2. One of the most unusual incidents took place in Tatnall County, Georgia on July 25, 1886. According to the Atlanta *Constitution* (July 27, 1886, 2), an unnamed black female was lynched after she had killed a young child and then cooked the remains and served them to the family for dinner. The rest of the body was found salted down in a barrel.

3. See Ayers (1992, ch. 6), for an account of how southern blacks and whites adapted to life after the Civil War.

4. A conflict perspective has been used to examine a wide variety of other social control techniques, including sizes of police forces, certainty of arrest, and use of deadly force by police. See Liska (1992), Olzak (1990, 1992), Phillips (1986), Quinney (1977), and Turk (1969) for elaborations on the conflict perspective.

5. Blalock (1967).

6. Blalock (1967, 148–49) points out that these different forms of non-

linear relationship between minority group size and discrimination will exist only under certain conditions. The weakening economic threat at higher levels of minority concentration assumes that the majority group can successfully regulate minority competition (at lower levels of minority population concentration) through discrimination. Thus, there would be no need to intensify discrimination as the minority population becomes larger. The power threat model, on the other hand, assumes that the majority group must intensify its mobilization to blunt minority political influence as the minority population increases. Blalock acknowledges that the expected relationships may not emerge in all situations. If the majority can successfully neutralize political competition when the minority group is relatively small (e.g., through slavery or disenfranchisement), then the political threat will not increase as the minority population grows proportionately larger.

7. Bloom (1987).

8. See Mandle (1978, 1992).

9. White (1929 [1969], 103).

10. See Bonacich (1972, 1975).

11. Cutler (1905, 224–25).

12. See Tolnay et al. (1989b) and Wright (1990).

13. See Raper (1933) and Shapiro (1988, 368) for discussions of "legal" lynchings.

14. Memphis *Commercial Appeal,* March 18, 1901, 1.

15. New Orleans *Times-Picayune,* April 19, 1918, 1.

16. Tampa *Sunday Tribune,* May 9, 1920, 1A.

17. Jacksonville *Times-Union,* August 19, 1888, 1.

18. Charleston, S.C., *Sunday News,* June 4, 1882, 1; Charleston *News and Courier,* June 13, 1882, 1, July 27, 1882, 1, September 15, 1882, 1.

19. New Orleans *Daily Picayune,* September 22, 1900, 1.

20. New Orleans *Daily Picayune,* September 9, 1891, 3.

21. See Kousser (1974) and Woodward (1966).

22. See Gaither (1977) and Woodward (1951).

23. As cited by Shapiro (1988, 74).

24. Columbus *Daily Enquirer-Sun,* August 22, 1882, 1; also see Huntsville *Gazette,* September 2, 1882, 2.

25. Atlanta *Constitution,* July 30, 1930, 12.

26. New Orleans *Daily Picayune,* July 26, 1890, 8.

27. Williamson (1984, 229); Ayers (1984, 239).

28. Reed (1972); Corzine et al. (1983); Tolnay et al. (1989a).

29. Olzak (1990); Soule (1992).

30. Ayers (1992); Myrdal (1972); Wilson (1978).

31. U.S. Bureau of the Census (1975, 465).

32. U.S. Department of Labor (1919, 41).

33. Hovland and Sears (1940).

34. Raper (1933, 31); White (1929 [1969], 11–12).

35. Charleston *News and Courier,* February 23, 1898, 1.

36. New Orleans *Times-Democrat,* March 28, 1892, 6.

37. Bloom (1987, 5); Shapiro (1988, 219).

38. *The Messenger,* July 1918, 14.

39. For example, see White (1929 [1969]).

40. Atlanta *Constitution,* August 6, 1908, 2.

41. Atlanta *Constitution,* June 25, 1909, 3.

42. See Beck and Tolnay (1990), Hovland and Sears (1940), and Raper (1933).

43. Unfortunately, they used the NAACP inventory of lynchings, which has significant flaws, making their findings questionable. Furthermore, their measure of the presence of cheap labor threat (number of black tenant farmers/number of white tenant farmers) is conceptually debatable, again undermining the usefulness of their findings. See Corzine et al. (1988).

44. Flynn (1983, 27).

45. For example, Hoffman (1896).

46. See Gould (1981) for an insightful history of the search for "objective" measures of racial superiority.

47. Newby (1965).

48. Smith (1905, 7–8).

49. Woodward (1951, 211).

50. Jacksonville *Times-Union,* June 2, 1929, 26.

51. New Orleans *Daily Picayune,* January 13, 1896, 1, 8.

52. See, for example, Ginsburg (1988) and NAACP (1919 [1969]).

53. Inverarity (1976). Criticisms of Inverarity's work focused on its inadequate and flawed conceptual framework (Pope and Ragin 1977) and its incomplete and insufficient statistical analyses (Wasserman 1977). Reanalyzing Inverarity's data, Bagozzi (1977, 358) found insignificant support for the linkage between his key concepts and lynching. Given the serious nature of these criticism, any linkage between boundary crises, populism, and mob violence remains unanswered.

54. As quoted by Henri (1975, 22).

55. Kousser (1984, 239).

56. Mandle (1978).

57. For example, in 1890, Alabama's and North Carolina's per-pupil expenditures for black and white students were equal, but by 1910, Alabama allocated black pupils only 31 cents for each dollar spent on white students. North Carolina was somewhat more generous, spending 54 cents

per black student for each dollar spent on white students. See Margo (1990, table 2.5, 21–22).

58. Johnson (1941).

59. Woodward (1966).

60. Tolnay et al. (1992).

61. See Beck et al. (1989) and Massey and Myers (1989). Phillips (1987) has suggested that legal executions and lynchings were substitutable forms of lethal sanctioning in North Carolina after disenfranchisement. Subsequent investigation by Beck et al., however, found very little covariation over time in the use of legal executions and lynching in North Carolina and Georgia between 1882 and 1930. Their results indicate that lynching was more likely to be used to punish suspected rapists and sex offenders, whereas legal executions were heavily restricted to punishment for murderers. Therefore, lynching and executions appear to have been reinforcing rather than substitutable forms of lethal sanctioning (chapter 4).

4

Lynching as Popular Justice

In virtually all cases, mobs claimed to have a legitimate grievance against the victims they lynched. Usually, but not always, it was a serious charge such as murder or rape. For most southern whites during the lynching era, these allegations were sufficient enough to justify severe punishment. The popular justice explanation accepts, relatively uncritically, the white community's justification for lynching—that black criminal behavior was out of control and exceeded the capacity of the formal justice system. However, alternative threat perspectives maintain that the southern social landscape was not that simple (chapter 3). Rather, multiple undercurrents of black-white tension or conflict either encouraged the white community to invent excuses for violence where no legitimate criminal justice grievance existed or led whites to intervene in the prosecution and punishment of bona fide black offenders. In either case, the mobs were engaged in extraordinary and illegal behavior. Before we embrace the alternative threat perspectives, however, it is useful to attempt an assessment of the merits of the popular justice model.

Had opinion polling been as common during the lynching era as it is now, there can be little doubt about what it would have revealed about the southern public's perception of black lynchings. Most likely, average white southerners would have described lynching as an exercise in popular justice. Indeed, many whites believed that a social contract existed between the races. That contract sharply defined the limits of acceptable behavior and permitted whites to punish transgressions of those limits. In certain instances, southern whites perceived the formal, legally constituted mechanisms for enforcing this social contract as being too unreliable or too anemic. In those cases, the white community felt compelled and justified to intervene. To resort to the rope and faggot to reinforce the unwritten contract was considered a solemn civic duty, and to shirk this duty was to endanger the very foundations of southern culture.

Almost certainly the mob in Tiptonville, Tennessee, that stormed the courtroom and lynched Ike Fitzgerald after a jury had failed to convict him believed it was fulfilling this social contract. Likewise, the mob of whites in Poplarville, Mississippi, that seized and lynched Claud Singleton after he was given a life sentence rather than the expected death penalty also believed that its intervention was justified. The same argument could have been made by countless other mobs that took the law into their own hands to murder southern blacks for alleged serious, and sometimes not-so-serious, violations of the southern code of conduct. The lynching record is replete with incidents in which the victim was kidnapped from sheriffs or abducted from courtrooms, seemingly out of impatience and frustration in the white community.

Few institutions were as effective at perpetuating the image of black lynchings as popular justice as were southern newspapers, which ran detailed rationalizations of mob activity. This was particularly true if the victim had been accused of a sexual assault on a white woman. A typical example appeared following the lynching of John Jones, who had been accused of "outraging" an infant girl. The Memphis *Commercial Appeal* reported, "Last Sunday morning, in the Mormon Springs neighborhood in this county [Monroe], a black brute in human form outraged D. Smithson's little infant daughter, not 2 years old until next August. The brute's name was John Jones. . . . It will be known in the course of time that all such crimes as these always meet justice at once, by hanging to the first limb available. Monroe County is ashamed to realize that such a demon had an existence within her borders."[1]

Another example is provided by a white mob's murder of Reeves Smith in October 1886 for allegedly attempting to rape a well-respected white woman in DeSoto Parish, Louisiana. Smith had been arrested by the sheriff, bound over for trial after a preliminary hearing, and was being held in the local jail. An estimated crowd of eighty of the "best people in the parish" rode into town, disassembled Smith's jail cell, and hung him from a shade tree in front of B. F. Jenkin's store. The *De Soto Democrat* observed, "While we deplore the necessity for mob law, we must commend it in this instance, for if the accused had been convicted of an 'attempt at rape,' the penalty would only have been two years in the Penitentiary, which is worse than farce. . . . the action of the mob is approved by the best people in the parish. As we have said before, 'the will of the people is the law of the land,' and all such monsters should be disposed of in a summary manner."[2]

In some situations, especially if the victim was not a social outcast or had been snatched from the hands of the formal justice system, newspapers would lament the unfortunate event.[3] But even then the press was often reluctant to fully exonerate black victims or enthusiastically condemn members of the white mob. Editorials about lynching, or the perennial "Negro Problem," also painted a picture of mob violence as a necessary evil when black offenders violated the sensibilities of southern white society. To judge from the southern press, lynchings as popular justice served an important purpose for maintaining control over the African-American population, which had become increasingly problematic throughout the late nineteenth century.[4]

At its simplest, popular justice really means nothing more than ordinary people punishing society's deviants outside the bounds of the established legal order. But somehow the expression carries more respectability than appropriate synonyms such as "vigilantism" or "mob rule." The difference, no doubt, lies in the word *justice,* which implies that a law was broken, that the perpetrator was identified, and that the offender did deserve to be punished. These are strong assumptions to make in the case of lynching. Generally, there was woefully little proof that lynch victims actually committed the offenses for which they were killed, or that most mobs were more than mildly concerned with systematically establishing guilt or meting out truly proportionate punishment. Nonetheless, it is likely that the members of mobs firmly believed that their grisly behavior was an exercise in justice and thus served the larger social good.

Two, probably related, factors are useful for explaining this conviction. First, the collapse of slavery required a new method of exercising social control over African-Americans. Second, popular images of blacks during the late nineteenth and early twentieth centuries portrayed a criminally inclined, mentally inferior, morally deprived, and predatory population.[5] As the postbellum South attempted to fashion new ways to punish black law violators and come to grips with what it considered the atavistic population in its midst, all strategies for survival were considered legitimate, including citizen participation. Many rationalized that extraordinary times required extraordinary measures.

Before emancipation, southern society concentrated immense power in the hands of slave owners. They were primarily responsible for controlling the behavior of their slaves and for punishing them when they committed crimes or violated informal behavioral rules. Although punishment was sometimes harsh and inhumane, owners rarely executed slaves, who constituted a sizable percentage of their wealth. The principles of rational economic behavior dictated that at least some restraint be exercised in the physical abuse of valuable property.

This pecuniary protection for blacks evaporated along with the hopes and dreams of the Confederacy. After the war, the southern criminal justice system assumed responsibility for black offenders and white offenders alike. Quite swiftly, the racial composition of southern jails and prisons was transformed. Before the war, jail populations had been overwhelmingly white. After the war, they became disproportionately black.[6] Just as quickly, legal executions began to claim proportionately more African-Americans. Despite its clearly discriminatory treatment of blacks, many white southerners remained extremely skeptical of the formal justice system's ability to become the region's foremost agent of social control. Some viewed the system as slow and inefficient in apprehending, trying, convicting, and punishing black criminals, concerns sometimes expressed in the form of mob intervention.

Aggravating this lack of confidence was the way in which the image of blacks was transformed. Williamson has provided a fascinating account of the rise of "radical racism" during the later years of the nineteenth century and early years of the twentieth century. According to Williamson, the conservative paternalistic attitudes that prevailed during the slavery era were replaced by a more malignant image of blacks as a subhuman species incapable of absorbing the full measure of civilized society. According to the doctrine of radical racism, black behavior was driven by urges and instincts more characteristic of "lower" animals than of humans. These urges and instincts often resulted in criminal behavior or norm violations, as blacks pursued their sexual appetites or economic interests while disregarding the rules that society had established for such behavior. The image is vivid in the following excerpt from Bruce's *The Plantation Negro as a Freeman:*

> Their [black males'] disposition to perpetrate it [rape] has increased in spite of the quick and summary punishment that always follows . . . There is something strangely alluring and seductive to the negro in the appearance of a white woman; they are roused and stimulated by its foreignness to their experience

of sexual pleasures, and it moves them to gratify their lust at any cost and in spite of any obstacle. . . . Rape, indescribably beastly and loathsome always, is marked, in the instance of its perpetration by the negro, by a diabolical persistence and a malignant atrocity of detail that have no reflection in the whole extent of the natural history of the most bestial and ferocious animals.[7]

The very racial characteristics that presumably predisposed African-Americans to violate the rules of southern society also required that same society to resort to extraordinary measures to control the behavior of blacks. Many believed that black criminals simply could not be dealt with in the same way as white criminals. The special nature of the black population raised the stakes of social control even higher by heightening the concern that black offenders be punished. Thus, according to Williamson, "For Radicals, the 'Negro Problem' was how to control the blacks as they passed through bestiality and into extinction."[8] The lynch mob was one extreme technique for supplementing the efforts of the southern justice system to deal with this "problematic" population.

To reiterate a point made in chapter 3, we can suggest two general interests that might have translated the concerns over a criminally threatening black population and inadequate social control mechanisms into lynch mob activity. First, whites strove desperately to assure that specific black offenders were punished, especially those who had committed particularly heinous crimes or who had violated caste restrictions. This describes the "specific deterrence" function of lynching. Second, in many cases the white mob also sought to send a threatening message to the African-American community to reinforce "appropriate" rules of behavior. This was the "general deterrence" function of lynching.

These two different motivations for popular justice lynchings lead us to expect somewhat different relationships between the efficiency of the formal justice system and the frequency of lynching. To the extent that lynchings were exercises in popular justice, motivated by an interest in specific deterrence, we would expect lynching to be less common when and where the formal justice system was relatively efficient. If the courts were punishing black offenders apace, and with a level of certainty and severity acceptable to whites, then mobs could put away their ropes and guns. However, it is possible that formal justice mechanisms were not capable of accomplishing the same general deterrence purpose as lynchings, given the greater "expressive" potential of lynch mobs. If that were the case, the activity of white mobs likely persisted even when efficient, formal alternatives for the punishment of specific offenders were available.

Popular Justice and the Reasons for Lynching

As a first step toward evaluating the popular justice explanation for lynchings, we return to the reported reasons for black lynchings that occurred between 1882 and 1930. These reasons are probably incapable of revealing the mobs' intentions to achieve general deterrence among the black population as a whole. Without additional information, such as the extent of torture or mutilation of the victim, those intentions can only be inferred. However, the reported reasons for lynching may prove useful for describing the types of offenders that were specifically deterred from repeating their "offensive" behavior. If the dominant reasons for lynching were for offenses that, in all probability, would also have been punished by the formal criminal justice system, then the need for lynching to assure specific deterrence is questionable. On the other hand, if the bulk of lynchings were sparked by behavior that violated uncodified caste rules of conduct, and therefore were unlikely to be adequately punished by the formal justice system, then the specific deterrent explanation cannot be rejected.[9]

Virtually all types of norm violations by southern African-Americans were potentially punishable within the formal criminal justice system. Thus, the argument could be made that there was never a real need for popular justice lynchings to achieve specific deterrence. This assumes, however, that the severity of the punishment handed down by the formal justice system would have satisfied the white community's appetite for appropriate vengeance. To circumvent this problem, we shall adopt a conservative approach in examining reported reasons for lynching by distinguishing between those that may be considered capital offenses and all others. We consider capital offenses—murder, rape, and rape-murder—to be those that carried a reasonably high probability of execution had the lynch victim been processed through the formal justice system rather than dispatched informally by mobs. Most people executed legally during this era had been convicted of these crimes. Noncapital offenses are all other reported reasons and have been collapsed into the following categories: other personal crimes, property crimes, other reasons, and unknown reasons. The distinction between capital and noncapital reasons seems appropriate given the many basic similarities between legal executions and lynchings as extreme forms of social control.

The reported reasons for lynching (Table 2-5) have been regrouped according to this classification scheme and are reported in Table 4-1. Once again, we maintain the Deep South–Border South distinction despite the trivial differences between the reasons for lynching reported in the two subregions. The evidence in Table 4-1 demonstrates very clearly that the majority of black lynch victims—more than two-thirds—were accused of crimes that were frequently punished by legal execution. Although they did occur, lynchings for relatively trivial reasons (e.g., speaking disrespectfully to whites) constituted only a small minority of all instances of mob violence.

The evidence would suggest that in the majority of cases mobs really had no legitimate concern about the potential punishment of black offenders. If, indeed, the lynch victim had been guilty of the capital crime, the mob could simply have turned the victim over to the authorities for processing through the formal justice system. Given the discriminatory practices of the southern justice system, there can be

Table 4-1. Justifications for Lynching of Southern Blacks by White Mobs: Capital versus Noncapital Offenses, by Region

Alleged Offenses	All South (%)	Deep South[a] (%)	Border South[b] (%)
Capital Offenses			
Sexual assault	29.2	28.7	30.2
Murder	37.3	38.7	34.3
Rape and murder	1.9	1.3	3.1
Subtotal	68.4	68.7	67.6
Noncapital Offenses			
Other personal offenses[c]	14.2	13.3	16.1
Against property[d]	8.3	9.2	6.3
Other[e]	6.0	5.7	6.9
Unknown	3.2	3.2	3.1
Subtotal	31.7	31.4	32.4
Total	100.1	100.1	100.0
Number of black victims	2,314	1,573	741

a. Alabama, Georgia, Louisiana, Mississippi, and South Carolina.
b. Arkansas, Florida, Kentucky, North Carolina, and Tennessee.
c. Nonsexual assaults, miscegenation, and other sexual norm violations.
d. Theft, robbery, and arson.
e. Incendiarism, race prejudice, and miscellaneous.

little doubt that blacks accused of murder and rape would have been dealt with harshly. The fact that these lynchings occurred anyway suggests one of two possibilities. First, it is possible that the white community in general, and mobs in particular, doubted the criminal justice system's ability to carry out its responsibilities. The feeling was that the formal mechanisms of social control did not guarantee punishment that was sufficiently certain or severe. This concern would also help to explain the many instances in which blacks were lynched after having been snatched from sheriffs or extracted from courtrooms. Even when the wheels of justice had begun to grind, the white community remained jittery over the prospects of an appropriate outcome. The second possibility is that mobs were less concerned about the punishment of particular individuals and more interested in sending a message to the black community at large. While the legal execution (or imprisonment) of a convicted offender also sent a message of sorts, it lacked the exclamation point of a lynching. As Phillips has noted,

> An execution is an awesome exhibition of the law's true power: its ability to take the most precious of commodities—life. The law responds to the most heinous events with a killing, but it does so with no excess of passion. Instead it responds with standard procedures, general rules, and some good measure of solemnity. A lynching, the quintessence of passion, stands in stark contrast. It is composed of a crowd gathering in the dark, high emotion mixed with hard liquor, and a frightening lust for blood vengeance.[10]

The motivation for sending a message to the African-American community may have been the particular offense for which the victim was lynched or it may have had deeper roots in the white community's perceptions of threat and competition. In either case, lynching became more than a pure exercise in popular justice.

White Victims of White Mobs and Black Victims of Black Mobs

For some southern lynchings, race or racial threat was unlikely to have been a major contributing factor. For example, white mobs lynched 284 white victims, and black, or integrated, mobs lynched 148 black victims during the era.[11] If, in fact, some lynchings were exercises in popular justice, then these incidents, essentially uncomplicated by racial tension and conflict, were the most likely to qualify. Although relatively rare when compared to white mob activities, which claimed 2,314 African-Americans during the same period, within-race incidents offer an interesting contrast with the most typical white-on-black violence.

If vigilante justice really played a role in mob violence, then it would likely have been more common during earlier eras when legal authority in the South was inchoate. In fact, that seems to have been truer of the same-race lynchings. Although only 47 percent of white mob lynchings of blacks occurred before 1900, fully 75 percent of white-on-white violence took place before the turn of the century, as did 68 percent of the black-on-black lynchings. Clearly, lynchings with a racial dimension were much more evenly distributed throughout the lynching era than were nonracial incidents and far more likely to extend into the modern period.

The same-race lynchings were also distributed somewhat differently across the southern landscape. Relatively few occurred in the eastern parts of the region, which had been settled the longest (Figure 4-1a, b). Indeed, a marked concentration of both types of within-race lynchings occurred either in the extreme southwest or in the border states of Kentucky, Tennessee, and Arkansas. Black mobs were very active in the Delta region of Mississippi and Arkansas but only scattered elsewhere throughout the South, even in the Black Belt areas of Georgia and Alabama.[12] In concert with their temporal distinctiveness, these geographic patterns are consistent with a higher concentration of same-race lynchings in more remote areas, possibly those where criminal justice agencies were formed less fully.

Finally, some intriguing differences emerge when we compare the reported reasons for same-race lynchings with those for inter-racial incidents (Table 4-2). The most common explanation that white mobs cited for lynching other whites was murder; almost 60 percent of white victims were accused of that crime. The sensational lynching of Leo M. Frank in 1915 for the murder of Mary Phagan and the mob killing of eleven Italians in New Orleans in 1891 are probably the best known examples of white-on-white mob violence, but the killing of Hal English was more typical in some ways.[13] English stood accused of brutally murdering his wife, and he had been placed in the Bakersville, North Carolina, jail for safe keeping. A mob of more than a hundred men rode into town early on the morning of Sunday, April 1, 1894, broke into the lockup, and spirited him away. A mile north of Bakersville, he was hung from an apple tree.[14]

Assaults, both sexual and nonsexual, were major factors in white-on-black lynchings (Table 4-1), but assaults were a relatively rare allegation in white-on-white lynchings, although not unheard of. Louis P. Mullens, a brakeman on the St. Louis, Avoyelles and Southwest-

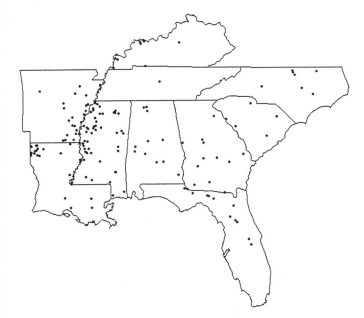

Figure 4-1a. Map of Black Victims of Black or Integrated Lynch Mobs.

Figure 4-1b. Map of White Victims of White Lynch Mobs.

ern Railway, had been accused of criminally assaulting a five-year-old girl in the summer of 1896.[15] While Mullens awaited trial in Bunkie, Louisiana, a mob overpowered the jailer, dragged Mullens from his cell, and hung him from a nearby tree.

Although it was even less common for them to do so, white mobs were not above murdering white victims for lesser violations of the normative order. In the winter of 1893 two Mormon preachers were seeking converts in Lewis County, Tennessee. Their proselytizing alarmed some of the local residents, and the Mormons were warned to leave the county. In mid-February the preachers were conducting

Table 4-2. Justifications by Region for Lynching of Black Victims by Black or Integrated Mobs and White Victims by White Mobs

	White Victims of White Mobs			Black Victims of Black or Integrated Mobs		
Alleged Offenses	All South (%)	Deep South[a] (%)	Border South[b] (%)	All South (%)	Deep South (%)	Border South (%)
Capital Offenses						
Sexual assault	8.5	8.1	8.7	25.7	32.0	19.2
Murder	59.5	51.2	65.8	46.0	44.0	48.0
Rape and murder	2.8	0.8	4.4	2.0	1.3	2.7
Subtotal	70.8	60.1	78.9	73.7	77.3	69.9
Noncapital Offenses						
Other personal offenses[c]	4.9	6.5	3.7	6.1	4.0	8.2
Against property[d]	10.6	17.1	5.6	8.1	6.7	9.6
Other[e]	9.9	10.6	9.3	10.8	12.0	9.6
Unknown	3.9	5.7	2.5	1.4	0.0	2.7
Subtotal	29.3	39.9	21.1	26.4	22.7	30.1
Total	100.1	100.0	100.0	100.1	100.0	100.0
Number of victims	284	123	161	148	75	73

a. Alabama, Georgia, Louisiana, Mississippi, and South Carolina.
b. Arkansas, Florida, Kentucky, North Carolina, and Tennessee.
c. Nonsexual assaults, miscegnation, and other sexual norm violations.
d. Theft, robbery, and arson.
e. Incendiarism, race prejudice, and miscellaneous.

a meeting in a friendly house when a gang of masked men rode up, shot through a window, and killed both men instantly.[16]

A second distinctive pattern of reported justifications for lynchings is found for African-American victims of black or integrated mobs (Table 4-2, last three columns). Once again, murder was the most frequent reason given for blacks lynching other blacks; 46 percent of the victims were accused of that crime. The case of Joe Scott is illustrative. Scott and another black, Sam Houston, were working at a logging camp in Bibb County, Alabama, in the summer of 1904. On June 23, Houston and Scott became entangled in a confrontation concerning Houston's wife. Armed with a shotgun, Houston attacked Scott, but his aim was faulty. Joe Scott then drew his pistol and shot Houston to death. Seeking revenge, friends and relatives of Sam Houston lynched Joe Scott by "riddling him with bullets."[17]

The second most common reason for black-on-black lynchings was sexual assault, which accounted for a surprisingly high percentage of black-on-black lynchings, 25.7 percent. In fact, a somewhat larger percentage of black victims of black mobs (32 percent, Table 4-2, fifth column) were lynched in the Deep South for sexual assaults than were black victims of white mobs (28.7 percent, Table 4-1, second column). The killing of Henry Abrams in 1897 is representative. Abrams, of Montgomery County, Alabama, was accused of incest with his two daughters. On November 25, 1897, as the local constable was escorting Abrams to jail, they were overtaken by a party of three armed black men. Ten miles from the city of Montgomery, the three men forced Henry Abrams into the woods and shot him to death.[18]

There are two potential but sharply contrasting explanations for this intriguing pattern of lynchings for sexual assaults. First, contemporary observers might have claimed that this evidence of black-on-black violence exonerates the popular justice explanation of inter-racial lynchings. That is, the problem of sexual attacks by African-American males may have been so serious that the black community itself felt compelled to resort to extralegal violence. Is it any wonder then that whites did the same? a lynching apologist might ask. On the other hand, critics of the southern caste system might argue that the black community had no alternative but to assume responsibility for punishing black rapists. Surely authorities were unlikely to treat any sexual assaults on black women seriously. For example, between 1882 and 1930, the state of Georgia legally executed forty-four black men charged with rape; seven were accused of raping a black woman. Over the same period, Georgia executed only one white man for rape, and he was convicted of assaulting a white woman.

As with some white-on-white lynchings, blacks were occasionally victimized by their own race for relatively minor offenses. According to the Little Rock *Arkansas Gazette,* Ernest Williams of Parksdale had made himself very unpopular in his community because of his irreverent use of obscene language.[19] A locally organized group of indignant black women took matters into their own hands and hanged Williams from a telephone pole on June 19, 1908, for his offensive behavior. Another example of extreme action is provided by an incident in Pine Level, North Carolina, in early January 1908. Portraying himself as an "advance agent," an unknown black man peddled tickets in the black community for a "big stage show." Eager ticket holders arrived for the anticipated event only to discover that the big stage show was a one-man performance by the self-styled advance agent himself. Apparently the hoax was not well-received in Pine Level; later that night, a mob of masked black men entered the agent's boardinghouse and carted him off. His body was found on the nearby railroad tracks at daylight.[20] It would appear, however, that these kinds of incidents of mob violence for seemingly minor infractions of the normative code were relatively rare in both black-on-black and in white-on-white lynchings.

In general, it appears that same-race lynchings differed in important respects from the inter-racial violence that is the focus of this book. Their distribution over time and across space, as well as their justification by the mobs, seems somewhat more consistent with a popular justice explanation. Still, this is a tentative conclusion based on relatively meager evidence. Whatever the underlying explanations for black-on-black lynchings, however, it is important to keep the frequency of such violence in perspective. For every African-American lynched by other African-Americans, sixteen others were lynched by whites.

Varieties of Lethal Social Control

It is impossible to determine definitively what motivated lynch mobs a century ago. The best that can be done is to identify potential explanations and test them against the surviving evidence of mob behavior. Those that fail to receive support must be abandoned, and alternative explanations sought. In the case of the popular justice explanation, a useful basis for such an evaluation is available. The explanation's credibility can be evaluated by examining concomitant trends in two forms of lethal social control: legal executions and ex-tra-legal lynchings. There would seem to be a good deal of similarity between the two. Both, for instance, exact the ultimate penalty—death. And the majority of offenses involved were the same—primarily murder and rape. Furthermore, both forms were often equated in the minds of white southerners, as indicated by those cases in which mobs abducted victims after it became clear that the formal justice system would fail to execute them.

What would the popular justice hypothesis predict for the relation-ship between lynchings and executions over time? Perhaps the most obvious expectation from the popular justice model is for the two forms of lethal sanctioning to be associated negatively. That is, when the formal justice system was relatively inactive in punishing capital crimes, mob behavior should have been more frequent. As formal punishment intensified, the need for informal sanctions should have weakened. This form of association between different varieties of so-cial control has become known as the "substitution model." In essence, it assumes that a fixed amount of punishment is "required" given the level of deviant behavior or rule breaking. When formal mechanisms are sufficient to provide the required punishment, supplementary methods are not required.[21]

James Cutler, a professor of political economy at the University of Michigan in the early 1900s, and one of the first social scientists to study lynching behavior, was among those who subscribed to the substitution model of social control. In addition to believing that blacks existed on a different moral and ethical plane than did whites, Cutler also recognized that formal executions satisfied a strong desire for vengeance among southern whites. He observed, "It is not too much to say that to abolish capital punishment in this country is likely to provoke lynchings. Whenever unusually brutal and atrocious crimes are committed, particularly if they cross racial lines, nothing less than the death penalty will satisfy the general sense of justice that is to be found in the average American community."[22] The substitution mod-el would seem especially applicable where specific deterrence was the primary motivation for popular justice lynchings.

To the extent that popular justice lynchings were motivated by an interest in general deterrence, however, we might anticipate a posi-tive, rather than negative, association between executions and lynch-ings over time. This expectation is based on the key differences in the character of legal executions and extra-legal lynchings. The number of incidents in which victims were severely tortured and mutilated, or in which the corpses of victims were displayed prominently in the

African-American community, illustrate that lynchings had the potential to be considerably more "expressive" than executions. Even if the formal justice system could have executed every black person who committed a capital offense (thereby achieving 100 percent effective specific deterrence), it would have done so in a comparatively facile and unexpressive manner. A residual need may have existed for the white community to continue lynching in order to teach the black community a lesson. This would especially have been the case had the white community perceived that the behavior of blacks seriously threatened the southern social order. Naturally, legal executions should also have been relatively more common in such an environment. The reinforcement model of social control depicts lynchings and executions as complementary methods of punishment rather than as alternatives.[23]

By describing the relationship, if any, between legal executions and lynchings during the period from 1882 to 1930, we should be able to assess the support for these models of social control. If years during which large numbers of blacks were marched to the gallows also tended to have relatively few lynchings, then the substitution model will seem to apply. On the other hand, if intensive lynching and execution activity tended to occur simultaneously, then the reinforcement model is more plausible. If lynchings and executions were unrelated throughout the era, then we must conclude that formal and informal methods of lethal punishment operated independently and look to alternative explanations for the observed temporal variation.

Black Executions in the South

Southern blacks visited the executioner in truly prodigious numbers during the "lynching era." Between 1882 and 1930, 1,977 African-Americans were legally executed in the ten southern states included in our study, an average of forty executions a year. During this same period, only 451 whites were legally executed. Clearly, there was a significant racial imbalance in southern lethal sanctioning; 81 percent of the legal executions involved a black offender, and 87 percent of the victims of white mobs were black. When combined, the two forms of lethal sanctioning claimed the lives of 4,291 blacks during the forty-nine-year period.[24] Put differently, an African-American was put to death somewhere in the South on the average of every four days.

Like lynchings, however, southern executions were not distributed evenly over time or across space. Two-thirds of all black executions between 1882 and 1930 took place in the states of the Deep South

Table 4-3. Black Lynching Victims and Black Legal Executions
by State, 1882–1930

State	Lynching Victims	Executions
Deep South		
Mississippi	462	173
Georgia	423	407
Louisiana	283	247
Alabama	262	264
South Carolina	143	217
Border South		
Florida	212	106
Tennessee	174	99
Arkansas	162	169
Kentucky	118	100
North Carolina	75	195

(Table 4-3). Georgia, where 407 blacks were legally put to death, was
by far the most active. Mississippi, with the largest number of lynchings during the period, ranked last. Although executions were carried
out at a somewhat slower pace in the Border States, North Carolina
and Arkansas still claimed a substantial number of victims. Like Mississippi, North Carolina presents an intriguing (although reversed)
pattern of lethal sanctioning. It had the fewest lynchings during the
period but the most active record of capital punishment among Border States. Could the patterns in Mississippi and North Carolina indicate that executions and lynchings truly were substitutable forms
of lethal sanctioning?

Executions also varied in intensity throughout the period, although within a much narrower range than lynchings (Figure 4-2).[25]
African-American executions peaked shortly after the turn of the
century but declined steadily, eventually bottoming out near the end
of World War I. Following the war, however, executions once again
rebounded modestly. Throughout the forty-nine years, it was unusual
for the number of executions to exceed sixty a year, and rarely did
the total dip below twenty.[26] In contrast, much wider swings occurred
with lynchings, which claimed more than ninety victims a year in
the early 1890s and fewer than fifteen a year in the late twenties
(chapter 2).

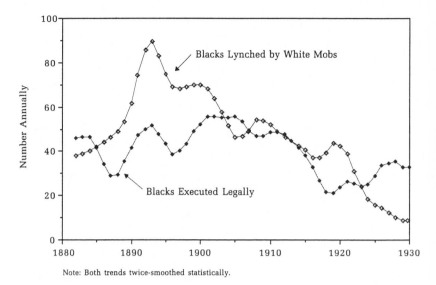

Note: Both trends twice-smoothed statistically.

Figure 4-2. Trends in Black Victims of Lynchings and Black Legal Executions, 1882–1930.

General Patterns of Covariation: Lynchings and Executions

We can obtain our first evidence with which to evaluate the substitution and reinforcement models of social control by examining, together, the temporal patterns of black lynchings and executions (Figure 4-3). The smoothed curves seem to tell a somewhat mixed story. During some periods lynchings and executions appear to have tracked each other closely. For example, during the early 1890s both lynchings and executions experienced rather impressive surges. Similarly, both forms of lethal sanctioning declined modestly after about 1910. On the other hand, during some periods, most notably during the 1920s, lynchings and executions moved in opposite directions. As a summary measure of the relationship between the two raw data trends during this forty-nine-year period, we may use the Pearsonian Correlation Coefficient. The correlation of $r = +0.44$ indicates a positive association between lynchings and executions, suggesting modest initial support for the reinforcement model of social control.[27]

However, it is possible that the evidence presented in Figure 4-3 is somewhat contaminated by the inclusion of lynchings for noncapital offenses that blacks committed. Despite Cutler's argument, lynchings were not totally reserved for "unusually brutal and atrocious crimes."

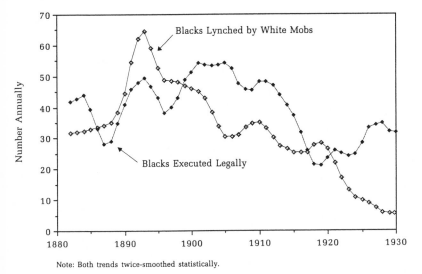

Note: Both trends twice-smoothed statistically.

Figure 4-3. Trends in Black Victims of Lynchings and Black Legal Executions for Capital Crimes Only, 1882–1930.

Although they constituted a definite minority of all lynchings, some victims were dispatched for even the most trivial violations of behavioral norms. Legal executions really cannot be considered to have been a substitute form of punishment for such trivial breaches of conduct as "insulting a white woman," "grave robbing," or "running a bordello" (Table 2-4). Indeed, fully 97.5 percent of the victims of all 1,977 legal executions represented by Figure 4-2 had been convicted of murder or rape.[28]

When the trends in executions and lynchings are confined to those carried out for murder or rape, we obtain the patterns in Figure 4-3. Because the overwhelming majority of executions were for murder or rape, the execution curve is virtually identical to that observed in Figure 4-2. The major difference is for the trend in lynching which, of course, is reduced somewhat in level because of the removal of lynchings for noncapital offenses. As in Figure 4-2, we can observe certain periods lynchings and executions moved in sync (e.g., the early 1890s) and periods during which the two trends diverged (e.g., the 1920s). Once again, however, the correlation ($r = +0.44$) between the two trends suggests a modest positive association between lynchings and executions during the period, supportive of the reinforcement model of social control.[29]

Lynchings and Executions: A Time-Series Analysis

The general trends in lynching and executions are suggestive of the association between the two forms of lethal punishment during the era (Figures 4-2, 4-3). They cannot be considered definitive evidence because of the complexities involved when attempting to assess the "true" relationship between simultaneous time trends for two phenomena. Because a more complete treatment of these "complexities" is available elsewhere, a brief, nontechnical discussion will suffice.[30] First, it is possible for two variables (e.g., lynching and executions) to follow similar time trends while being causally independent. There may be other explanations for why the two series follow the same trend over time. As a first step toward avoiding premature conclusions of causation from two time series we must "detrend" the series by "differencing."[31] Second, it is possible for the observed level of a variable at one point to be influenced by its value at an earlier point. This is a problem of serial correlation, which also can be dealt with statistically. Third, other social forces may have experienced temporal swings during this period and be partially responsible for the observed trend in lynching and also related to the level of executions. By introducing those social forces into the analysis explicitly, it is possible to take their influence into consideration.

With these issues in mind, we have conducted a more sophisticated statistical analysis to describe the relationship between lynchings and executions between 1882 and 1930. In technical terms, we have estimated a time-series regression model that regresses the number of black lynchings in any given year (t) on the number of black executions that occurred during the previous year ($t - 1$). We have introduced a one-year lag between executions and lynchings in the belief that any response by southern whites to perceived weaknesses in the formal justice system would have been based on events during the recent past. In addition to the number of executions, we have included two control variables as predictors of black lynchings. First, the relative size and absolute size of the black population were included in light of the expectations of social conflict theory, which predicts greater racial oppression in the face of a larger minority. Second, the number of white lynchings was included to account for social forces that may have promoted mob violence but were independent of race. The formal analytical model is specified as:

$$\text{Lynchings}_t = \beta_{\text{exec}}(\text{Black Executions}_{t-1}) + \beta_{\text{wht}}(\text{White Lynchings}_t)$$
$$+ \beta_{\text{\%blk}}(\text{Percent Population Black}_t)$$
$$+ \beta_{\text{blk}}(\text{Size of Black Population}_t) + \varepsilon_t$$

where lynchings$_t$ is the number of black victims of white lynch mobs in year t, β_ks are parameters indicating the effects of the four predictor variables on the number of black victims, and ε_t is a disturbance term to account for extraneous variables excluded from the model.[32]

If the effect coefficient for the number of black executions (β_{exec}) is negative in sign and statistically significant, then the analysis supports the substitution model of lethal social control. If the coefficient is positive in sign and statistically significant, then the findings support the reinforcement model. A statistically nonsignificant coefficient for the number of executions suggests that the two forms of lethal sanctioning moved independently of one another during the forty-nine-year period.

The findings from the time-series analysis imply that executions had a negative effect on black lynchings throughout the period (Table 4-4).[33] Our model suggests that it would take an increase of eleven black executions in year ($t - 1$) to reduce the number of lynching victims by about one ($[-0.096][11] = -1.06$) in the following year (t). Because of this small effect and the magnitude of its t-ratio (only -0.63), we conclude that the effect of executions on all black lynchings throughout the period is negligible.[34]

Virtually the same conclusion must be reached concerning lynchings and executions for only the most serious of capital crimes (columns 3 and 4). Once more, the overall effect of executions falls far short of both sociological and statistical significance.[35] Thus, we cannot infer empirical support for either the substitution or reinforcement

Table 4-4. Time-Series Regression of Number of Black Lynching Victims on Black Executions, White Lynchings, and Composition of Population and Black Population Size[a]

Predictor Variable	Black Lynchings for All Offenses		Black Lynchings for Capital Offenses	
	Coefficient	t-ratio	Coefficient	t-ratio
Number of black executions$_{t-1}$	−0.096	−0.63	0.020	0.18
Number of white lynchings$_t$	0.521	1.47	0.149	0.55
Percent population black$_t$	9.207	1.29	5.344	1.01
Size of black population$_t$ (1,000s)	0.019	0.77	0.008	0.40
Moving-average coefficient	−0.271	−1.81	−0.239	−1.57
Durbin-Watson statistic	1.86		1.89	

a. First-order moving-average models; all variables differenced once; $N = 47$.

models from the findings presented in Table 4-4. Other coefficients in Table 4-4 indicate that white and black lynchings followed similar trends and were more frequent when the African-American population was relatively larger. In both cases, however, the strength of these associations was considerably weaker for lynchings for capital offenses only. And in both equations none of the variables has a statistically significant effect on black lynchings.

An important limitation to the findings from this time-series analysis, however, is that they implicitly assume that the same processes were operating throughout the forty-nine-year period. Although that may be an accurate assumption, it is also possible that the overall patterns that the coefficients in Table 4-4 describe are masking a variety of different episodes within shorter intervals during the longer time series; in this sense, traditional time-series analysis is "ahistorical," to use Isaac and Griffin's term.[36]

With no clear theoretical basis for specifying when the nature of the relationship between executions and lynchings should have shifted, we have simply divided the entire series into thirty-three shorter, overlapping series of fifteen years each. For example, the first series runs from 1884 to 1898, the second from 1885 to 1899, and so on. For each fifteen-year period we have estimated separate time-series equations of the kind reported in Table 4-4. The advantage of this "moving" time-series technique is that it allows the emergence of historically meaningful variation in the effect of executions on lynchings.[37] For each of these thirty-three periods, we estimated the coefficient that describes the effect of executions at time $(t-1)$ on the number of lynchings at time (t), controlling on size of the black population, population composition, and frequency of white lynchings. In Figure 4-4 we have plotted these execution coefficients from the thirty-three moving time-series regressions.

Allowing for historical variation in the effect of executions on lynching yields some interesting information. Most notably, for periods starting after 1894, the effect of black executions is consistently negative, although only in two periods, 1897–1911 and 1908–22, did this effect attain statistical significance. Nevertheless, we believe that the consistent pattern of negative effects of executions is intriguing. Although these findings must not be overinterpreted, they suggest that during the years between 1894 and 1930, there may have been a very modest substitution effect and that years of frequent executions of blacks were followed by years of reduced lynchings.

When a similar analysis is conducted for lynchings and executions carried out for capital offenses (rape and murder), a less interpretable pattern of coefficients is obtained (Figure 4-5). Unlike the findings in

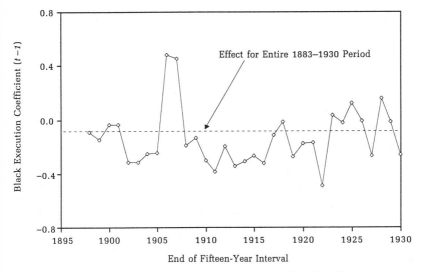

Note: Blacks lynched for all reasons. The x-axis represents the end year of the fifteen-year interval (e.g., 1900 for the 1886–1900 interval, etc.).

Figure 4-4. Effect of Black Executions on Black Lynchings by Time Period.

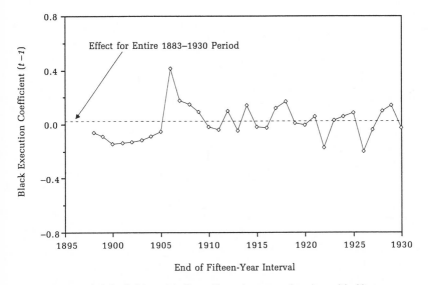

Note: Blacks lynched for capital offenses. The x-axis represents the end year of the fifteen-year interval (e.g., 1900 for the 1886–1900 interval, etc.).

Figure 4-5. Effect of Black Executions for Capital Crimes on Black Lynchings for Capital Offenses by Time Period.

Figure 4-4, there is no series of consecutive time intervals during which the effect of executions on lynchings was consistently positive or negative and sizable. When considered in conjunction with the findings in Figure 4-4, these results would suggest that any depressing effect of executions on lynchings shortly before and after the turn of the century must have been due to a negative effect of executions on lynchings for less serious offenses.

In summary, the time-series analyses indicate a meager effect of executions on black lynchings throughout the era. When considering the entire forty-nine-year period, we observe virtually no effect of the number of executions in one year on the intensity of lynching during the next year. Although the moving-regression analysis provides an intriguing hint of a substitution process operating for all lynchings and executions around the turn of the century, the effects are really too weak to warrant much emphasis or speculation. Thus, the time-series findings are incapable of providing support for either the substitution or reinforcement models of lethal social control.

Lynchings and Executions: A Cross-Sectional Analysis

An alternative approach to evaluating the popular justice model involves spatial covariation between the two forms of lethal punishment. It is possible that the time-series analysis—aggregated over the entire South—is not sensitive enough to discern a trade-off between formal and informal punishment that may have been occurring within individual communities. In light of this possibility, we turn now to an analysis of the frequency of legal executions and black lynchings within southern counties between 1882 and 1930 (chapter 2).

The basic question addressed by the following analysis concerns whether local areas that executed a larger number of blacks experienced fewer lynchings. The popular justice model would suggest that they did because a more vigorous imposition of the death penalty within a county would indicate a reduced need for mob intervention in the punishment process. Although our primary focus is the roughly eight hundred counties in these ten southern states, we also examine the relationship between executions and lynchings during five separate periods: 1882–89, 1890–99, 1900–1909, 1910–19, and 1920–29.[38] This separation allows the relationship between executions and lynchings to fluctuate, thereby increasing the chances of discerning periods when the two may have been related cross-sectionally.

In order to investigate these associations, it is first necessary to specify a formal model linking the number of African-American victims of white lynch mobs to the explanatory factors discussed earlier. Because our data consist of counts of black victims in each county, the most suitable statistical approach is to model the number of victims as a Poisson process.[39] Specifically, if Y_i is the number of black lynch victims in the ith county during a particular period of t years, the probability that the ith county would experience exactly y_i victims is given by:

$$\text{Prob } (Y_i = y_i) = e^{-\lambda_i} \frac{\lambda_i^{y_i}}{y_i!} \qquad y_i = 0, 1, 2, \ldots n$$

which has a single distribution parameter λ_i that governs how many black lynch victims the ith county would experience in t years; λ_i can be interpreted as the intensity of antiblack violence within the ith county. Under this specification, spatial variation in the number of black victims is due to intercounty differences in λ.

This spatial variation in the λs—and hence variation in the number of black victims—is due to differences in the size of the county's black population, racial composition of the population, number of white lynchings, the county's historical proneness to inter-racial violence, and, of particular interest, the number of black legal executions.[40] Given these considerations, we specify that the Poisson parameter λs are linked to a function of the predictor variables and a disturbance term,[41]

$$\begin{aligned}
\text{Log } \lambda_i = {} & \beta_0 + \beta_{exec}(\text{Black Executions}_i) + \beta_{wht}(\text{White Lynchings}_i) \\
& + \beta_{\%blk}(\text{Percent Population Black}_i) \\
& + \beta_{\%blk2}(\text{Percent Population Black}_i^2) \\
& + \beta_{blk}(\text{Log Size of Black Population}_i) \\
& + \beta_{prone}(\text{Proneness to Antiblack Violence}_i) + \varepsilon_i
\end{aligned}$$

where λ_i is the ith county's Poisson parameter, β_0 is a constant, β_ks are parameters indicating the effect of the predictor variables, and ε is a random disturbance assumed to have a Gamma distribution.

Our focus will be on the coefficient β_{exec}, which indicates whether the frequencies of legal executions and black lynchings within counties were related—net of the other variables—and whether there is cross-sectional support for the substitution or reinforcement models. As in the time-series analyses, we also include controls for the number of white lynchings and the racial composition of the county. In this case, however, we allow for the relative size of the black population to have a nonlinear effect on lynchings within counties by including both linear (Percent Black) and quadratic (Percent Black[2]) terms.[42]

The second row in Table 4-5 shows a reasonably consistent pattern of relationship between legal executions and black lynchings across the five decades.[43] In four of the periods (1890–99, 1900–1909, 1910–19, and 1920–29), there was no statistically strong relationship be-

Table 4-5. Poisson-Gamma Regression of Number of Black Lynching
Victims of White Mobs on Black Executions, Racial Composition, and
Related Variables for Counties in the South, by Decade

Predictor Variable[a]	1882–89[b]	1890–99	1900–1909	1910–19	1920–29
Constant	−2.360	−1.409	−2.193	−2.858	−3.745
	(−7.37)	(−6.93)	(−8.86)	(−10.43)	(−10.48)
Number of black					
executions	−0.216	0.046	0.068	0.034	0.016
	(−2.27)	(0.99)	(1.71)	(0.54)	(0.23)
Percent population					
black	0.044	0.039	0.056	0.056	0.089
	(2.31)	(2.92)	(3.60)	(3.47)	(4.17)
Percent population					
black^2	−0.0005	−0.0004	−0.0005	−0.0004	−0.0009
	(−2.58)	(−2.94)	(−3.00)	(−2.58)	(−3.95)
Log size of black					
population (1,000s)	0.544	0.266	0.126	0.174	0.139
	(4.04)	(2.84)	(1.16)	(1.52)	(1.02)
Number of white					
lynchings	0.451	0.150	0.623	0.827	0.402
	(3.34)	(2.39)	(2.30)	(2.15)	(0.99)
Proneness to anti-					
black violence	—	0.146	0.093	0.104	0.073
		(3.18)	(3.25)	(5.03)	(3.25)
Number of					
observations	786	804	809	830	858

a. Percent population black and the size of the black population measured in 1880,
   1890, 1900, 1910, and 1920. White lynchings refer to the total number in each period: 1882–89, 1890–99, 1900–1909, 1910–19, 1920–29. Proneness is the cumulative
   number of black victims of white mobs from 1882 to the beginning of the period.
b. Asymptotic t-ratios in parentheses.

tween the two forms of punishment, although the direction of the
association in all four cases was positive rather than negative as predicted by the popular justice model. During the remaining period,
1880–89, executions and lynchings were significantly related negatively, as would be expected with the popular justice hypothesis.
However, because we have no data on lynchings before 1882, we cannot include the measure of antiblack violence proneness in the equation for the 1880–89 period. This raises the possibility that, if this

measure could have been included, the coefficient of black executions might have been reduced to insignificance. In any regard, it is quite clear that the evidence in Table 4-5 does not lend broad support to the popular justice model.

Many of the other relationships presented in Table 4-5 are reasonably consistent across decades and therefore worthy of brief comment. First, the intensity of mob violence against whites is strongly related to the number of black lynchings within counties.[44] It appears that some counties were simply more prone to generalized mob violence than others and that blacks and whites alike were victimized in such settings; of course, the level of mob violence against blacks was much greater. Second, the county's historical proneness toward antiblack violence is a consistently important predictor of current patterns of mob violence. Third, the relative size of the black population for counties has a significant curvilinear effect on lynchings during all decades. A positive relationship exists between percent black in the county and black lynchings, but it grows weaker as black concentration increases. In general, counties where more than 54 percent of the population was black experienced fewer lynchings than did counties with relatively smaller black populations.[45] This type of relationship is consistent with Blalock's economic threat hypothesis (chapter 3) and suggestive of the operation of underlying economic processes not included in this analysis. The issue will be explored more thoroughly in chapter 5.

Empirically then, we can discern little solid basis for the popular justice model of African-American lynchings. Neither the time-series analysis nor the cross-sectional approach suggest that a more vigorous implementation of the death penalty reduced the level of mob violence. Neither, however, is there strong evidence that formal and informal lethal sanctioning were driven by the same social forces. Rather, in light of the evidence, we must conclude that executions and lynchings were largely independent forms of social control in the South. Of course, it is still possible that the two types of lethal punishment were connected in the minds of the members of some southern lynch mobs.

Conclusions

When reading the accounts of specific lynching incidents, there can be little doubt that many mobs acted in response to some offense (real or perceived) that African-Americans committed. Thus, in the strictest sense, those lynchings might be considered episodes of popular justice in which ordinary citizens decided to assume the responsibilities of all legal agents in the formal criminal justice system—the sheriff, the prosecutor, the judge, the jury, and the executioner—in order to impose punishment. The mob's decision to do so and the necessity for it to do so are two very different issues, however.

It seems from the evidence presented in this chapter that the intensity of lynching bore little systematic relationship to the legitimate activities of the formal justice system, at least to the extent that the number of legal executions of blacks taps those activities. Lynchings were neither particularly common nor especially rare when or where the state executioner was busy. In fact, lynch mobs appear to have been impressively insensitive to the vigor with which the state imposed the death penalty on blacks.

A couple of possibilities exist for interpreting this insensitivity. First, perhaps the white community was too poorly informed about state-sanctioned executions to know with what frequency black offenders were being executed. Thus, perceptions of the efficiency of the formal justice system may have been based on incomplete information. Although possible, this explanation seems somehow inadequate in light of the number of cases in which mobs lynched blacks following a jury's failure to convict or the imposition of a sentence it considered too lenient. In those cases at least, the white community seems to have followed quite closely the operation of the formal justice system. It is difficult to argue that whites were ignorant of the relative frequency of executions when we have good evidence to suggest that they were all too aware of cases in which the death penalty was not forthcoming. A more reasonable conclusion is that lynch mobs went about their business with the realization that legal channels existed through which they could have operated, and, because they knew how willing those official channels were to impose discriminatory punishment, whites also realized that blacks could be marched to their deaths at the hands of the state executioner. As Raper observed, "Lynchers and their apologists cannot justify their actions on the grounds that unless they dispose of accused Negroes the courts will likely dismiss their cases or treat them lightly. In should be observed, too, that any group which can execute a lynching could place the accused in the custody of peace officers."[46]

The second possible interpretation builds on the assumption that white mobs knew that they had alternatives, that the formal justice system would have been all too eager (in most cases) to satisfy their appetites for vengeance. Instead, they chose to circumvent the formal mechanisms for punishment in order to accomplish a variety of useful purposes. They could terrorize specific blacks under the pretext of punishment for criminal activity when in fact they had little or no proof of such activity. In addition, they could exploit the lynching's potential to engender generalized terror in the African-American community. By conducting the lynching in a circuslike atmosphere, by subjecting the victim to torture and mutilation, and by prominently displaying the corpse, preferably near the black community, they could convey a clear message to the general black population. That message was not necessarily restricted to a simple admonition to obey the law. Rather, it was capable of achieving far broader objectives. Through their actions, white mobs demonstrated the ability to run roughshod over the rights, lives, and property of the black community. Mob action etched clearly in the minds of blacks their relative standing in the southern social hierarchy. The message was given additional emphasis by the notorious reluctance of legal authorities to arrest, prosecute, and punish members of lynch mobs despite the fact that such people were often easily identifiable. Finally, it gave the white community the ability to respond to a wide variety of noncriminal threats from the black community and to do so with dispatch and a veneer of respectability. How could any self-respecting white southerner object to periodic mob violence as long as the myth was perpetuated that a weak and ineffective justice system required it, or at least made it inevitable?

Casting doubt on the viability of the popular justice explanation for lynching leaves a void that needs to be filled. If white mobs were not responding to weaknesses in the formal justice system, then why did they lynch blacks? As we entertain possible answers to this question we must keep in mind that criminal activity by blacks is not an explanation. As Raper noted, even if a clear criminal offense had been committed, the mob had choices. It could either impose its own punishment or allow the formal system of justice to run its course. Thus, even in the aftermath of a particularly heinous crime, the occurrence of a lynching requires explanation. Why the rope and faggot rather than the courtroom? To answer this question, it is necessary to turn first to the possibility that the frequency of black lynching was a product of the South's dependence on King Cotton. It was a dependency that had effects on the region's race and class relations.

NOTES

1. Memphis *Commercial Appeal,* April 15, 1896, 2.
2. The quotes are from an article appearing in the October 23 edition

of the *De Soto Democrat,* as reported by the New Orleans *Daily Picayune,* October 25, 1886, 8.

3. Brundage (1993) presents an interesting discussion of how the community's reaction to lynching varied by the characteristics of the victim, the nature of the mob, and the events leading up to the incident.

4. Not all newspapers were tolerant of mob violence; some actively condemned lynching and called for its eradication. After a lynching in Mississippi on one day and another in Georgia on the next, on May 18, 1919, the Atlanta *Constitution* editorialized: "Brutal business; barbaric business; dangerous business; intolerable business! And it is a type of business which must be stopped by the States which now permit its practice" (as quoted by Skaggs 1969, 326–27).

5. See Dixon (1907), Smith (1905), and Hoffman (1896).

6. See Ayers (1984) for a thoughtful discussion of this transition in the racial composition of the incarcerated southern population.

7. Quoted sympathetically by Hoffman (1896, 231).

8. Williamson (1984, 182).

9. When considering the reported reasons for lynching, it should be kept in mind that the reasons generally cannot be substantiated. The southern press rarely speculated about the guilt or innocence of lynch victims. Usually, guilt was taken for granted. For this discussion, we shall also assume the accuracy of the reported reasons.

10. Phillips (1987, 362).

11. A few whites were murdered for miscegenation or other prohibited liaisons with blacks of the opposite gender. Race clearly would have played an important part in their demise. See Brundage (1993) for a description of white-on-white lynchings.

12. Black residents of the Mississippi Delta region enjoyed a surprising degree of affluence. According to Ayers (1992, 195), they were more likely to own land and have greater access to nonagricultural jobs than their counterparts elsewhere in the South: "It was no wonder the Delta exercised a strong hold on the imagination of many blacks in less favored parts of the South." An interesting question, which will not be pursued in this book, concerns why so many blacks were lynched by black mobs in the Delta.

13. See Dinnerstein (1968) and Frey and Thompson-Frey (1988) for examinations of the Leo Frank lynching, and Gambino (1977) for a description of the mass lynching of Italian Americans in New Orleans in 1891.

14. Asheville *Daily Citizen,* April 3, 1894, 1.

15. Alexandria *TownTalk,* August 3, 1896, 2.

16. Memphis *Appeal-Avalanche,* February 19, 1893, 16; Macon *Telegraph,* February 19, 1893, 1.

17. Atlanta *Constitution,* June 24, 1904, 8.

18. Montgomery *Advertiser,* November 27, 1897, 7.

19. Little Rock *Arkansas Gazette,* June 21, 1908, 1.

20. Atlanta *Constitution,* January 10, 1908, 2.

21. The substitution model of social control is clearly evident in the work of Black (1976).

22. Cutler (1907, 626).

23. What we refer to as the "reinforcement model" has been linked to a social conflict perspective of lynchings. That is, both lynchings and executions are viewed as forms of repression that the white population used to hold the black population in check. When whites felt particularly threatened by the behavior, or even the presence, of blacks, all forms of repression were invoked. Thus, the conflict perspective predicts that the frequency of lynchings and executions will covary positively. Discussions of the substitution and social conflict (or reinforcement) models can be found in Phillips (1987) and Beck et al. (1989).

24. The number 4,291 equals 1,977 blacks legally executed plus 2,314 black victims of white lynch mobs. The data on southern executions have been obtained directly from Espy's Capital Punishment Research Project in Headland, Alabama. Espy's inventory is widely acknowledged as the most complete enumeration of legal executions currently available (Bowers 1984). He has created the inventory through detailed examination of local records and archival collections, and the data are also available through the Interuniversity Consortium for Political and Social Research (ICPSR). However, personal communication with Espy indicates that the execution data available through ICPSR are less complete than the data he provided directly to us. Several executions have been added since the data were provided to ICPSR. It is uncertain whether the ICPSR version of Espy's data would yield patterns identical to our version of his data.

25. Both trends are twice smoothed statistically for clarification. See chapter 2, note 34 for a discussion of the smoothing of time-series trends.

26. The largest number of executions occurred in 1905, when sixty-seven blacks were put to death. There were also sixty-four executions in 1902 and sixty-two in 1906. The fewest number of executions, fourteen, took place in 1919. The years 1888 and 1924 also claimed fewer then twenty victims of capital punishment.

27. The zero-order correlation between the raw, unsmoothed data trends in black lynching victims and black executions is 0.44.

28. Of those executed blacks not convicted of murder or rape, eight were convicted of robbery, two of riot, seven of arson, fourteen of burglary, and four of multiple offenses. Information on the offense of fifteen of those executed is missing.

29. The zero-order correlation between the raw, unsmoothed data trends in black lynching victims and black executions, when both are limited to capital offenses, is 0.44.

30. See Gottman (1981) and McCleary and Hay (1980).

31. Differencing involves transforming the time series by taking first-differences; for example, if Y_t is the number of black lynchings in year (t), the first difference is : $\Delta Y_t = Y_t - Y_{t-1}$. By analyzing the series of first differences rather than the original time series, we are able to remove any confounding factor due to time and avoid spurious conclusions.

32. All variables have been differenced once, and there is no intercept or constant term in the model. We considered two specifications for the disturbance term in the time-series model. First, we entertained a model where the disturbance term was assumed to follow a simple (AR1) autoregressive scheme, hence:

$$u_t = \rho u_{t-1} + \varepsilon_t \qquad t = 1, 2, \ldots, n \text{ years}$$

where ρ is the first-order autocorrelation coefficient and ε_t is random error. The second specification assumed the disturbance term followed a first-order (MA1) moving average process, hence:

$$u_t = \varepsilon_t + \phi \varepsilon_{t-1} \qquad t = 1, 2, \ldots, n \text{ years}$$

where ϕ is the first-order moving-average coefficient and ε_t is random error. For discussions of the differences between the auto-regressive and moving-average specifications, see McCleary and Hay (1980) and Gottman (1981). To ensure that our substantive conclusions were robust with regard to the specification of the disturbance term, we estimated our models first assuming an AR1 process and then reestimated assuming an MA1 process. The substantive conclusions were identical under each specification. Here we report only the empirical results from the MA1 model.

33. We used iterative nonlinear least squares to estimate the moving-average models, using the Box-Jenkins routine in the R.A.T.S. (Regression Analysis of Time Series) software produced by Estima, Inc.

34. The coefficient for executions at time $(t-1)$ falls far short of statistical significance if we use the common rule of thumb requiring that a coefficient be twice as large as its standard error.

35. We have also estimated the two models described in Table 4-2 without lagging the execution variable. Although the substitution model would expect a lagged effect of executions on lynchings, the reinforcement model would not. That is, if both lynchings and executions were responding to social forces that required the exercise of control over the

black population, then their relationship, if any, should be simultaneous, not lagged. The supplementary models that specify a simultaneous effect did yield positive effects of executions on lynchings for all reasons as well as for rape and murder only. Although these effects are in the expected direction, like the coefficients reported in Table 4-4 they fell far short of statistical significance.

36. For an excellent discussion of the need to consider historical variation within longer time series, see Isaac and Griffin (1989).

37. The procedure we followed is the same as the diagonal model discussed by Isaac and Griffin (1989).

38. The specific number of counties represented in the analysis varies across the periods because of changes in county boundaries—including the creation and elimination of counties—and because of missing data for variables included in the analysis.

39. For discussion of Poisson processes and examples of their use, see Balkwell (1990), Cameron and Trivedi (1986), Maddala (1983), and McCullagh and Nelder (1983).

40. Antiblack "proneness" effects are operationalized as the total number of African-Americans murdered by white lynch mobs in the county in periods before the period being analyzed. For example, for the period from 1900 to 1909, the proneness measure would be the number of blacks lynched between 1882 and 1899.

41. The linking function is logarithmic to insure the non-negativity of the λs. In the simple Poisson regression model there is no disturbance term (ε) in the specification. Although having the virtue of simplicity, this model is highly restrictive and of limited value because count data are often "overdispersed" and cannot meet the rigid assumptions of the simple Poisson model. By adding a disturbance term to the model, we are able to gain considerable analytical flexibility. When this disturbance follows a Gamma distribution—a highly adaptable and flexible probability distribution—a compound model results: the Poisson-Gamma regression model specified here. For a description of Poisson regression, its limitations, and its modifications, see Cameron and Trivedi (1986), Hinde (1982), Maddala (1983), and Lawless (1987). The parameters of the Poisson-Gamma regression were estimated by Bennett's algorithm (Bennett 1988) in GLIM (Aitkin et al. 1990; McCullagh and Nelder 1983). The county-level Poisson parameters, the λs, are not actually estimated. The GLIM estimation procedure uses the raw number of black victims of white mobs in each county as the dependent variable.

42. We were unable to include percent black squared in the time-series equations because of extreme collinearity with the linear vari-

able, percent population black. This collinearity is more problematic for the time-series analysis because it is based on a much smaller number of observations (forty-nine years versus approximately eight hundred counties).

43. Because our data cover the years from 1882 through 1930, we have no information on the amount of antiblack violence before 1882, thus the proneness variable could not be included in the regression for the 1882–89 period.

44. The exception to this pattern was in the decade from 1920 to 1929, when the number of white lynchings had no statistically significant effect on the number of black lynch victims. This is likely due to the fact that by 1920 the lynching of whites by white mobs was a rare event.

45. To find the point at which the relationship between percent black and antiblack violence changes direction, we differentiate the regression model with respect to percent black and set it equal to zero,

$$\partial \text{Victims}/\partial \text{Percent Black} = \beta_{\%blk} + 2\beta_{\%blk2}(\text{Percent Population Black})$$
$$= 0.$$

Solving, the point at which percent black reverses direction is found to be $-\beta_{\%blk}/2\beta_{\%blk2}$. Solving this equation for each period produces 44.0 percent for the period from 1882 to 1889; 48.8 percent for the period from 1890 to 1899; 56.0 percent for the period from 1900 to 1909; 70.0 percent for the period from 1910 to 1919; and 49.4 percent for the period from 1920 to 1929.

46. See Raper (1933, 36).

5

The Role of King Cotton

The geographical concentration of black lynchings has intrigued commentators for a long while. It has been obvious to all that lynchings were primarily a southern phenomenon, and many have noted that lynchings within the South were further concentrated in certain locales while virtually unknown in others (chapter 2). The land bordering the Mississippi River and the Black Belt of South Carolina, Georgia, and Alabama claimed more than its proportionate share of African-American lynch victims (Figure 2-4). However, these regions not only produced many black lynchings, but they also were prime cotton growing areas, which raises the possibility of a connection between cotton agriculture and racial violence.[1] We have mapped the locations of black victims of white lynch mobs and superimposed them on the prime cotton growing areas of the South (Figure 5-1).[2] Although the correspondence between the cotton regions and antiblack violence is not exact, there appears to be a broad correlation between cotton-dominated areas and black lynchings. In fact, black lynching victims were almost twice as likely to be from cotton-dominant areas than those less dedicated to cotton production.[3] At least on the surface, this suggests a potential link between the cotton culture and antiblack violence.

The suspicion that King Cotton may have had an important role in affecting racial violence has a long history. Exactly how the cotton culture of the South could have fostered an environment within which mob violence flourished has remained an intriguing mystery. Was it because of a particularly virulent racist ideology? Were blacks and whites engaged in especially keen economic competition? Did the

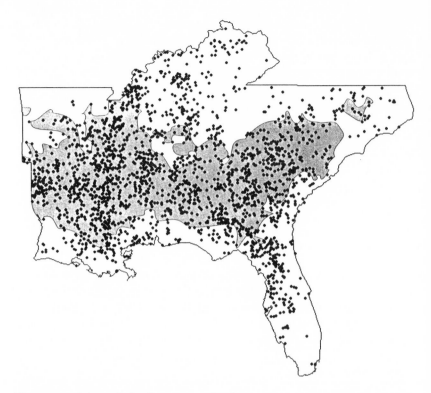

Figure 5-1. Map of Black Victims of White Mobs and Cotton-Dominant Areas of the South.

white elite, who benefited most from King Cotton's profits, need to exercise terroristic control over the cheap labor force upon which it relied? Was the agricultural economy of the Cotton South susceptible to wide swings between prosperity and destitution, driven by the vagaries of cotton prices? Here, we hope to fashion a reasonably convincing conceptual framework describing exactly how the southern cotton culture accounted for temporal and spatial variation in the intensity of black lynching.

Mob Violence and the Price of Cotton

In his classic *The Tragedy of Lynching* (1933) Raper presented evidence apparently linking the incidence of lethal mob violence against southern blacks to variation in the value of southern cotton crops. He concluded that "periods of relative prosperity bring reductions in lynching and periods of depression cause an increase. Mathematically, this relationship is shown by the correlation of −0.532."[4] According to Raper, economic competition between marginal black and white laborers accounts for the association between economic conditions and lynching. The economic hardship caused by a poor profit from the cotton crop leads to an effort by whites to replace black workers with unemployed white laborers. Mob violence was a form of intimidation used to facilitate this labor substitution.

Seven years later, Hovland and Sears used similar data to again demonstrate an association between swings in the southern economic cycle and lynching.[5] They reported impressive evidence that lethal mob violence against blacks became more acute during years of economic stagnation when the value of cotton was depressed. Unlike Raper, however, Hovland and Sears interpreted the association as support for a goal-frustration model of aggression.[6] When low cotton prices frustrated southern whites in their quest for economic security, they lashed out violently at the subordinate black population. The goal-frustration interpretation was buttressed by Hovland and Sears's observation that "by no conceivable stretch of the imagination could the victims of lynchings, either Negro or white, be considered responsible for the value of cotton or the general level of business activity."[7] Clearly, Hovland and Sears underestimated the imagination of the average white southerner, who had a well-documented history of blaming blacks for social and economic problems for which they were not responsible. It was the empirical evidence offered by Hovland and Sears, however, that was challenged.

Alexander Mintz found Hovland and Sears's study methodologically wanting.[8] By reanalyzing the lynching data using a different measure of association and allowing for nonlinearities and other methodological complexities, Mintz found that the relationship between the value of southern cotton and black lynchings was still negative but substantially weaker than reported by Hovland and Sears. He concluded that the evidence does not support a linkage between the value of the southern cotton crop and lynching.

Despite the serious questions raised by Mintz, the assumption that black lynchings were partially a function of swings in the southern economic cycle (primarily the fortunes of cotton) persists in the social science literature. Reed and his colleagues surveyed this literature and found the cotton price-lynching association cited routinely and uncritically as an example of the frustration-aggression process.[9]

They dubbed the presumed relationship as "too good to be false." Still, a definitive assessment of the form or strength of association between southern cotton production and black lynchings has yet to be offered.

White Class Structure and Economic Explanations for Lynchings

The hypothesized link between temporal swings in the price of cotton and black lynchings assumes that southern whites responded to economic stress by resorting to racial violence. Their motives may have been "instrumental," as suggested by Raper, or "emotional" as described by Hovland and Sears's frustration-aggression model. Is it naive, however, to believe that southern whites were unanimous in their economic interests and responses? Bonacich argues that rural southern white society was divided into three major classes: the dominating white planters and employers; a class of white day laborers, sharecroppers, and tenants; and a class of black landless workers.[10] Planters and employers were dependent on the cheap labor that blacks provided, but white laborers were threatened by the competition from the cheaper black labor force. Although the economic interests of the two classes of whites diverged in many important respects, periods of economic distress may have created a potential for convergence, at least with respect to racial violence. When cotton profits were down, all whites may have perceived certain advantages to heightened racial hostility and mob violence.

The late nineteenth and early twentieth centuries were years of shrinking fortunes for many southern rural whites. The rate of white farm tenancy increased, and black and white labor was thrown into direct competition on a significant scale for the first time.[11] This was an undesirable situation for marginal whites during the best of times; it was virtually intolerable when the cotton economy was slack. Poor whites, suffering from reduced incomes, perceived neighboring blacks to be competitors for a shrunken economic pie as well as challengers to the superior social station "guaranteed" by the caste system.

In some cases, the response of poor whites to financial stress was clearly instrumental and driven by a desire to reduce competition from blacks.[12] As Williamson notes, "The history of bust and boom [in the cotton economy] had something to do with the history of Radicalism. Heated antiblack sentiment in the early nineties was related to the fact that black men sought places that white men felt they needed in order to live and support their wives and children."[13] Marginal whites used violence to force black tenant farmers off desirable land or to drive away successful black businessmen or landowners.

Worsening economic conditions for poor rural whites also emphasized the relatively small difference between their level of financial well-being and that of nearby blacks. This made more salient the superior social status that even desperately poor whites took for granted. As White observed, "It is not difficult to imagine the inner thoughts of the poor white as he sees members of a race he has been taught by tradition, and by practically every force of public opinion with which he comes into contact, to believe inferior making greater progress than his own."[14] Thus, violence in response to economic distress sometimes took on an expressive nature as well. In some cases, poor whites reacted out of frustration to the contradiction between their objective economic status and the expected benefits of white supremacy. In other cases, lynchings were intended as messages to the black community, reminders of its inferior position in white society.

The white elite also benefited from a heightened sense of racial antagonism and the violence that accompanied it. Most important was the perennial fear of a coalition between black and white labor. Such a coalition was perhaps the greatest threat to the social, economic, and political hegemony that the southern white elite enjoyed. It was in the interest of the white elite, therefore, to perpetuate hostility between black and white laborers. Raper noted this function of lynching when he wrote, "Lynchings tend to minimize social and class distinctions between white plantation owners and white tenants."[15] Shapiro put it more directly, "When those committed to racial subordination saw the possibility of blacks and whites coming together for common purposes, their response most often was to reach for the gun and the rope."[16] The threat of a coalition between black and white laborers likely increased when the poor of both races suffered from reduced cotton prices.

Thus the economy of the Cotton South was often critically dependent upon the fortunes of the cotton crop. As King Cotton went, so went the region. Declining prices had serious consequences for all groups involved in the production of cotton. Rural blacks were the most vulnerable; there is reason to believe that racial hatred and the violence it spawned served the interests of poor whites and the white elite during periods of economic stress. Of course, the motives and objectives of the two classes were not necessarily the same. For poor whites, violence was a response to fear of black competition for economic and social position. For the white elite, violence prevented a coalition between black and white laborers. Thus, the relationship between swings in the cotton economy and black lynchings does not assume participation by a single class of southern whites, nor does it assume a coordinated response by all whites.

King Cotton and Mob Violence: General Patterns

The broad historical sequence is uncontested: The peak of black lynchings in the early 1890s coincided with a softening demand for southern cotton, the rise of populism and agrarian protest, and the birth of radical racism.[17] The bloody 1890s were followed by several years of rising cotton prices and an apparent decline in violence against southern blacks. Following World War I, however, there was a significant reversal of this trend when an alarming bottoming of the cotton market was accompanied by another wave of radical racism signaled by the dramatic rebirth of the Ku Klux Klan and the popular acclaim lavished on D. W. Griffith's epic *Birth of a Nation.*

The basic data are displayed in Figure 5-2.[18] Between the early 1890s and mid-teens, there was a broad downward trend in the num-

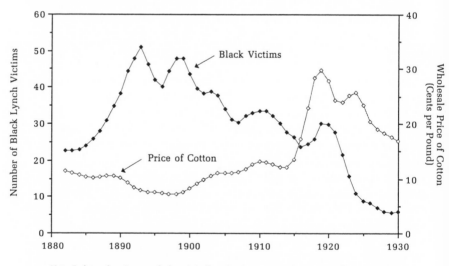

Note: Both trends twice-smoothed statistically using three-year moving averages. Cotton prices per pound are unadjusted for inflation.

Figure 5-2. Trends in Black Lynch Victims in the Cotton South and the Wholesale Price of Raw Cotton, 1882–1930.

ber of black lynch victims concurrent with a general upward swing in the nominal wholesale price of raw cotton. The two smoothed trends are linearly correlated −0.64 over the entire period. Using the raw, unsmoothed series, the correlation is still a respectable −0.53. Similar correspondence between trends in lynching and cotton prices led Raper and Hovland and Sears to conclude that the fortunes of the cotton economy played an important role in determining the intensity of mob violence.

However, before endorsing such a conclusion it must be demonstrated that this general historical correspondence is something more than coincidence. Several problems must be considered before concluding that swings in the price of cotton actually drove corresponding swings in the level of mob violence against blacks. First, a correlation between any two time series is insufficient to establish a functional relationship (chapter 4). To reach conclusions about the covariation of two time trends, their joint dependence on time must be removed by detrending both time series.

Second, the overall negative correlation suggests that as prices rose, the frequency of black lynchings diminished. But increasing cotton prices may reflect inflationary trends as well as changes in the constant dollar price of cotton. Would black lynchings decline if cotton prices increased solely as a result of inflation? Between 1919 and 1920, the average wholesale price for raw cotton increased by 1.4 cents per pound, but the deflated price actually fell close to 1.6 cents per pound.[19] Thus an apparent increase in wholesale price masked what actually was a worsening condition for cotton producers and others whose livelihoods depended on a healthy King Cotton.

To the degree that inflation in the cost of staples matched advances in cotton prices, marginal whites experienced no net gain and thus there would be no softening of racial antagonism. In fact, if inflation were sufficiently high, the plight of many agrarian whites would harden, and their tenuous position become even more precarious. Under these conditions, the frustration-aggression model predicts that increased hostility would be directed toward blacks even though the apparent price of cotton was increasing. Thus, increases in the constant dollar price of cotton should be correlated negatively with lethal violence against blacks, whereas increases due to inflation should have the opposite effect. To consider the cotton price-lynching hypothesis adequately, price data must be decomposed into two parts, the deflated price and an inflationary component, and each component related separately to the frequency of lynching.

The third problem is the lack of any consideration of the concentration of black population living in the Cotton South. Although there is no logically necessary relationship between black population concentration and the frequency of black lynchings, dwindling black population might produce some lessening of black-white competition as well as offer fewer targets for white aggression, resulting in fewer African-Americans killed by mob action.[20]

Fourth, Figure 5-2 ignores the effects of changes in agricultural productivity that are not translated into real price shifts. Changes in cotton productivity may affect lynchings net of their impact on prices. During the period from 1882 to 1930, the amount of cotton harvested in the Cotton South varied from a high near 8,300,000 bales in 1911 to a low of fewer than 3,200,000 bales in 1923. The total income derived from the cultivation of cotton is determined by both the price per pound paid to farmers and the number of pounds produced. The potential economic hardship implied by declining cotton prices could be offset by higher yields, resulting in relatively stable total income.

Finally, while previous interpretations of the link between cotton prices and lynching assume a process of black victimization (either expressive or instrumental) at the hands of southern whites, alternative interpretations are imaginable. An increase in the number of lynchings during periods of economic distress could be a white reaction to increasing crimes committed by blacks during these periods. If so, we would expect a significant attenuation in the association between cotton prices and lynching after controlling for the level of black crime. If the relationship persists, then the black victimization theory cannot be dismissed. Of course, it is conceivable that both processes operated simultaneously.

In sum, the apparently straightforward evidence demonstrating a linkage between the value of cotton and lynching (Figure 5-2) is far from conclusive. In light of the preceding issues, it is important to formulate an analytical model of black lynchings that incorporates (1) a distinction between the deflated wholesale price of cotton and changes in inflation; (2) a control for changes in the size of the black population; (3) a measure of cotton productivity; and (4) a proxy measure of the level of crime committed by blacks.

The Effects of Cotton Price, Cotton Productivity, and Black Demography on the Lynching of Blacks by White Mobs

In consideration of the issues discussed earlier, our analytical time-series model is:[21]

$$\text{Lynchings}_t = \beta_{\text{blk}}(\text{Population Black}_t) + \beta_{\%\text{blk}}(\text{Percent Black}_t)$$
$$+ \beta_{\text{price}}(\text{Price of Cotton}_t) + \beta_{\text{inf}}(\%\Delta\text{CPI}_{t-1})$$
$$+ \beta_{\text{bales}}(\text{Cotton Bales Produced}_t)$$
$$+ \beta_{\text{wht}}(\text{White Lynchings}_t) + \beta_{\text{crime}}(\text{Black Crime}_t) + \varepsilon_t$$

where Lynchings_t is the number of black victims of white lynch mobs in year t, the β_ks are effect parameters for the explanatory factors (size of black population, percent population black, deflated price of cotton, rate of inflation lagged one year, cotton bales produced, number of white lynchings, and the black crime rate proxy),[22] and ε is a disturbance term.[23]

The results of the time-series analysis of the effects of cotton prices, cotton productivity, and demographic factors on the frequency of black lynchings by white mobs for the period from 1884 to 1930 are presented in Table 5-1.[24] Model A includes the effects of the predictor variables, excluding the black crime rate proxy. In regard to Model A, several findings are noteworthy. First, the analysis indicates that

Table 5-1. Time-Series Regression of Number of Black Lynching Victims on Cotton Price and Production and Related Variables for Five Cotton South States[a]

Predictor Variable	Model A	Model B
Size of black population$_t$ (1,000s)	0.018	0.018
	(2.26)	(2.09)
Percent population black$_t$	4.533	4.418
	(3.79)	(3.32)
Wholesale deflated price of cotton$_t$	−1.578	−1.459
	(−2.47)	(−2.24)
Percent change in CPI$_{t-1}$	0.753	0.736
	(2.88)	(2.79)
Cotton bales produced$_t$ (1,000s)	−0.002	−0.002
	(−1.30)	(−1.31)
Black crime rate proxy$_t$	—	22.890
		(0.47)
Moving-average coefficient	−0.818	−0.792
	(−8.03)	(−7.35)
Durbin-Watson statistic	1.82	1.91

a. First-order moving-average models; all variables differenced once; t-ratios in parentheses; $N = 47$; five cotton states: Alabama, Arkansas, Georgia, Mississippi, and South Carolina.

changes in the constant dollar price of cotton are statistically significant and have the expected negative effect on black lynchings, whereas
the rate of inflation has the anticipated positive relationship. This
suggests that when the constant price was climbing, the likelihood of
black lynchings declined. During hard times, when the price of cotton stagnated or when inflation had become a significant problem,
black lynchings in the Cotton South were more frequent.

Second, changes in the racial composition of the population influenced the likelihood of lethal mob action. Net of price factors, increases in the absolute and relative sizes of the black population are
associated with more frequent black lynchings. This finding is consistent with a conflict perspective of social control that suggests that
a high proportion of blacks in the population represented a "threat"
to white hegemony and led to stern measures of social control, such
as lynching.[25]

Third, net of price shifts, cotton productivity had a negative relationship with lynchings, but this effect is not large relative to the
amount of variation in the time series, as shown by the coefficient's
modest size relative to its standard error (t-ratio of −1.30 in Model A).

The findings reported in the first column of Table 5-1 are consistent with an interpretation of lynching behavior that stresses the victimization of blacks at the hands of whites. It is likely that low market prices threatened the life chances of many southern whites,
especially those on the margins of society. Economic distress also
raised the potential for a coalition between black and white labor,
which threatened the social, economic, and political advantages held
by the white elite. The combination of these forces, which cut across
class lines, generated aggressive and hostile behavior directed at the
most vulnerable and powerless targets—southern blacks. The most
radical form of this aggression was lethal mob violence—lynching.

The Role of Crimes Committed by Blacks

While these findings are consistent with the black victimization
model of lynchings, they are also consistent with a radically different perspective that rests on the victimization of whites at the hands
of black criminals. This interpretation rests on a different presump-
tion, one that permeated the mentality of many whites.[26] Contemporary newspaper accounts and editorials often refer to crime committed by blacks and to fears within the white community of the black
"brute" criminal. Popular wisdom viewed lynching as a morally justified solution to virtually all crimes, ranging from insolence and petty
theft to murder and rape, perpetrated by blacks against whites. If

worsening economic conditions produced more crime by blacks against whites, and if there was little confidence in the criminal justice system, then increases in the frequency of lynching could be a logical although radically reactionary consequence. In this scenario, the role of commodity market factors is, therefore, indirect.

Model B in the second column of Table 5-1 includes the proxy for the black crime rate as an additional predictor of lynchings. If the black crime hypothesis is correct, inclusion of this factor should eliminate, or substantially attenuate, the net effect of cotton prices on black lynchings. We can see from the results offered in Table 5-1 (column 2) that including the crime proxy does not weaken significantly either the impact of the deflated price of cotton or the effect of the rate of inflation. Thus the link between cotton price, inflation, and black lynchings is substantively not reduced when a control for black crime is introduced.

The findings reported in Models A and B of Table 5-1 suggest that black lynchings by white mobs were not a simple reflection of criminal activity and that economic factors played an important and independent role in affecting mob violence. The black crime explanation also suffers from two other conceptual weaknesses. First, the southern criminal justice system was not lax in punishing blacks convicted of crime. Blacks received the same discriminatory treatment in southern courts that they received in the rest of society, including disproportionate imposition of the death penalty. Thus, it is unlikely that lynching was necessary to control crime. Second, if lynching was used to combat increasing crime, why was it used almost exclusively against blacks after 1900? Surely, criminal activity by whites should also have peaked during periods of economic stagnation or recession. Thus, despite the somewhat problematic measure of black criminality used in our empirical analyses, we are reasonably confident in rejecting the black crime model as an explanation for the strong association between cotton prices and black lynchings.

Historical Effects

Table 5-1 provides statistical evidence that between the early 1880s and 1930 the frequency of blacks lynched by white mobs was influenced by the market for cotton and the rate of inflation. However, it may be premature to conclude that this relationship was stable over the forty-nine years. Specifically, it is possible that significant historical episodes altered the basic relationship.

The typical time-series model is ahistorical in the sense that it contains no provision for shifts in the functional relationship between black lynchings and the market for cotton over time. In other words, it precludes any interaction between time and the explanatory variables and implies that the relationship between mob violence against blacks and the southern cotton economy was the same, for example, during the 1920s as it was during the 1880s. This is a very restrictive assumption for a historical process, and one that we now relax.

One method for coping with this problem is to apply a moving time-series methodology, which involves obtaining estimates for the model parameters using successively incremented and overlapping time points over a fixed-length interval. Thus we first estimated the parameters for Model A in Table 5-1 for the fifteen-year interval from 1883 to 1897. We then computed a second set of parameter estimates using the incremented fifteen-year interval from 1884 to 1898, a third set for the interval from 1885 to 1899, and so forth until the parameters of the last fifteen-year interval (1916–30) had been estimated.[27] Using fifteen-year intervals and following this incremental procedure, we obtained thirty-four sets of coefficients. These coefficients were then plotted chronologically to show the longitudinal stability of the relationship between lynchings and the explanatory variables.

We have plotted the moving time series for the net effect of the deflated wholesale price of cotton on black lynchings (Figure 5-3) and also the net effects of the rate of inflation on black lynchings (Figure 5-4). The effects of these variables were not constant across time, but rather had more influence in some periods than in others. The figures show that the negative influence of the constant dollar price of cotton and the positive effect of the rate of inflation on mob violence were much stronger in the 1880s and early 1890s than in the following years. Using 1900 as a crude point to dichotomize the period, we found that the effect of cotton price on black lynchings was seven times more powerful before 1900 than after. Although not as dramatic, the effect of inflation on black lynchings was more than twice as strong before 1900 than during the later period.[28]

What social and economic trends might account for the weakening effect over time of the deflated price of cotton and inflation on black lynchings? First, by 1910, these states had enacted measures that effectively disenfranchised blacks.[29] Doing so may have allayed fears among the white elite about a political coalition between white and black labor.

A second viable explanation for the reduced influence of the cotton economy on black lynchings centers around the changing character of the southern economy during the late nineteenth and early twentieth centuries. If the grip of King Cotton relaxed, its salience for

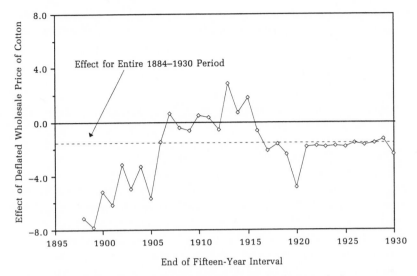

Note: The x-axis represents the end year of the fifteen-year interval (e.g., 1900 for the 1886–1900 interval, etc.).

Figure 5-3. Effect of Deflated Price of Cotton on Black Lynchings by Time Period.

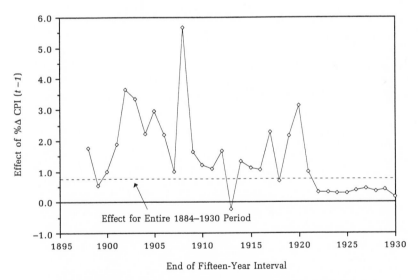

Note: The x-axis represents the end year of the fifteen-year interval (e.g., 1900 for the 1886–1900 interval, etc.).

Figure 5-4. Effect of Inflation (%Δ CPI) on Black Lynchings by Time Period.

lynchings would decline. To explore this alternative, we compiled trends in selected characteristics of the southern economy from 1880 to 1930 (Table 5-2). In general, the evidence is consistent with this perspective. Although the percent of improved land planted in cotton remained relatively stable, greater numbers of southern workers became engaged in nonagricultural occupations. The percent of all workers employed in agriculture dropped from 82.4 percent in 1880 to 51.9 percent in 1930. The number of wage-earners in manufacturing grew from 55,600 in 1880 to more than 459,100 in 1930, far outstripping the overall growth in the southern labor force.

A final potential explanation lies in the history of migration from the South during the period. Net out-migration for blacks and whites increased after 1890, with the pace accelerating sharply after 1900 (Table 5-2). This may have altered the association between swings in the cotton economy and black lynchings. White migration may have acted as a safety valve of escape for marginal whites, while black migration reduced competition between blacks and agrarian whites (chapter 7).[30]

In summary, using annual time-series data for the period from 1882

Table 5-2. Selected Characteristics of the Cotton South Economy, 1880–1930: Trends in Agriculture and the Work-Force Economy

Characteristic	1880	1890	1900	1910	1920	1930
Percent of workers in agriculture[a]	82.4	73.3	72.1	68.3	59.5	51.9
Percent of improved land in cotton[b]	34.4	36.4	33.7	37.0	32.5	34.5
Wage-earners in manufacturing (1,000s)[c]	55.6	112.9	229.3	323.9	385.8	459.1
Net migration of native whites (1,000s)[d]	−7.3	−87.1	−196.7	−148.3	−225.4	−455.4
Net migration of blacks (1,000s)[d]	2.3	19.4	−112.8	−118.7	−350.6	−660.1

a. Source: Lee, Miller, Brainerd, and Easterlin (1957), volume 1, Table L-4.
b. Source: Census Office (1883, 1895, 1902); U.S. Bureau of the Census (1913, 1922, 1931, 1932).
c. Source: Lee et al. (1957), volume 1, Tables L-4 and M-2.
d. Source: U.S. Bureau of the Census (1975). Net migration estimates for blacks and whites apply to the decade preceding the year shown. For example, net migration for 1900 refers to the decade 1890–1900.

to 1930 for five Cotton South states, we find evidence that advances in the constant dollar price of cotton were associated with fewer black lynchings, whereas inflationary shifts in the price of cotton were associated with increased mob violence against blacks. Furthermore, our analysis suggests that the association between lynchings and cotton prices was not invariant throughout the period. The response of black lynchings to shifts in the deflated and inflationary components of the price of cotton weakened considerably after 1900. Although this is consistent with a linkage between the southern cotton economy and racial violence, it introduces a need for more exhaustive exploration into the precise nature of the linkage.

Cotton Prices and Lynching: Further Consideration

In the frustration-aggression hypothesis, the health of cotton is taken as a convenient indicator of general economic conditions in the rural South; fluctuations in cotton prices really represent instabilities in the broader agrarian economy. There is, however, another interpretation of the role of cotton in affecting violent behavior. Daniel notes that cotton had its own distinctive culture and historical legacy; while sharing some features with the tobacco and sugar cultures, it remained somehow "different."[31] This raises the possibility that the price of cotton may have a dual role in the dynamics leading to mob violence: It may indicate general economic conditions and also represent a unique set of social relations and social values.

Three strategies can be used to investigate whether the relationship between the price of cotton and black lynchings is more than a mere reflection of broad economic conditions and whether it represents something unique between economics and social relations within the cotton culture. First, we could apply an empirical model similar to that reported in Table 5-1 to the lynchings of whites by whites. If our notions are correct, we would expect that, in the case of white-on-white mob violence, the price-lynching relationship would be attenuated, if present at all. The social and economic forces would be expected to have less influence on the trend of white lynchings than on the frequency of white mob violence against blacks. Second, we could apply the model to the lynching of blacks by black mobs in order to discover whether the price-lynching relationship is race-neutral or race-specific. Finally, we could apply the model to the lynching of blacks by white mobs outside the Cotton South to help determine if there is something unique about the Cotton South.

White Victims of White Mobs

Although the overwhelming number of victims of white lynch mobs in the Cotton South were black ($N = 1,452$), there were instances of whites being lynched ($N = 121$) during the years between 1882 and 1930, so we are able to explore our hypothesis empirically by reestimating the models in Table 5-1 substituting the trend in white lynchings for the trend in black lynchings.[32] Now the pattern of white victims of mob violence becomes the dependent variable to be analyzed. The first column of Table 5-3 reports the results of these additional analyses. A comparison of the effects of the deflated price of cotton in Table 5-3 for white lynchings with those reported for blacks lynchings in Table 5-1 reveals that, in the case of white victims, the effect of deflated wholesale cotton price is substantively weaker. For example, the cotton price effect for black lynch victims is –1.578 (Table 5-1, column 1), whereas the comparable effect for white lynch victims

Table 5-3. Time-Series Regression of Number of Intrarace Lynching Victims on Cotton Price and Production and Related Variables for Five Cotton South States[a]

Predictor Variable	White Victims of White Mobs	Black Victims of Black Mobs[b]
Size of white or black population$_t$ (1,000s)	–0.004	–0.001
	(–2.60)	(–0.36)
Percent population white or black$_t$	0.939	0.285
	(1.96)	(1.69)
Wholesale deflated price of cotton$_t$	–0.135	–0.083
	(–1.01)	(–0.56)
Percent change in CPI$_{t-1}$	0.059	0.015
	(1.06)	(0.25)
Cotton bales produced$_t$ (1,000s)	–0.0002	–0.0001
	(–0.06)	(–0.30)
Moving-average coefficient	–0.855	–0.956
	(–9.03)	(–11.27)
Durbin-Watson statistic	2.05	1.92

a. First-order moving-average models; all variables differenced once; t-ratios in parentheses; $N = 47$; five cotton states: Alabama, Arkansas, Georgia, Mississippi, and South Carolina.
b. Black or integrated mobs.

is only –0.135 (Table 5-3, column 1). Similarly, the effect of inflation on black victims of white mobs is 0.753 (Table 5-1, column 1), compared to only 0.059 for white lynch victims (Table 5-3, column 1). We take this as evidence that the economic and social forces that affected white mob violence against southern blacks had dramatically less effect on the frequency of whites being lynched by other whites.

Black Victims of Black Lynch Mobs

As a second strategy to explore the relationship between cotton price and lynching, we expanded our investigation to cover black victims of black or integrated mobs. Although the majority of black lynch victims in the Cotton South met their deaths in the hands of white mobs, a significant minority, 6.7 percent ($N = 97$), were victims of intraracial violence. Findings reported in Table 5-1 suggest that white mob violence toward African-Americans was affected by economic conditions, but what about black-on-black violence? Would the behavior of black mobs be influenced by these same economic conditions? To answer this question, we applied the regression model to the time series of black lynch victims of black or integrated mobs. These results are presented in the second column of Table 5-3. Neither the deflated wholesale price of cotton, the rate of inflation, the amount of cotton produced, nor the size of the black population had any statistically significant effects on the trend of black-on-black mob violence, although the coefficients of the price variables are in the expected direction.

White mob violence toward African-Americans was influenced by economic conditions, in particular the changes in the real price of cotton and the general rate of inflation (Table 5-1). Yet economic conditions appear to have played no significant role in affecting trends in black-on-black mob violence or in the pattern of white-on-white violence (Table 5-3).

Black Victims of White Mobs outside the Cotton South

The third strategy for exploring the relationship between the cotton culture and the lynching of blacks would be to take the statistical models reported in Table 5-1 and apply them to black lynchings by white mobs outside of the Cotton South. If the cotton price variable is simply reflecting general economic conditions, we might expect that it would continue to have an influence on black lynchings, yet if there was something unique about the cotton culture, the price-lynching relationship should be altered significantly.

In Table 5-4, we present the results of estimating the effects of cot-

ton price and the other predictor variables on the time trend of the 862
black victims of white mobs that occurred in the five noncotton states
from 1882 to 1930. Comparing the coefficients in Table 5-4 with those
reported initially in Table 5-1 reveals that the effect parameters for
cotton price are smaller in states outside the Cotton South than in the
Cotton South, regardless of which model is contrasted. Comparing
Model A's, for example, shows that the effect of deflated cotton price
in the Cotton South (−1.578) is almost four times larger in magnitude
than its effect elsewhere (−0.418). Perhaps it is not surprising that
cotton price had less influence on antiblack violence because the rest
of the South was less dependent upon cotton agriculture. But this same
argument does not seem to apply to the effect of inflation. Here we
find the impact of inflation on mob violence is more than four times
larger in the Cotton South than in the rest of the South, 0.753 compared to 0.173 in the Model A's.

Contrasting the estimated effects in Table 5-1 with those in Table
5-4 clearly demonstrates that economic conditions influenced lethal

Table 5-4. Time-Series Regression of Number of Black Lynching Victims on Cotton Price and Production and Related Variables for Five
Non-Cotton South States[a]

Predictor Variable	Model A	Model B
Size of black population$_t$ (1,000s)	−0.003	−0.002
	(−0.07)	(−0.04)
Percent population black$_t$	1.461	1.680
	(0.21)	(0.25)
Wholesale deflated price of cotton$_t$	−0.418	−0.406
	(−0.72)	(−0.69)
Percent change in CPI$_{t-1}$	0.173	0.175
	(0.69)	(0.69)
Cotton bales produced$_t$ (1,000s)	−0.002	−0.002
	(−0.56)	(−0.57)
Black crime rate proxy$_t$	—	−13.349
		(−0.25)
Moving-average coefficient	−0.353	−0.380
	(−2.32)	(−2.49)
Durbin-Watson statistic	1.81	1.80

a. First-order moving-average models; all variables differenced once; t-ratios in parentheses; $N = 47$; five noncotton states: Florida, Kentucky, Louisiana, North
   Carolina, and Tennessee.

mob violence against blacks more strongly in the Cotton South than in the rest of the South. The evidence presented thus far suggests that general economic conditions influenced aggressive behavior of whites toward southern blacks, and that within the Cotton South the linkage between the fortunes of the cotton economy and mob violence was stronger than in bordering states. We are also able to conclude from Table 5-3 that even within the Cotton South fluctuations in the price of cotton and inflation had little impact on the pattern of lynchings with white victims, or in the pattern of blacks lynched by black mobs. Thus it would appear that economic conditions did not affect the likelihood of mob violence in general, but rather affected the likelihood that whites in the Cotton South would engage in mob violence against their African-American neighbors.

Cotton Dominance and the Lynching of Blacks

The preceding evidence demonstrates that year-to-year fluctuation in the number of black lynchings by whites was partially due to concomitant changes in the fortunes farmers enjoyed from their cotton crops. Moreover, it seems that shifting cotton prices had a much stronger impact on black lynchings in states of the Cotton South before 1900. Although these findings suggest a special relationship between the production of southern cotton and racial violence, it is possible to go even further for corroborating evidence. If, in fact, there is merit to the cotton culture explanation for racial violence, then we should be able to demonstrate that subregions of the South that depended more heavily on King Cotton also experienced more racial violence.

It is also appropriate to maintain an interest in the temporal dimension of racial violence even as we examine cross-county variation in black lynchings. As we found in the examination of longitudinal patterns of lynching, the association between cotton prices and lynching weakened considerably after the first decade of the twentieth century. We would anticipate, then, that any cross-sectional correspondence between the dominance of cotton within the agricultural economy and racial violence would also become weaker as the twentieth century progressed. We shall consider two periods: 1890 to 1909 and 1910 to 1929. The first corresponds, roughly, to the time that black lynchings were very responsive to cotton profits. The later period witnessed a weakening association between King Cotton and lynching.

Great variation occurred within the South in both the degree of cotton dominance and in the number of lynchings of African-Americans (Table 5-5). During the earlier period, the average southern county planted almost 19 percent of its improved land in cotton, and the intensity of cotton cultivation changed relatively little over time, remaining at an average of 19 percent from 1910 to 1929. During both periods, however, these averages masked considerable variation within the southern states. Although some counties planted no cotton, more than 82 percent of the improved land in Marshall County, Mississippi, was planted in cotton during the earlier period, while Coahoma County, Mississippi, devoted more than 75 percent of its improved land to cotton between 1910 and 1929.

Table 5-5. Cotton Dominance and Black Lynchings in the South, 1890–1909 and 1910–29[a]

County Characteristic[b]	1890–1909			1910–29		
	Mean	Max.	Min.	Mean	Max.	Min.
Cotton dominance (%)	18.8	82.6	0.0	19.2	75.2	0.0
Black lynching victims	1.47	15	0	0.72	11	0
Percent population black	34.1	94.0	0	31.0	91.0	0.0

a. The South includes the counties of Alabama, Arkansas, Florida, Georgia, Kentucky, Louisiana, Mississippi, North Carolina, South Carolina, and Tennessee.
b. Cotton dominance and percent population black measured in 1900 and 1920.

Unlike cotton dominance, the intensity of lynching changed substantially across the time periods. The average number of blacks lynched per county dropped from 1.47 during the earlier era to less than half that number (0.72 per county) in the 1910–29 span. Still, during each period there was impressive variation in the intensity of lynching across southern counties. In both periods, many counties experienced no lynchings at all. At the other extreme, however, between 1890 and 1909, white mobs from Bossier Parish, Louisiana, compiled the bloodiest record of racial violence by lynching fifteen blacks.[33] Caddo Parish, Louisiana, claimed the dubious distinction of lynching the most blacks (eleven) between 1910 and 1929. Caddo and Bossier parishes are adjacent, together defining the northwest corner of Louisiana. Bossier Parish ranked in the top 5 percent of all southern counties in the percent of land planted in cotton from 1890 to 1909, and Caddo Parish was similarly ranked during the later period.

However, our first indication of the overall relationship between cotton dominance and black lynching at the county level throughout the South comes from the zero-order correlations between these two variables.[34] Cotton dominance and black lynching are positively and significantly related during both periods ($r = +0.32$ and $r = +0.26$ for 1890–1909 and 1910–29, respectively). The correlations suggest that southern counties that planted a greater percentage of improved farmland in cotton also tended to be the site of more black lynchings. While this evidence is encouragingly consistent with the cotton culture interpretation of black lynchings, it cannot be considered definitive. First, it is possible that counties with cotton-dominated economies also had larger black populations, in absolute terms, and that the greater number of lynchings in those counties was simply due to the racial composition of their populations. Second, it is also likely that the black populations of cotton-dominant counties were larger relative to the coresident white population. If so, then the significant correlations between cotton dominance and black lynchings might only reflect the frequently observed effect of percent black and all it represents on lynchings (chapter 3).

In order to investigate these associations, it is necessary to specify a formal model linking the number of black victims of white lynch mobs to the explanatory factors (chapter 4). Here we use the same kind of Poisson model that we employed previously. Under the Poisson specification, spatial variation in the number of black victims is due to intercounty differences in λ, the implied Poisson parameter for each county. These county-level λs are a function of cotton dominance, racial composition (both linear and quadratic terms), size (log) of the county's African-American population, and the county's historical proneness to antiblack violence:

$$\begin{aligned} \text{Log } \lambda_i = \beta_0 &+ \beta_{cotdom}(\text{Cotton Dominance}_i) \\ &+ \beta_{\%blk}(\text{Percent Population Black}_i) \\ &+ \beta_{\%blk2}(\text{Percent Population Black}_i^2) \\ &+ \beta_{blk}(\text{Log Size of Black Population}_i) \\ &+ \beta_{prone}(\text{Proneness to Anti-Black Violence}_i) + \varepsilon_i \end{aligned}$$

where λ_i is the ith county's implied Poisson parameter, β_0 is a constant across counties, the β_ks are effect parameters for the explanatory factors, and ε is a random disturbance assumed to have a Gamma distribution.[35]

In order to account for the competing explanations of the relationship between cotton dominance and lynchings, we have first estimated this relationship without statistical controls for the black population and racial composition of the county's population (the Model A's), and then with controls for the racial demographic structure within each county (the Model B's). The results of these Poisson-Gamma regressions (Table 5-6) show that, in each period, a county's dependence on cotton was a significant predictor of the number of black lynchings occurring within the county (the Model A's). In both periods, a one-point increase in cotton dominance was associated with an approximate 2.7 percent increase in the number of black victims of white lynch mobs.[36]

In the Model B's, we have reestimated the relationship, controlling statistically for the size of the local black population, the racial mix, and the county's historical record of violence toward blacks. As expected, all three factors are significantly related to the number of blacks killed in each period. It is important, however, to note that the

Table 5-6. Poisson-Gamma Regression of Number of Black Lynching Victims of White Mobs on Cotton Dominance and Related Variables for Counties in the South, 1890–1909 and 1910–29

Predictor Variable[a]	1890–1909		1910–29	
	Model A[b]	Model B	Model A	Model B
Constant	−0.170	−0.999	−0.901	−2.408
	(−2.10)	(−6.15)	(−9.12)	(−11.31)
Cotton dominance (percent improved acreage in cotton)	0.028	0.009	0.026	0.004
	(9.64)	(2.36)	(7.63)	(1.03)
Percent population black	—	0.034	—	0.062
		(3.12)		(4.83)
Percent population black[2]	—	−0.0003	—	−0.0005
		(−3.28)		(−4.05)
Log size of black population (1000s)	—	0.323	—	0.186
		(4.38)		(2.33)
Proneness to antiblack violence	—	0.134	—	0.101
		(3.51)		(6.08)
Number of observations	809		858	

a. Cotton dominance, percent population black, and the size of the black population measured in 1900 and 1920. Proneness is the cumulative number of black victims of white mobs from 1882 to the beginning of the period.
b. Asymptotic t-ratios in parentheses.

net effect of cotton dominance remains a significant predictor of black lynchings during the 1890 to 1909 period, although at a much reduced level (0.009 in Model B compared to 0.028 in Model A). In the 1910–29 period, after controlling on racial composition, size of the black population, and proneness to antiblack violence, cotton dominance no longer has a statistically significant effect on black lynchings.[37] This attenuation over time in the net impact of cotton dependency on antiblack violence is consistent with the findings of the time-series analyses presented earlier.

It is also worthy of note that the relative size of the black population in a county has a significant curvilinear effect on lynchings in both periods. There is a positive relationship between percent black in the county, but it grows weaker as black concentration increases. This type of relationship is consistent with Blalock's economic threat hypothesis and is congruent with the findings reported in chapter 4 (Table 4-4).

In sum, the findings from our cross-sectional analysis of the relationship between cotton dependency and black lynchings in southern counties agree—for the most part—with the evidence from the time-series investigation reported previously. There appears to have been a reasonably strong association between the dominance of cotton cultivation in the local agricultural economy and the level of racial violence in the county, and this effect persists when the other county characteristics are introduced. However, the cross-sectional evidence indicates that the strength of this relationship faded over time and that by World War I the extent of concentration in cotton production had significantly less effect on levels of racial violence.

Two caveats are worth mentioning at this point. First, it is likely that the net impact of cotton dominance on lynchings described in Table 5-6 actually understates the overall importance of the cotton culture. The net effect was estimated by holding constant the racial composition of southern counties. However, it is likely that one way in which the cotton culture influenced the climate for racial violence was by shaping the racial composition of local areas. That is, cotton production was heavily dependent upon cheap, exploitable labor, that is, black labor. Thus, the true effect of the cotton culture on black lynchings really should include some undetermined part of the effect of the absolute and relative size of the county's black population. Second, although the analytical model used in Table 5-6 was adequate for estimating the net effect of cotton dominance on black lynchings, it is too simplistic to do justice to all social forces operating at the county level.

Production Cycle of Cotton and Black Lynchings

The preceding sections linked the price of cotton and cotton domination to the frequency of lethal mob attacks against blacks. In this section we expand our exploration by investigating one further connection between the cotton culture and violence—the seasonality of lynchings.[38]

An assumption that the intensity of mob violence varied with the seasons has long been part of the conventional wisdom of mob violence.[39] For example, in 1932 the Southern Commission on the Study of Lynching noted that lynchings were most prevalent during the summer. The commission provided two viable explanations for this pattern. First, it blamed the idleness of the rural population: "During the midsummer months, after cultivating is done and before harvesting begins, there is little to occupy the time of Negro and white workers on Southern farms, nearly two-thirds of whom are wage hands or tenants. During the slack-work summer months, there is a great deal of visiting, loafing, gambling, and general 'carousing about', and inevitably an *unusually large amount of crime."* Second, the commission offered an economic interpretation that stressed the "need" for greater supervision of farm laborers by landlords during the summer,

> relations between landlords and tenants in summer account for an unusually large amount of major strife. During the winter, the tenant is disposed to conduct himself so as to get a 'place' for the coming year. With summer, the tenant has received about all he can get from the landlord, and often owes the latter practically all his equity in the crop, a situation that tends to lessen the tenant's industry. . . . Thus, *in summer, tenants are likely to be more hopeless and antagonistic and the landlords and their overseers more domineering, than at other periods of the year.*[40]

It is important to note that the quotations suggest very different explanations for seasonal patterns. Was the seasonality of lynching due to summertime crime or to a reflection of the need to control agrarian black labor?

The first implied model stresses the opportunity for mischievous and criminal behavior by the agrarian labor force when the demands for agricultural work were slack. This line of reasoning argues that idleness led to increased criminal activity among black laborers. In response to these threats, whites resorted to mob violence to punish black law violators. If accurate, this hypothesis suggests that lynchings should display roughly the same seasonal pattern as other serious crimes and vary directly with the opportunity for such crimes to be committed.

The second implied model—the labor control interpretation—argues that landlords and planters were required to exercise greater supervision over their work force during the peak periods of labor demand. Although the Southern Commission on the Study of Lynching appeared to connect this motive among landlords to the slack agricultural season, we believe that it may have misinterpreted the situation somewhat. Rather, we suspect that landlords were inclined to exercise greater oversight during the periods of most intensive need for labor. And cotton cultivation required considerable labor input during some summer months.

The agricultural production cycle for cotton set the pace for much of life in the South.[41] In winter, field hands would break land with mule-driven plows, clear last season's cotton stalks, start compost heaps, and prepare the soil for planting. As warmer days arrived in late March and April, cotton seed would be planted. Then, after the seeds sprouted in May, field-workers would be set to "chop out" (thin) cotton plants and weeds with a hoe, a highly labor-intensive process that continued until the "lay-by" in midsummer. May was the most repetitive and costly part of farm cultivation, not only because of cotton "chopping," but also because the corn and other crops demanded attention as well.[42]

By late July or early August, the most intensive work was completed, and the cotton crop would be laid-by, meaning that the bulk of the fieldwork was finished until early fall, and there was now time for more relaxed activities. In September the handpicking would begin and continue through November until all bolls had burst and the fields had been stripped. After each picking, raw cotton was carted to the gin to be cleaned of seed and baled for market. During the early winter, the fields would again lay fallow until it was time to start the next season's plowing.[43] Thus, in the cotton culture there were two periods of intense work activity: The first was in the early summer, when the cotton had to be chopped and weeded, and the second fell during the fall harvest. If the labor control interpretation of seasonality is correct, we should expect lynchings to be relatively more frequent during these two periods when labor demand was strong.

Violence can be used to influence and control labor in two different ways. The first, and most direct, is where mob action is aimed toward laborers refusing to work, workers who are organizing for collective bargaining, or workers who are otherwise trying to subvert the labor extraction process. A classic example of such direct action was the killing of Robert Collins. According to reports in the Atlanta *Constitution,* Collins, a resident of Oglethorpe County, Georgia, was lynched on February 9, 1894, for trying to entice African-American workers away from local plantations and creating conflict and strife between black servants and their employers. A mob of masked white men forced Collins from his home and then beat him unconscious. He died from the wounds a few hours later.[44] A second example comes from the Lee County, Arkansas, cotton pickers' strike.[45] In September 1891, Ben Patterson came to Lee County to organize black cotton pickers for a strike against local plantation owners. Following days of conflict among organizers, striking and nonstriking pickers, and agents of the plantation owners, a posse of whites rode to hunt down Ben Patterson and his supporters. The wounded Patterson was discovered and killed by white vigilantes while he hid aboard a steamboat docked at Cat Island in the Mississippi River. Other whites continued to hunt and murder escaping strikers.

Although the motive behind the violence that ended the lives of Robert Collins and Ben Patterson is unambiguous, it was relatively infrequent. It was rare that a specific black would be killed by indignant whites for violating a labor contract or refusing to work or encouraging others to strike. Accounts of southern lynchings reveal that most had apparently little to do with the labor market, at least in any direct fashion. Most blacks were lynched for alleged violations of the criminal codes, such as murder, rape, arson, or theft, or for infractions of the de facto code of racial etiquette, such as being insolent, making suggestive comments to white women, or being surly. But this, in itself, does not mean that violence had no impact on the labor market, nor that larger issues were not at stake. Quite to the contrary, for mob violence to be an effective means of social control of black labor, victims did not have to stand accused of work-related transgressions. The lynching of a black for any offense would have the effect of tightening or reinforcing white domination over the entire local black population. For this reason, we suspect that the linkage between mob violence and the labor market was, for the most part, indirect and diffuse as opposed to being direct and specific, yet no less real in its consequences. In many ways, this point is similar to the distinction between the specific and general deterrent functions of lynching (chapter 4).

Seasonal Patterns of Antiblack Mob Violence

In Table 5-7 we tabulate the monthly percentage distribution of black lynching victims for southern counties that were and were not

Table 5-7. Black Lynching Victims of White Mobs by Month in Cotton-Dominant and Non-Cotton-Dominant Counties[a]

Month	Cotton-Dominant (%)	Non-Cotton-Dominant (%)
January	6.87	7.20
February	6.53	5.91
March	7.27	9.64
April	6.20	5.91
May	8.53	9.64
June	10.20	9.64
July	10.40	9.00
August	10.47	9.64
September	9.07	8.87
October	8.00	9.13
November	7.47	6.94
December	8.33	8.23
Month unknown	0.00	0.26
Total	100.01	100.01
Number of black victims	1,500	778

a. Aggregated over the years 1882–1930.

cotton-dominant, aggregated over the period from 1882 through 1930.[46] In plotting the numbers of black victims in each month in each region over the same period (Figure 5-5a), the seasonal nature of black lynching is clearly evident. In each area, monthly variation occurs in the number of black victims, and, in general, lynchings were more frequent in the warmer summer months than during the cooler times of the year. Of particular interest, however, are the regional differences in this periodicity.

First, there is considerably greater monthly variation in lynching activity in the cotton-dominant counties than in those areas where cotton was less important. In fact, seasonality in the cotton areas is almost twice that of the other regions.[47] Second, the pattern of seasonality is much clearer in the areas dominated by cotton. To clarify this trend even more, we have plotted in Figure 5-5b the monthly trend for the cotton-dominant region in standard scores.[48] In the major cotton-producing areas, black lynchings were relatively infrequent between January and April; about 17 percent fewer victims than would be expected were there no seasonality. After April, however, the fre-

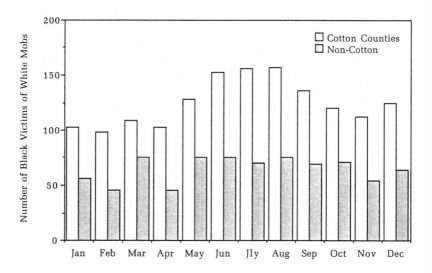

Figure 5-5a. Frequency of Black Lynching Victims by Month in Cotton-Dominant and Non-Cotton-Dominant Counties.

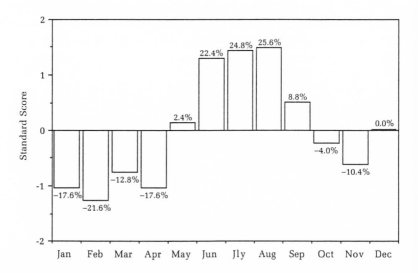

Figure 5-5b. Monthly Pattern of Black Lynching Victims in Cotton-Dominant Counties.

quency of lynching increased through the summer; June, July, and August experienced more than 20 percent more lynchings than the monthly average. The peak in lynching activity occurred in August, when 25 percent more blacks were lynched than were there no seasonality present. After summer, the frequency of lynching declined through the winter. What is unique about this pattern, which is generally consistent with previous descriptions?[49]

As suggested earlier, the patterns observed in Figure 5-5b may reflect a confounding of two analytically separable yet correlated patterns. The first is the seasonal trend of generalized violent crime, and the second is a seasonal trend that is a function of the need to influence, if not dominate, the market for black labor. Lethal mob violence, or the threat of violence, was one of the ways that whites could maintain some leverage over the black agrarian labor force. The brutal treatment of some blacks sent a powerful message that reinforced the racial caste system. If this second seasonal periodicity exists, we expect that lynchings would have been relatively more common during peak periods of labor demand when control over the black work force was critical.[50]

In order to isolate the contributions of the black crime and labor control explanations for the periodicity of lynching, we must expunge that component of the seasonality of black lynching that other violent crimes share. Optimally, we would have liked to purge the monthly variation in lynching of any generalized pattern of violent crime unrelated to mob violence against blacks. This would require, in the ideal case, monthly data on the incidence, by race, of all violent crime in the South over the entire period from 1882 to 1930. Unfortunately, such data do not exist. Instead, we use the seasonal pattern of white lynching victims from 1882 to 1930 as a proxy indicator of generalized violence. By using the corresponding monthly pattern of white lynchings as an adjustment factor, the observed monthly pattern of black lynchings can be corrected for the seasonal trend in generalized violence. If a monthly pattern of lynching persisted after this adjustment procedure, there would be evidence to suggest the operation of forces unique to the seasonality of black lynchings.

The most straightforward statistical procedure for adjusting the monthly lynching data is to regress the number of black victims occurring each month on the frequency of white victims in that month, then use the residuals from this brief time-series regression as the amended seasonal lynching data.[51] Employing this procedure, we have amended the monthly lynching data (Figure 5-6).

The revised pattern shows some similarities and differences from

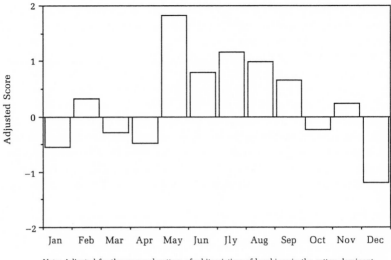

Note: Adjusted for the seasonal pattern of white victims of lynchings in the cotton-dominant counties.

Figure 5-6. Adjusted Seasonal Pattern of Black Lynching Victims in Cotton-Dominant Counties.

the original profile reported in Figure 5-5b. In particular, in Figure 5-5b, the winter and spring months (January through April) experienced a below-average number of lynchings. In Figure 5-6, we find that, after adjusting for the seasonal pattern of white lynchings, the frequency of blacks killed by white mobs in the winter and early spring was closer to the annual average. On the other hand, the summer season had an above-average number of lynchings. Even after controlling on the pattern of white-on-white mob violence, substantially more blacks were lynched from May through September than would be expected.

The adjusted pattern in Figure 5-6 suggests that a periodic component to black lynchings existed over and above the general seasonal effects of lethal southern mob violence. The labor control model may provide insights into why black lynchings would be more common in summer. The model hypothesizes that any unique seasonal variation in lynching may be due to the agricultural production cycle. Although plantation production was extremely labor intensive, the demand for labor was not uniform throughout the year. It is likely that landlords and planters perceived greater need to maintain control over workers during periods of peak labor demand. The pattern reported in Figure 5-6 is partially supportive of this notion. Lynchings increased during the May chopping time, then declined through the lay-by. On the other hand, using this same logic we would have expected an increase in lynchings during the fall harvest season, but, as the data show, that was not the case.

One explanation for the lack of a pronounced increase in lynchings during the harvest is that the terroristic effect of the summer lynching season would have been sufficient to maintain white supremacy and the racial caste system. This carry-over effect may have reduced the need for lethal sanctioning during the cotton harvest season. Another possibility, and one we prefer, is that there was little need for sanctioning during the harvest season because field workers, sharecroppers, and farm renters and tenants were strongly motivated to work. Their efforts had immediate economic payoff as the cotton was ginned and marketed.

In the American South from 1882 to 1930, the lynching of blacks for "crimes" against whites was a common spectacle, yet mob violence was not random in either time or geography. Like many other violent crimes, lynchings were more frequent in the hot summer months than in cooler seasons. This seasonality was not a direct reflection of climate, but rather due to changing labor requirements over the agricultural production cycle. Mob violence was more frequent during times of stronger labor demand than during slack periods. Although the manifest function of lynchings might well have been to rid the white community of offending blacks who violated the moral order, the latent function was to tighten the reins of control over the black population, especially during times when whites most needed black labor to work fields of cotton. Yet, empirical support for a labor control interpretation is not as clean as might have been hoped. Although there is some correspondence between lynchings and the peak of preharvest work in the cotton fields, there is no strong evidence of a similar correspondence between mob violence and the intense labor demands of the cotton harvest.

White Landlessness and Black Lynchings

Students of southern history have long noted the massive transformation of agriculture that began to accelerate after Reconstruction—the expansion of farm tenancy as a means for coping with chronic labor shortages in the agricultural sector.[52] The breadth of these changes was dramatic.

The plots graphed in Figure 5-7a confirm that during the period from 1880 to 1930 the percentage of owner-operated farms declined strikingly in both subregions.[53] In the states outside the cotton culture,

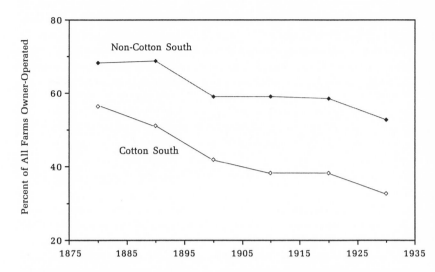

Figure 5-7a. Rates of All Farm Ownership in the Cotton and Non-Cotton South, 1880–1930.

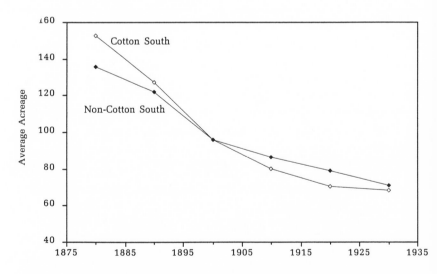

Figure 5-7b. Average Size of All Farms in the Cotton and Non-Cotton South, 1880–1930.

the average rate of decline in ownership was 3.11 percentage points per decade, whereas in the Cotton South the decline in ownership was even more dramatic, averaging 4.62 percentage points per decade. In 1880, the percent of owner-operated farms in the Cotton South was 56.3 percent, compared to 68.3 percent in the rest of the south. By the end of the period, however, the gap had widened. In 1930 only 32.6 percent of farms in the Cotton South were owner-operated, compared to 52.7 percent in the rest of the region.

Another way of demonstrating this critical transformation is to consider changes in the average size of farms. In both subregions, the numbers fell precipitously over the period from 1880 to 1930, especially in the Cotton South, where the average fell from 152 acres in 1880 to a mere 68 acres in 1930 (Figure 5-7b). In the non-Cotton South, the decline was somewhat more moderate yet still significant, from 136 acres in 1880 to 71 acres in 1930. It has been suggested that the rapid decline in owner-operated farms and the corresponding expansion in farms operated by tenants and sharecroppers from 1880 through 1930 had profound consequences for social relations between the races as well as social, political, and economic relations within the white caste itself.[54]

Because our attention is focused on the role of King Cotton, in subsequent analyses we concentrate on the relationship between land tenure and antiblack violence; in particular, it is necessary to examine what was occurring to white and black farm operators at the turn of the century.[55] Given de jure and de facto discrimination and the extent of black poverty, it is not surprising that the rate of ownership was substantially less among black farmers than white farmers (Figure 5-8a), but what is significant is the change in farm ownership. In 1900, only 17.8 percent of black farms were owner-operated compared to 61.5 percent of white farms, a racial gap of 43.7 percentage points. By 1930, however, the racial differential declined to only 31.5 percentage points.

The shift in the relative status of black and white farmers was primarily due to the decline of farm ownership among whites; during the period from 1900 to 1930, the percentage of black owner-operated farms remained relatively stable, varying only from 17.8 percent in 1900 to 14.9 percent in 1930. On the other hand, the decline in white farm ownership was more precipitous and fell from 61.5 percent in 1900 to 46.3 percent in 1930. The average size of both black and white-owned farms declined between 1900 and 1930, but the decline was most obvious for white farms (Figure 5-8b). In 1900, the average size was 131 acres, but by 1930 it was only 89 acres, a significant 32 per-

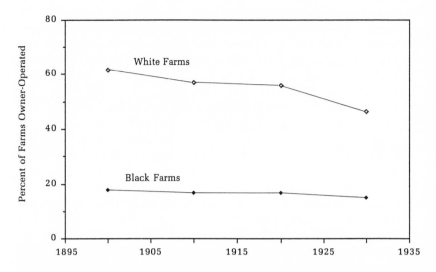

Figure 5-8a. Rates of Farm Ownership in the Cotton South by Race, 1900–1930.

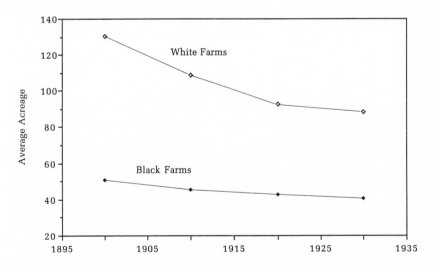

Figure 5-8b. Average Size of Farms in the Cotton South by Race, 1900–1930.

cent decline. Over the same period, the size of black farms also fell, but much less dramatically, from 51 acres in 1900 to 40 acres in 1930.

The message is unambiguous: after 1900, transformations in southern agriculture were eroding the status of many southern whites, and some of the apparent gap between agrarian whites and blacks was diminishing. Although this pattern is clear, it is less obvious whether the shifts were recent or whether they represent longstanding trends.

Because the Bureau of the Census did not compile data on farm operators by race before 1900, it is not known whether the trends noted in Figure 5-8 existed before the turn of the century. This is a significant obstacle; if we want to argue that changes in land tenure affected violence against blacks, the lack of race-specific ownership data covering the period of peak black lynching (the 1890s) represents a serious liability. There is, however, a possible solution, or at least a hint of one. For their seminal investigation of the consequences of emancipation Ransom and Sutch sampled the manuscript census for 1880 data on farm ownership, size, crops produced, and race of farm operator in the Cotton South.[56] Using these data they were able to estimate farm tenancy by race for 1880.

Thus we can use—with appropriate caveats—Ransom and Sutch's data to speculate about the trends in ownership by race before 1900.[57] In Figure 5-9, we have augmented the census data originally presented in Figure 5-8a with Ransom and Sutch's ownership data for 1880. These additional data suggest that the decline in the relative status of agrarian whites in the Cotton South was well under way before 1900. In fact, the Ransom and Sutch estimates, combined with census data, imply that a massive reorganization of agriculture in the Cotton South occurred throughout the lynching era, and that the restructuring involved the downward slide of many whites into tenancy and sharecropping.[58] This shift could mean that increasingly more whites would have entered into competition with blacks, and there would have been some erosion in the apparent status advantage of being white. Given the historical ideology of white racial superiority, this slippage in the status of some whites created a volatile environment and may have produced the necessary conditions for racial conflict. In this regard, Flynn concludes, "Friction [between black and whites] increased during the late nineteenth century as some blacks achieved a measure of independence and as the number of landless whites increased rapidly."[59]

To explore whether such changes in land tenure affected violence toward blacks, we exploit cross-sectional county-level data on lynch-

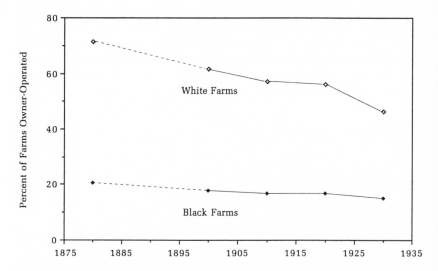

Figure 5-9. Rates of Farm Ownership in the Cotton South by Race, 1880–1930

ings and tenancy. The analytical strategy was to estimate a Poisson-Gamma regression model for black lynchings for three periods: 1900–1909, 1910–19, and 1920–29.[60] For each period, we first regressed the total number of black lynching victims of white mobs during the period on the rate of white farm tenancy and white farm tenancy squared (see Model A for each period).[61] The results of these regressions are presented in Table 5-8.

The findings from the Model A's indicate a significant nonlinear relationship between white farm tenancy and blacks killed by white mobs in the 1900–1909 and 1920–29 periods. For the 1910–19 period, however, there is little evidence at this stage that white tenancy and black lynchings were related. For the two other periods, however, our results suggest a nonlinear relationship such that, at low levels of white tenancy, increases in tenancy were associated with fewer black lynchings. At higher levels, the reverse held: Rising rates of white farm tenancy were associated with greater numbers of blacks being lynched. The point at which this relationship reversed direction was at about 32 percent white tenancy in the 1900–1909 period and 38 percent for the 1920–29 period.[62] In other words, after the rate of white tenancy reached about 32–38 percent in a county—approximately the average level—further increases in white landlessness were

associated with more lynching activity (Figure 5-10).[63] The figure
clearly shows the nonlinear relationship between tenancy and mob
violence, especially for the period from 1900 to 1909. The graph for
the period from 1920 to 1929 is less pronounced, but the nonlineari-

Table 5-8. Poisson-Gamma Regression of Number of Black Lynching
Victims of White Mobs on White Tenancy and Related Variables for
Counties in the South

Predictor Variable[a]	1900–1909		1910–19		1920–29	
	Model A[b]	Model B	Model A	Model B	Model A	Model B
Constant	0.259	−0.840	−1.017	−2.608	−0.333	−2.271
	(0.67)	(−1.69)	(−2.28)	(−5.05)	(−0.87)	(−4.66)
Rate of white farm tenancy	−0.045	−0.070	−0.004	−0.018	−0.069	−0.079
	(−1.91)	(−2.93)	(−0.16)	(−0.79)	(−3.26)	(−4.15)
Rate of white farm tenancy^2	0.0007	0.0008	0.0003	0.0002	0.0009	0.0008
	(1.98)	(2.38)	(0.94)	(0.66)	(3.29)	(3.41)
Cotton dominance (% acreage in cotton)	—	0.013	—	0.020	—	0.002
		(2.16)		(3.13)		(0.22)
Percent population black	—	0.037	—	0.048	—	0.083
		(2.27)		(2.88)		(4.04)
Percent population black^2	—	−0.0003	—	−0.0004	—	−0.0008
		(−2.05)		(−2.58)		(−3.74)
Log size of black population (1,000s)	—	0.253	—	0.161	—	0.226
		(2.26)		(1.44)		(1.84)
Proneness to anti-black violence	—	0.098	—	0.110	—	0.073
		(3.44)		(5.32)		(3.48)
Number of observations	809		830		858	

a. Rate of white farm tenancy, cotton dominance, racial composition, and size of the
    black population measured in 1900, 1910, and 1920. Proneness is the cumulative
    number of black victims of white mobs from 1882 to the beginning of the period.
b. Asymptotic t-ratios in parentheses.

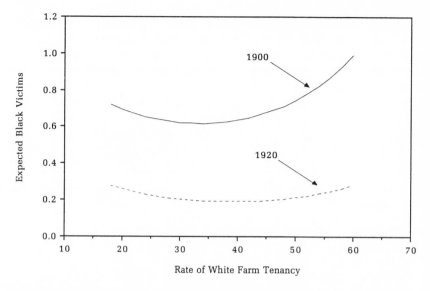

Figure 5-10. Relationship between Black Lynch Victims and White Land-lessness, 1900–1909 and 1920–29.

ty is significant nevertheless. This flattening of the 1920 curve rela-tive to the 1900 curve reflects the lessening of overall mob violence during the latter period.

To further explore this relationship, we next reestimated the mod-els, adding cotton dominance, percent black, the log size of the black population, and the county's proneness to antiblack violence as con-trol variables. Not surprisingly, cotton dominance, racial composition, size of the black population, and proneness to violence had signifi-cant effects on black lynchings. In general, the larger the absolute and relative sizes of the local black population, the greater the dependence on cotton, and the stronger the legacy of antiblack violence, the greater the number of black lynching victims, although the effect for cotton dominance is insignificant in the later period (see Model B for each period). The important finding is, however, that even after controlling on these factors, the effects of white farm tenancy are statistically sig-nificant from 1900 to 1909 and from 1920 to 1929, with the same u-shaped nonlinear pattern noted earlier.[64]

The results of the Poisson regressions in Table 5-8 indicate a rela-tionship between white landlessness and mob violence directed to-ward blacks, and the linkage existed over and above any association between white farm tenancy, cotton dominance, size of the black la-bor force, and the county's historical tendency toward antiblack vio-

lence. Consistent with these findings is the view that the last part of
the nineteenth and early twentieth centuries witnessed a decline in
the relative position of many southern whites and a narrowing of the
racial status gap. This change created conditions where some whites
competed more directly with blacks, and those not in direct competition were in indirect rivalry for status claims.[65] Every time white
mobs were able to kill offending blacks with impunity—if not com-
mendation—their act highlighted and reinforced the dominance of the
white caste and the inferiority of the black caste, thus emphasizing
the status differences.

Conclusions

Gains in the real price of cotton in the Cotton South between 1883
and 1930 were associated with years of reduced lynching activity
against blacks, a relationship that remains intact even after we control for the effects of population composition, generalized violence,
and black crime. This cotton price-lynching relationship was more
pronounced between 1883 and 1906 than in later years. However, the
price of cotton generally affected neither the frequency of the lynching of whites in the Cotton South nor the lynching of blacks outside
the Cotton South. The lynching of blacks was more common in southern counties dominated by cotton agriculture than in counties less
dependent upon King Cotton, a relationship not attributable to the fact
that cotton-dominated counties tended to have larger black populations, both relatively and absolutely. Patterns of land tenure also had
important independent effects on violence directed toward blacks in
the Cotton South, and blacks were lynched more frequently during the
warmer months when labor demand was strong and less commonly
during the colder times of the year when labor was less necessary.

We have hypothesized a conceptual model by which these findings
may be interpreted based on the labor requirements of plantation cotton production, the historical legacy of slavery in cotton-growing areas, and economic stresses produced by declining cotton prices in the
late nineteenth century (Figure 5-11). The southern cotton culture was
historically founded on plantation production that exploited black
labor held captive through chattel slavery. Along with the plantation
economy grew a racist ideology of innate white superiority and inborn
black inferiority that rationalized white dominion and the South's
racial caste structure. After the Civil War, the South's dependence on
cotton as a primary cash crop—as well as the persistent need for a
controllable black labor force to plant, tend, and harvest cotton—con-

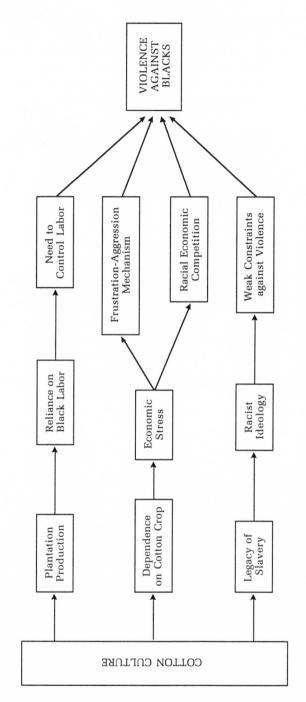

Figure 5-11. Possible Linkage between the Cotton Culture and Racial Violence.

tinued to grow. Because the Thirteenth Amendment abolished formal slavery, alternative forms of social control emerged to maintain white domination of southern blacks, and one of those forms was the widespread use of verbal and physical violence.

The civil rights that whites enjoyed were rarely extended to blacks because of the racism that permeated so much of southern culture. This meant, among other things, that whites could harass and assault blacks with little fear of the legal consequences of aggression.[66] Southern racist ideology produced a moral and legal system that had only weak constraints against violence targeted at blacks. Often blacks were considered legitimate, and even deserving, objects for white wrath.

Southern dependency on cotton not only meant a concomitant reliance on black labor, but also a dependency upon the world commodity market for cotton. Soft cotton prices negatively impacted all cotton producers, but small farmers, sharecroppers, or tenants suffered disproportionately because of a lack of capital resources. The economic squeeze not only threatened the current standard of living, but also jeopardized the future. In Hovland and Sears's view, this represents "goal-frustration" and produces aggressive behavior. Although Hovland and Sears impute no rational motive to such aggressive behavior, Raper suggests that it was related to attempts by white laborers to reduce competition from black laborers and to replace blacks with unemployed whites.

Although there were marginal blacks as well as whites, blacks were relatively powerless to protest their plight or externalize their aggression. Marginal whites, on the other hand, had options. They could direct their rage toward the powerful class of whites—large landowners, merchants, and bankers—although the costs of such hostility were clear. This is not to argue that no hostility existed between marginal whites and local elites. As early as the 1870s, there was growing conflict between these groups, and yeoman farmers began to organize for collective action. The swelling membership of the Southern Farmers' Alliance during the 1870s and 1880s is testimony to the conflict.[67] The point is, however, that those who acted hostilely toward the white elite risked retribution, whereas penalties for hostility against blacks were minimal.

Perhaps it is reasonable to think of the cotton culture as representing a constellation of factors including arrangements of land tenure, a strong dependency on cotton as the primary cash crop, and a reliance upon black labor. To be sure, many blacks died at the hands of white mobs outside the boundaries of the cotton culture, yet it is unmistakable that the demographic, social, and economic conditions that defined such a culture were important factors influencing the likelihood of lethal violence directed toward southern blacks.

NOTES

1. Brundage (1993) includes an interesting discussion of the geography of Georgia and Virginia and offers compelling explanations for the uneven distribution of lynchings within the two states. The economic organization of local areas and the role of blacks within the agricultural economy are prominent in his framework for understanding the distribution of lynchings across regions.

2. We defined a prime cotton growing area as a county dominated by cotton production. A county was designated as being "cotton-dominant" if its average percent of improved acreage dedicated to cotton production equalled or exceeded 25 percent for the years 1890, 1900, and 1910.

3. Of these 2,314 black victims of white lynch mobs, we have a county location for 2,278. Of these, 1,500 (65.9 percent) were killed in, or by mobs from, cotton-dominant counties. Thus the odds favoring a victim coming from cotton-dominated areas are 1,500 divided by 778, or 1.93—almost 2 to 1.

4. Raper (1933, 30).

5. Hovland and Sears (1940).

6. For a thoughtful critique of the frustration-aggression framework, see McPhail (1991, 33–49).

7. Hovland and Sears (1940, 348).

8. Mintz (1946).

9. Reed, Doss, and Hulbert (1987).

10. Bonacich (1972, 1975).

11. Jaynes (1986).

12. Brundage (1993) describes several lynching incidents in Georgia that were clear attempts by whites to intimidate, or drive off, successful blacks.

13. Williamson (1984, 441–42).

14. White (1969, 11–12).

15. Raper (1933, 47).

16. Shapiro (1988, 219).

17. See Gaither (1977), Hahn (1983), Shapiro (1988), White (1929 [1969]), Williamson (1984), and Wright (1986).

18. Both time series have been twice-smoothed statistically using three-year moving averages in order to simplify the underlying trends visually. The cotton price data refer to average nominal prices for wholesale raw cotton (U.S. Bureau of the Census 1975, series E 126, 208).

The "Cotton South" is defined as the five states of Alabama, Arkansas,

Georgia, Mississippi, and South Carolina. Elsewhere we have included Louisiana and labeled the six states the "Deep South" (Beck and Tolnay 1990). For this chapter we use an empirical criterion for state inclusion. Exploiting agriculture census data for 1899 and 1909, we found that in Alabama, Arkansas, Georgia, Mississippi, and South Carolina cotton revenues comprised more than 50 percent of the total value of acreage crops, so we identified these five states as being the Cotton South. In the remaining states, cotton was of minor economic importance. In 1899, for example, it comprised only 14.3 percent of acreage revenues in Tennessee, less than 1 percent in Kentucky, and 28.9 percent in North Carolina. These states were clearly outside the Cotton South. The one case that caused some difficulty was that of Louisiana. There, cotton accounted for 44.3 percent of the value of acreage crops in 1899. Although this fell short of the 50 percent criterion, it still shows that Louisiana's dependency on cotton was not trivial. Thus, although we excluded Louisiana from the category of Cotton South states, a counterargument could be made that it should have been included.

19. Wholesale prices were deflated using the Bureau of Labor Statistics Consumer Price Index for All Items (U.S. Bureau of the Census 1975, series E 135, 210–11). In principle, the BLS Wholesale Price Index for All Commodities might seem a more reasonable deflator, but it covers only the years since 1890. The BLS Consumer Price Index, however, can be applied to prices extending back to 1800.

20. For example, Blalock (1967) and Tolnay and Beck (1990).

21. See Beck and Tolnay (1994) for a somewhat different specification of the relationship among these variables. Even though a different specification is employed, the substantive conclusions concerning the relationships among the variables are consistent with the conclusions reached in this section.

22. Two measures of the size of the black population are included: the absolute size of the black population and the percent of the population that is black. Statistics on the size of the black population were obtained from decennial census data. Black population for intercensal years was estimated by linear interpolation.

The rate of inflation is the annual percentage change in the Consumer Price Index. Exploratory research revealed that the effect of inflation on the number of black lynch victims was lagged by one year; that is, it was the rate of inflation experienced during the prior year that affected the likelihood of mob violence in the current year.

Total annual production of cotton is measured by the number of bales of cotton (in 1000s) ginned in the Cotton South. These data are from U.S. Department of Agriculture 1951–52.

Our measure of the annual level of black crime is necessarily less precise than the other explanatory variables. Annual statistics on crimes committed by blacks in all five states are not available for this historical period. We constructed a somewhat imperfect proxy based on the number of blacks legally executed annually in the Cotton South: black crime rate$_t$ = 10,000 (black executions$_{t+1}$ / black population$_t$).

This proxy has two weaknesses: (1) by using executions we capture only the most serious crimes and thus underestimate the actual amount of crime committed by blacks; and (2) blacks were executed for crimes against blacks as well as crimes against whites, so using black executions overestimates the rate of black against white crime. This variable must be interpreted with caution.

23. The term ε is modeled as a first-order moving-average process (chapter 4).

24. Because the variables in the empirical models in Table 5-1 have been differenced once, and the rate of inflation variable is lagged one year, the actual time period covered is 1884 to 1930, rather than 1882 to 1930. Further, because all variables have been differenced there is no need to include an intercept (constant) parameter in these time-series models.

25. For example, see Blalock (1967).

26. Du Bois (1969); Williamson (1984).

27. Model A was chosen to conserve degrees of freedom. Like the time-series findings reported in Table 5-1, the variables in the moving regressions were differenced once, and the model estimated assuming a first-order moving-average specification.

28. We estimate that in the period 1882–99, the net effects of cotton price and inflation on black lynchings to be –7.4308 and 1.6490, respectively. For the period 1900–1930, these effects are estimated to be –1.0582 and 0.7077, respectively.

29. For some southern states, the "official" dates of voter disenfranchisement postdate actual measures to reduce black political participation. For example, 1908 is generally considered the date of disenfranchisement for Georgia because several restrictive voting statutes were approved in that year. In fact, long before 1908 very small numbers of blacks had voted in Georgia (Kousser 1974).

30. Also see Tolnay and Beck (1992) for a discussion of the effect of black out-migration on the southern economy and lethal violence against blacks.

31. Daniel (1985).

32. For the geographical distribution of white victims of white lynch mobs, see Figure 4-1b.

33. In addition to fifteen black victims, white mobs also killed two

whites during this period; black or integrated mobs lynched six black victims. In total, twenty-three people were victims of lynch mobs in Bossier Parish between 1890 and 1909.

34. Cotton dominance is measured as the county's percentage of improved agricultural land dedicated to cotton production.

35. See note 41 in chapter 4 for the justification of this particular specification. A county's proneness to antiblack violence is measured as the number of black lynch victims of white mobs in the county between 1882–89 for the 1890–1909 period, and the number between 1882–1909 for the 1910–29 period.

36. A 2.8 percent increase occurred for the 1890–1909 period, and a 2.6 percent increase for the 1910 to 1929 period.

37. The coefficient's asymptotic t-ratio is only 1.03, which would not be considered to be statistically significant by conventional standards.

38. See Beck and Tolnay (1992) for a further investigation into the seasonality of black lynchings.

39. For example, see Ames (1942, 13–14), and Williamson (1984, 186).

40. Southern Commission (1932, 12), emphasis added.

41. See Daniel (1985, 3–22), Phillips (1929, 112–15), and Vance (1929).

42. *Southern Cultivator, or Dixie Farmer* 49, nos. 1–12 (1891).

43. Not coincidentally, it was during this slack time that traveling carnivals, fairs, and tent shows visited Dixie, taking advantage of fresh cotton money in pants pockets and purses throughout the South (Vance 1929, 306).

44. Blacks were not the only victims of mob violence against labor, however. In mid-January 1923, E. C. Gregor, a white male, was hung from a railroad trestle in Harrison, Boone County, Arkansas. He had been involved in a militant strike against the railroad and, when questioned, refused to identify those who might have been implicated in sabotaging it. Mrs. Ella May [Wiggins], also white, was killed by a mob near Gastonia, North Carolina, in early September 1920. She had joined a textile union and was trying to arrange a mass meeting in Gastonia in support of the union's efforts to organize workers. Her efforts were not appreciated by textile employers and some of the locals who may have feared for their jobs.

45. For more detailed descriptions of the cotton pickers' strike, see Harris (1982, 33–36), and Holmes (1973).

46. In this section we used counties to define the cotton-dominant versus nondominant areas of the South. A county was defined as being "cotton-dominant" if its average percent of improved acreage dedicated to cotton production equaled or exceeded 25 percent for the years 1890, 1900, and 1910.

47. For each group of states we computed the χ^2 statistic comparing the observed monthly distribution of black victims with the pattern that would be expected if no seasonality existed. The χ^2 for the cotton-dominated counties was 40.4. For the noncotton areas, the χ^2 was dramatically smaller, 21.7, indicating substantially weaker seasonality.

48. The scores are normalized with a mean of zero and a standard deviation of unity.

49. See, for example, Ames (1942) and the Southern Commission on the Study of Lynching (1932).

50. It could be reasoned that lynching was counterproductive because it removed labor from the supply pool by (1) killing the able-bodied black workers, and (2) by encouraging them to migrate from areas of frequent mob violence. We believe that there is some evidence of the latter effect (Tolnay and Beck 1990, 1992), but, as for the former, the absolute number of blacks lynched would have represented a very small fraction of the total black labor force available for work.

51. That is, the adjusted monthly lynching score is:

Adjusted $Y_i = (Y_i - Y_i^*)/\sigma_\varepsilon$ $i = 1, 2, \ldots, 12$

where Y_i is the observed number of black lynching victims occurring in the ith month, Y_i^* is the predicted number of black victims occurring in the ith month based on a first-order moving-average regression with white lynchings as a predictor, and σ_ε is the square root of the mean square error.

52. We use the terms *farm tenancy* and *sharecropping* interchangeably to mean the class of farm operators who were not owners. In reality, there were significant differences among tenants, renters, and sharecroppers. For discussions of the growth and meaning of farm tenancy, see the work of Ayers (1992), DeCanio (1974), Flynn (1983), Hahn (1983), Ransom and Sutch (1977), Reid (1981), Shlomowitz (1979), Woodman (1968), Woodward (1951), and Wright (1978, 1986).

53. Unless otherwise noted, all data come from various bulletins and reports of the U.S. Bureau of the Census.

54. See in particular Flynn (1983) and Hahn (1983).

55. Data on the race of farm operators was not published before the 1900 census, thus we are unable to extend our discussion back to the 1880s.

56. See Ransom and Sutch (1977, 283–94) for a discussion of their sample of southern farms from the Cotton South. Their definition of the Cotton South is based on county-level characteristics and is more geographically restrictive than our state-level definition of the Cotton South. See Ransom and Sutch 1977, xx.

57. Data for 1880 is computed from Ransom and Sutch (1977, 295, Table G.12).

58. For an interesting discussion of the evolution of black and white tenancy in one southern state, see McKenzie (1993).

59. Flynn (1983, 182).

60. Here again the lack of race-specific ownership data before 1900 prohibits extending the analyses into the earlier periods.

61. Exploratory research suggested that white tenancy might have a nonlinear effect on lynchings, so white tenancy entered the model both as a linear and a quadratic (squared) term.

62. Specifically, differentiating our regression model with respect to white tenancy, we find ∂Victims/∂Tenancy = β_1 + 2 β_2(White Tenancy), where β_1 is the linear effect of white tenancy on victims and β_2 is its quadratic effect. To find the point at which the tenancy-lynching relationship reverses, we set ∂Victims/∂Tenancy equal to zero and solve for the implied value of tenancy, that is, point of reversal equals $-\beta_1/[(2)(\beta_2)]$. Using the coefficients reported in Table 5-8, we find that for lynchings between 1900 and 1909, the point of reversal in Model A is $-(-0.045)/[(2)(0.0007)] = 32.1$. Thus, for this period, in counties where the percentage of white farm tenancy was less than 32.1, increases in tenancy were associated with fewer lynchings, yet in counties where the percentage white tenancy was greater than 32.1, increases in tenancy were associated with greater lynching activity. For the 1920–29 period, the point of reversal is: $-(-0.069)/[(2)(0.0009)] = 38.3$ percent.

63. We have plotted these figures using the coefficients of the Model A's in Table 5-8.

64. After controlling on cotton dominance, percent black, log size of the black population, and proneness to antiblack violence, the point of reversal for the 1900–1909 period is = $-\beta_1/[(2)(\beta_2)]$ = $-(-0.070)/[(2)(0.0008)] = 43.8$. For the other two periods, the points of reversal are 45.0 and 49.4, respectively. These are rightward shifts relative to the pattern found previously.

65. Doob (1937, 466) vividly describes white reactions to increased competition between landless whites and blacks, especially aggression and hostility. He notes that even though few lynchings actually took place, "Every 'peckerwood' [poor white] asserts that it is 'a good thing' to lynch 'a nigger' occasionally."

66. In Georgia, for example, of the 492 legal executions that occurred between 1882 and 1930, 83 whites were executed for crimes against other whites, but only 2 whites were executed for crimes against blacks. Such an imbalance did not exist for blacks; 206 blacks were executed for crimes against other blacks (notably murder); and 192 were executed for crimes against whites.

67. See Hahn (1983), and Wright (1986).

6

Southern Politics and Lynching, 1880–1900

After the Civil War, southern politics became a very messy affair. Contributing to the turmoil was the newly franchised African-American population. Even a casual reading of the history of southern political life between 1865 and 1900 reveals a complex and confusing cast of parties and interest groups maneuvering upon a stage whose dimensions were defined by class and race. Most of the political actors were native to the South, but external political and economic forces from the West and the Northeast also played a role in the ongoing drama.

The political fortunes of southern blacks shifted dramatically during the closing decades of the nineteenth century. During some periods they either exercised considerable influence or at least were considered important enough to have been exploited by more established political forces. Whenever African-American voters were in a position to help determine the outcome of a political contest, they were also in danger of antagonizing a group of southern whites who believed that the political interests of the black population were orthogonal to their own. Naturally, this danger would not have been so keen had race not been such a pivotal issue. But it was, so the political participation of blacks was potentially threatening to the perceived well-being of some segment of the southern white community.

The competition theory of racial and ethnic relations tells us that dominant social groups, when they feel threatened, will invoke a wide variety of methods to preserve their privileged access to society's scarce resources.[1] Whites were clearly the dominant political group within the South. Furthermore, their impressive repertory of discrim-

inatory weapons for perpetuating their advantage included gerrymandering, election fraud, bribery, disenfranchisement, and other forms
of skulduggery designed to neutralize the black vote. A number of
scholars have also suggested that southern whites were willing to resort to violence (including lynching) in order to assure the continuation of white political supremacy.

Surveying the Evidence for a Political Threat Model

The political threat model of lynchings emphasizes the struggle for
control over southern politics and government during the last quar-
ter of the nineteenth century. It contends that African-Americans,
when armed with the vote, assumed the potential to influence southern political institutions. Their ability to translate this potential into
reality depended upon a number of things, including the character of
local political life, their relative numbers in the electorate, and their
propensity to exercise their newly obtained political freedom. When
the conditions were right, the black vote represented a significant
threat to certain segments of the white population, especially (but not
exclusively) the dominant Democratic party. And racial violence was
one technique that whites used to discourage and punish black political participation.

Previous efforts to examine the validity of the political threat model
of black lynchings generally have proceeded under one of two kinds
of assumptions. The first, and more robust, is that lynchings should
have declined in frequency after the widespread disenfranchisement
of southern blacks, which was accomplished by the early twentieth
century. We consider this to be a robust assumption because it is insensitive to the specific nature of the threat that voting blacks posed
and to the source of racial violence within the white population. For
example, disenfranchisement should have reduced lynchings, whether it was poor whites or the white elite that was most threatened by
the black vote.

The second assumption is that lynchings should have been more
common where the African-American population was proportionately
greater. Accordingly, whites were more likely to perceive blacks as a
political threat where blacks' numbers gave them a larger relative influence over the outcome of local elections. We consider this assumption more volatile because its validity is highly vulnerable to the character of local politics as well as to the class-specific behavior of local
whites. For instance, would we expect a large or small number of
lynchings in a predominately black county that was firmly in control

of well-to-do whites and the Democratic party, which fraudulently "purchased" the votes of blacks? Would we expect a large or a small number of lynchings in a predominately black county that lent its overwhelming support to a dominating Populist party? These complicating issues might reduce the usefulness of findings emanating from research carried out under the second assumption and to which we will return later in this chapter.

One of the simplest ways to determine whether disenfranchisement affected the frequency of black lynchings is to look at the trends in lynching before and after the implementation of restrictive voting statutes. An immediate reduction, or a protracted decline, in lynchings after the South rescinded the black vote would support the political threat model. On the other hand, if there was no perceptible short- or long-term impact of disenfranchisement, then the validity of the political threat model remains in doubt. Phillips examined longitudinal patterns of lynching in North Carolina between 1889 and 1918 as part of a study of the relationship between legal and extralegal lethal punishment. His data showed a rather sharp decline in lynchings after North Carolina had effectively disenfranchised its black population by means of a constitutional amendment in 1900. As he observes, "The destruction of black political power in North Carolina made the extreme, highly visible, and somewhat dangerous act of lynching a costly and unnecessary form of repression."[2]

Beck and his colleagues replicated Phillips's analyses to correct for a variety of problems associated with the data and methodology and extended the analysis to include the state of Georgia, a better representative of the Deep South region. Like Phillips's, the results suggested a possible effect of disenfranchisement on lynching in North Carolina. The data for Georgia, on the other hand, contained no hint of an effect of disenfranchisement on lynchings. Although admittedly limited in geographic scope and methodological sophistication, the longitudinal investigations by Phillips and Beck and his colleagues yield only mixed support for the political threat model of lynching in its more general form.[3]

The alternative approach to exploring the political threat model of black lynchings has drawn heavily from the work of Blalock.[4] He distinguishes two primary forms of competition between minority and majority group members—political and economic. In both cases, competition is predicted to be stronger where the minority group represents a proportionately greater part of the total population. As the size of the minority group rises, the dominant majority group also becomes increasingly motivated to discriminate against the competing minority group in order to preserve its privileged social position. However, according to Blalock, the varying character of economic and political competition should produce somewhat different forms of relationship between minority concentration and discrimination (e.g., lynching). Although the relationship is predicted to be positive in both instances, the strength of the association is expected to increase with the relative size of the minority where competition is primarily political in nature but to become progressively weaker when the basis for competition is economic. The political threat model would be supported had we found that black lynchings were more common where the black population was relatively larger and had lynchings been especially frequent where blacks enjoyed a clear numerical superiority.

Reed was the first to conduct a systematic test of Blalock's articulation of the political threat model.[5] He found that the rate of black lynching in Mississippi was higher in counties with proportionately larger black populations. Importantly, Reed noted that the lynching rate rose to very high levels in counties where more than 80 percent of the population was black, thereby supporting the political threat model.

Corzine and his colleagues offered a fuller test of Blalock's political threat hypothesis by extending Reed's analysis to all eleven former Confederate states and by including a variety of relevant control variables.[6] Their results also showed a positive relationship between black population concentration and lynching, again with lynchings being especially frequent in counties with overwhelmingly black populations. However, they further refined the political threat model by showing that it applied only to the states of the Deep South, and only before the widespread adoption of African-American disenfranchisement.

Reacting to a variety of conceptual and methodological weaknesses in the research conducted by Reed and Corzine and his colleagues, Tolnay and his colleagues replicated both studies. Most problematic was the lynching index used in both previous studies, which was predisposed to yield exactly the type of curvilinear relationship between black population concentration and lynching predicted by the political threat model even if there was no variation in the intensity of lynching by percent black.[7] After correcting for this and a variety of other problems, Tolnay and his colleagues found that the intensity of lynching did, in fact, rise with the level of black population concentration. However, they failed to observe the especially high level of lynching in predominantly black counties that Reed and Corzine and his colleagues noted and that is critical for support of Blalock's political threat model. Although limited by the poor lynching data available in 1989, and therefore reluctant to claim a definitive conclusion, Tolnay and his colleagues inferred no support from their analyses for the political threat model of black lynchings.[8]

Additional inquiries into the relationship between southern politics and black lynchings have been conducted but do not fit neatly within the two general categories of research described. Inverarity observed that lynchings (not race-specific) in Louisiana increased sharply during election years in which the Populist party mounted spirited challenges to the dominant Democratic party. He concluded that this pattern suggested the operation of a kind of "boundary maintenance" as Louisiana whites reacted to the Populist threat. Olzak also observed an increasing level of lynching during years in which the Populist party was most active. However, her study was based on national-level political and lynching patterns and cannot speak directly to the dynamics of southern politics and lynching.[9] Looking only at the state of Georgia, Soule found no relationship between Populist voting behavior and black lynchings.[10]

It must be concluded, therefore, that the existing evidence regarding the political threat model of black lynchings is decidedly ambiguous. No solid, convincing evidence exists that disenfranchisement reduced the level of black lynchings. In addition, although the relationship between African-American population concentration and black lynchings appears to be positive, it is not especially supportive of the political threat model (as opposed, say, of the economic threat model). Piecemeal evidence does indicate that the level of black lynching may have been responsive to the activity of the Populist party, however it is certainly premature to conclude that such evidence is definitive.

Thus, given the complex nature of southern political life during the last decades of the nineteenth century—and the fluctuating position of African-Americans within it—more sophisticated conceptualization of the political threat model of lynching is required. Whom did southern blacks threaten by their political participation, and how was this "threatening" behavior translated into racial violence against African-Americans?

Southern Politics, 1865–1900

A comprehensive picture of southern politics, in all of its complexity during the last half of the nineteenth century, has been drawn elsewhere.[11] Here we intend to illuminate the potential linkages between southern political machinations and racial violence. The following discussion is organized according to four general eras of political history during the period: Reconstruction, redemption, populism, and disenfranchisement. The role that blacks played in southern politics varied substantially across these four periods, as did the potential for politically motivated lynchings.

Reconstruction: 1865–80

After the Confederacy collapsed, southern politics underwent a remarkable transformation. The intimidating presence of occupying federal troops and the offensive influx of carpetbaggers from the North set the stage for an even more humiliating insult to southern sensibilities—the political empowerment of the freedman. Socially, economically, and politically, white southerners saw their control of the region rudely wrested away by the two groups they despised the most, Yankees and blacks.

First, the Civil Rights Act of 1866, and the ratification of the Fourteenth Amendment to the U.S. Constitution in 1868, extended to freed blacks the full rights of citizenship, including due process. Then, ratification of the Fifteenth Amendment guaranteed southern blacks the right to vote. Armed with the franchise, African-Americans suddenly had the power to exert a strong influence on the shape of southern politics. In many counties, especially in the Black Belt that cut a swath across South Carolina, Georgia, Alabama, and Mississippi, blacks actually constituted a numerical majority of the population. And they exercised this new freedom with a vengeance. As a result of their political participation, blacks enjoyed measurable political success. They were elected to office at all levels of government and began to play an integral part in local affairs, including service on juries that sat in judgment of whites. The once politically impotent race was now a force to be reckoned with.

The traditionally dominant Democratic party sometimes found itself in the unusual position of political subordination. With the help of the black vote, the Republican party greatly expanded its influence in the South and fed the hysterical concern among many that the region was threatened by the prospect of "Negro domination." Southern Republican candidates were sent to state houses, as well as to the U.S. Congress and Senate, in unprecedented numbers. Race split the political landscape during Reconstruction by threatening the hegemony of the white supremacist Democratic party and added still another reason for southern whites to fear blacks.

Early during Reconstruction, whites attempted to institute a variety of measures to thwart the expanding freedom of blacks. These Black Codes varied from state to state but often dictated the separation of blacks and whites in rail cars, hospitals, jails, asylums, and schools. The codes were overturned relatively quickly by federal civil rights legislation and the Fourteenth and Fifteenth Amendments, however. Yet they were far from dead, only lying dormant to await a more sympathetic political climate after the turn of the century, when they were revived in the form of the notorious Jim Crow laws. Unfortunately, violence was one white response to increasing human rights for freed blacks that was more difficult to eradicate.[12]

The Ku Klux Klan and other self-appointed protectors of white supremacy did not feel especially obligated to honor the constitutional guarantees. Thus, Reconstruction witnessed a staggering increase in the amount of violence directed at blacks—often with an explicitly political motive. Indeed, Wright maintains that lynchings in Kentucky peaked during the 1870s as whites turned to violence to discourage African-Americans from voting or to guarantee that their votes advanced the interests of the white supremacist Democratic party.[13] Shapiro argues that "the evidence accumulated that violent acts against blacks were a major component of the economic and *political system* that now controlled the South. Blacks might be permitted to operate within well-circumscribed limits, but where black activity was seen as actually or potentially threatening, aimed at achieving genuine equality, the answer of the white supremacists was forcible repression."[14]

Politically active southern blacks, therefore, were potentially threatening to virtually any segment of the white community that desired to see the demise of "Negro domination" and the continuation of white political supremacy (and the Democratic party that embodied that sentiment). This group cross-cut all economic classes of the white population. African-Americans had ample opportunity to excite the dominant caste by their political participation. And there were virtually no limits to the numbers (or variety) of whites willing to get out the rope and faggot when they felt so inclined. Undoubtedly, this accounts for the obviously impressive, although still relatively undocumented and unexamined, level of black lynchings during Reconstruction.[15]

White Redemption: 1880–90

The end of the Reconstruction era and the beginning of white redemption of southern politics actually began before 1880. A key turning point for southern Democrats was the Compromise of 1877. The presidential election of 1876 between Rutherford B. Hayes (a Republican) and Samuel J. Tilden (a Democrat) ended with neither candidate garnering enough electoral votes for success. Tilden held 184 electoral votes, only one short of the number required for election, while Hayes trailed with 166. An impasse was reached, and the parties became hopelessly divided over how the deadlock should be resolved. After a good deal of back-room dealing and several false starts, southern Democrats threw their support to the Republican Hayes—assuring his election—in return for promises of support for internal reconstruction of the war-ravaged South and the appointment of a southerner to the position of postmaster general. Also implicit in the agreement was the northern Republicans' tacit approval of a greater voice for southern Democrats in the direction of race relations in Dixie.

Following the Compromise of 1877, Democrats began to implement a variety of policies designed to neutralize the black vote, thereby weakening the southern Republican party.[16] Among the weapons in their arsenal were gerrymandering political districts; appointing county-level officials sympathetic to their cause; establishing elaborate voting registration procedures and inaccessible polling places that discouraged black voters; and using fraud and bribery to exploit or attract black votes. Through the use of these methods and others like them, conservative Democrats often were able to elect their candidates and achieve their political objectives. The policies of the Democratic party tilted increasingly toward the interests of northern capitalists, including bankers and railroads (who maintained strong financial interests in the postwar South), and worked to the disadvantage of an increasingly disenchanted group of agrarian whites.

Although the Democratic party was relatively successful at redeeming southern politics for white supremacists, the era of redemption was far from placid. The challenges that Democrats faced from within their own party as well as from without were not trivial. Some white farmers (traditionally Democrats) began to bridle at such handicaps as the cost of transporting goods to market and the price, and conditions, of credit. Furthermore, they believed that the dominant conservative wing of the Democratic party was in league with the real villains—northern capitalists and industrialists. Although this agrarian wing hesitated to bolt the party of white supremacy during the 1880s, it did threaten to reshape the party's politics. But, as Woodward noted, "Agrarian mavericks were eternally taking off up the left fork followed by great droves that they stampeded. With the aid of the New-South propagandists, however, and by frequent resort to repressive or demagogic devices, the right-forkers continued to keep the South fairly faithful to the Eastern alignment—until the advent of the Populists."[17]

Although the relative success of the resurrected southern Democrats had weakened the Republican party, it was still able to mount successful challenges in some areas, particularly when the party was able to count upon the support of black voters. As the decade wore on, however, the probability of this grew increasingly dim as Democrats invoked fears of renewed "Negro domination" and fraudulently manipulated the black franchise. Ironically, the southern Republican party (like its northern counterpart) gradually began to abandon the very black voters upon whom it had depended and sought to establish other political alliances not necessarily sympathetic with the plight of southern blacks, including some within the incipient agrarian movement.

Woodward sums up the confusing world of southern politics that emerged during the era of white redemption well: "With the party of white supremacy in alliance with the Negro against lower class white men; with the Republican party of hard money and Negro rights in alliance with Greenbackers and repudiationists against the Negro and debt payers; and with agrarian anti-monopolists in alliance with the party of big business, what wonder is it that the average Southerner retreated into some form of political nihilism?"[18]

The politically cross-cutting dimensions of race and class during the 1880s had great potential to imperil southern blacks. Again, the basic questions are, Who might southern blacks have threatened politically? and Which segments of the southern white community might have been politically motivated to lynch blacks? These questions have many possible answers, largely because black voters were used as political pawns at the same time they pursued their own political ends. For instance, when conservative Democrats used blacks to establish a new hegemony during redemption, agrarian and lower-class whites may have been antagonized. Blacks were used to further the political and economic interests of the Bourbon Democrats, interests that again were not shared universally by all whites, even those within the party. On the other hand, when the black vote strengthened the hand of the Republican party (and thereby threatened the feared resurgence of "Negro domination"), southern whites of all classes may have been motivated to take action. In each case, it is possible that they resorted to lynching in response to a perceived political threat from black voters. It is also possible that lynchings could have resulted from the atmosphere of heightened racial tension that elite whites in the Democratic party created as they deliberately raised the specter of "Negro domination" to assure race solidarity and prevent political defections.

Clearly, the search for evidence supporting the political threat model of black lynchings is complicated considerably by the political realities of the 1880s. They also demonstrate why previous efforts to infer a political motive for lynchings simply by using the racial composition of the population have been disappointing. A relatively large African-American population would not necessarily have been politically threatening to all southern whites in all situations. The degree of threat would have depended heavily on how those blacks were voting and who their political behavior threatened within the community.

The Populist Movement: 1890–1900

The cracks that had always marred the "solid South" sought by the white supremacist Democratic party began to deepen and widen as the 1880s came to a close. As Woodward noted, by 1890, "The black man was beginning to feel toward his party much the same as the Southern white man was feeling toward his—that his vote was taken for granted and his needs were ignored."[19] For the first time, southern politics—and society, for that matter—faced the real possibility of a coalition built around common class interests rather than race. The vehicle for this potentially revolutionary development was the Populist movement and the third political party that it eventually spawned.

During redemption, southern farmers watched the power base within the Democratic party strengthen its allegiance to the financial and industrial interests of the Northeast and perceived an alarming neglect of their own problems. Many, blacks and whites alike, were virtually bound to the crop-lien system that required them to mortgage their maturing crops in exchange for credit from merchants and landlords to meet day-to-day expenses. The balance sheets at the end of the year often were written in red, and farmers saw the same cycle of debt and poverty continued annually. At the same time, the costs of transporting crops to market were so high, and the price received so unpredictable, that some farmers actually faced increased debt after their crops had been transported and sold. This agrarian penury was made even more distasteful by the special treatment and subsidies received by other sectors of the southern economy, especially the railroads and carpetbagging northern industries.[20]

Many southern farmers' grievances had a long history, and the populism of the 1890s really had its roots in the earlier agrarian movements of the late 1870s and 1880s.[21] Most notable was the Farmers' Alliance, founded in 1879 in Lampasses County, Texas. Not quite ready to challenge the southern caste system, the Farmers' Alliance established separate organizations for whites and blacks. The two groups shared most of the same economic concerns and worked together toward their common objectives. Their premier achievements involved cooperative buying and selling arrangements that allowed them to bypass the unpredictable and sometimes corrupted commercial markets. They also strove to construct alternative credit arrangements that would make them much less dependent upon the usurious lending practices of merchants and landlords. The Farmers' Alliance tried to remain loyal to the Democratic party for as long as possible. However, political involvement became inevitable as economic conditions worsened and Democratic candidates elected with the support of the Farmers' Alliance continued to ignore agrarian concerns.

Earlier renegade political parties in the South had also voiced agrarian concerns, but it was the Populist party that posed the first significant challenge to the dominant Democratic party. The decision for southern Populists to shift their efforts into the political arena was not an easy one. Formation of a third-party movement was a definite attack upon southern Democratic tradition and smacked of disloyalty to the memory of the Confederacy and endorsement of racial equality. As Woodward observed, "Changing one's party in the South of the nineties involved more than changing one's mind. It might involve a falling-off of clients, the loss of a job, of credit at the store, or of one's welcome at church. It could split families, and it might even call in question one's loyalty to his race and his people."[22] Above all, the greatest symbolic importance of the formation of the Populist party was the placement of class interests above race on the southern political agenda, a significant departure from the past.

The position of southern blacks within the Populist movement was fraught with difficulty and dissension from the very beginning. Despite public pronouncements by such Populists as Tom Watson of Georgia, who stressed the commonality of African-American and white economic interests, a persistent undercurrent of racism existed within the party. The Populists were strongest in the upland parts of the region, where racial antagonism had historical roots reaching back to the days of slavery. Many whites still resented black collaboration with the conservative Democrats of the redemption period, who were so efficient at ignoring the plight of upland whites. Others within the party were genuinely committed to a biracial political coalition that would improve the economic well-being of both races and reduce racial tension and conflict.

One factor limiting the potential for racial harmony within the Populist party was the differing class origins of blacks and whites. In some respects, it is not quite correct to say that the contest between Populists and Democrats was a clash of classes; class variation existed within the parties as well. However, among Populists this variation was highly correlated with race. Most whites in the party were landowners, but most blacks were landless, a fact that aggravated the effort to achieve commonality on economic matters. Policies that benefited tenants or agricultural laborers might actually hurt the white landlords who were so dependent upon those classes. Initiatives that benefited farm owners could, in turn, work to the disadvantage of the landless.

Early in the Populist Era, political pragmatism prevailed over racial animosity, and the party made a serious attempt to attract the black vote. Given the historical strength of the Democrats, the Populist party was virtually obligated to court black voters if it were to prevail. As Woodward observed, "In their platforms Southern Populists denounced lynch law and the convict lease and called for defense of the Negro's political rights. Populist officers saw to it that Negroes received such recognition as summons for jury service, which they had long been denied. White and black party workers organized Negro Populist clubs and indoctrinated them in party principles."[23] Gaither argues that black support centered around four primary concerns, "economic betterment, protection of person, a share in the patronage, and actual involvement in the political process." Of these, Gaither maintains that blacks were most concerned with the "protection of person."[24]

The Populist's ability to attract African-American voters by supporting those issues that most concerned them varied substantially from state to state. Gaither contends that Populists in North Carolina and South Carolina, for example, never really received much support from black voters. On the other hand, the party in Georgia was somewhat more successful. Some of the interstate variation was due to corresponding differences in the effort the party devoted to wooing black voters. Some was also due to varying Democratic success in subverting the electoral process by reducing black support for Populist candidates through the use of fraud, bribery, and violence.

Southern Democrats employed an impressive arsenal of techniques designed to derail the Populist juggernaut. Foremost was their resurrection of that favorite bogeyman, the fear of "Negro domination." Democratic race-baiting reached truly incredible proportions during the 1890s as the party tried to unify white voters under the banner of

white solidarity and supremacy. In addition to reminding whites of
the "nightmare" of Reconstruction, Democrats exploited increasing
national racism and intolerance. These efforts were assisted by a number of fortuitous events that were unrelated to the Populist challenge.
For example, the 1890s saw the rising popularity of theories of scientific racism that portrayed blacks as an inherently inferior race.[25] These
theories found a willing audience in the popular media and legitimized the invective of racial hatred spewing forth from the Democratic
party. Later in the decade, the nation's imperialistic forays in the Car-
ibbean and South Pacific further aggravated the racial atmosphere
within the country. Increasingly, national authorities referred to the
inherent inferiority of the nonwhite natives of the foreign lands (primarily Cuba and the Philippines) that the U.S. military occupied.
Although intended primarily to justify the acquisitive and exploitative
behavior of these foreign adventures, the arguments also reinforced
the racist message of the southern Democrats. Finally, the Democrats'
effort to shore up the barrier of white solidarity benefited from the
controversy over the "Force Bill" introduced into the U.S. Senate by
Henry Cabot Lodge of Massachusetts. Essentially, the proposed legislation provided for federal oversight of southern elections to assure
that blacks were not denied the right to vote. The timing of Lodge's
proposal was extremely unfortunate for the southern Populists because
it aggravated racial divisions, gave new life to Democratic warnings
of a "new Reconstruction," and drove many fence-sitting whites into
the Democratic camp out of fear of "Negro domination."

Ironically, race-baiting was also accompanied by an effort to appeal
to black voters. In some cases, this consisted of the nomination of
Democratic candidates who voiced genuine concern over the plight
of southern blacks. For instance, the Democratic candidate in Georgia's gubernatorial race of 1892, W. J. Northen, expressed concerns over
educational appropriations, voiced strong disapproval of lynching,
and promised to support antilynching legislation. Many black voters
in Georgia actually preferred Northen over the Populist candidate W.
L. Peek, whose own positions were not as appealing to them. Gaither
has also pointed out that the Democratic appeal to African-American
voters was bolstered by the subservient and subordinate position of
blacks in southern society, "More than any other group, the Negro,
member of a perennial debtor class, was subjected to economic and
physical coercion that literally compelled him to conform to Southern white majority opinion—notably, Southern white *Democratic*
opinion. The obvious result of such actions was not only to make a
mockery of public elections, but to give expression to Democratic

demands for unilateral conformity to the principles that the party deemed as representative of Southern politics."[26]

In some cases, the Democratic effort to garner black votes was not as honorable as the sincere expression of support for issues that concerned blacks. Democrats also bribed black voters with paltry sums of money or with alcohol, and they engaged in outright election fraud by stuffing or destroying ballot boxes from predominately black districts. Occasionally, their strategy turned to discouraging black voters through intimidation and outright violence. Whatever specific tactics were responsible, black support for the Democratic party played a critical role in the Democrats' fight against populism.

Ultimately, southern Democrats were successful in blunting the Populist offensive. Although the Populists did enjoy a degree of success in electing their candidates to office, in most cases the Democratic political hegemony remained intact either through legitimate or illegitimate means. By the middle of the decade (1896 and after), the southern Populist vote had declined sharply in most states, and Democrats had successfully co-opted many of the Populists' favorite issues or supporters. The Populist position on race also underwent an intriguing metamorphosis. In the later years, Populists favored a blatantly racist agenda that included the belief that true economic change, and a realignment of class interests within the southern white population, required that African-Americans first be disenfranchised. Perhaps this turnabout should not be surprising, given the central role of black voters in the Democratic victory over populism and the Populists' resentment of that role.

As in the redemption period, southern blacks during the Populist Era had ample opportunity to jeopardize themselves because of their political behavior. Again, however, the political motives for black lynching could not have been simple or straightforward. Some scholars have maintained that the Populist threat increased the political motivation for lynching in the South, and this is why the 1890s were an especially bloody decade.[27] One argument claims that racial violence during the era was intended to intimidate blacks and thereby discourage them from voting Populist. However, this argument identifies only one possible scenario and only one possible instigating force for lynchings. There are others.

Who did African-Americans threaten politically? What segments of southern society could have had political motives to lynch blacks? Obviously, Democrats could have benefited from black lynchings had violence discouraged blacks from voting for Populist candidates. The Democratic cause was also furthered by the atmosphere of heightened racial tension caused by race-baiting. This tension may have led to lynchings that were not explicitly political in nature and that could have been carried out by any segment of the white community. Ultimately, however, such violence did discourage a black-white political coalition, and thereby it benefited Democrats. Another possible scenario portrays disgruntled Populists as the instigators of lynching for political reasons. Surely it was discouraging for Populists to watch their efforts thwarted, sometimes with the help of the black vote. It is not unreasonable to suspect that racial intimidation could have originated in the Populist camp in an effort to discourage black collaboration with Democrats. After all, the strong racist heritage that some Populists carried into their political mobilization may have been triggered by perceived threats from the black franchise.

In sum, the political threat model of lynching cannot be distilled to a simple question of whether blacks were lynched in order to thwart Populist victories. Rather, whether blacks voted Populist, Democratic, or Republican, they represented a potential political threat to someone. And it is possible that threat was, on occasion, translated into racial violence. Only when most blacks were no longer able to vote did their potential to threaten southern whites politically evaporate.

African-American Disenfranchisement: After 1900

The turn of the twentieth century is a convenient marker for the transition to the fourth political era—black disenfranchisement. In fact, the movement toward disenfranchisement had begun considerably earlier. Some states implemented restrictive voting statutes well before 1900. Kousser has shown that the number of blacks voting in some southern states had dipped substantially even before those statutes were passed.[28] Some states, such as Georgia, did not impose full arsenals of disenfranchising measures until after 1900. Consequently, any single year chosen to demarcate the era of disenfranchisement will necessarily be somewhat ambiguous.

Although the political freedom and influence of southern blacks had been on shaky footing since the end of Reconstruction, their prospects dimmed even further during the waning years of the nineteenth century. The death knell for the black franchise was sounded when competing segments of the white electorate concluded—for somewhat different reasons—that their own ambitions were more likely to be realized if blacks were removed from the political scene.

On the one hand, the patriarchs of the conservative Democratic party believed that black disenfranchisement would reduce the threat of a political coalition between blacks and disenchanted whites. Without black support, political challenges like those mounted by the Populists were probably doomed to fail. On the other hand, politically estranged whites concluded that the political dominance of the conservative Democrats would be weakened if they could no longer exploit black voters, legitimately or illegitimately. Many within the Populist party argued that a satisfactory resolution to the political confrontation among different economic classes of whites could be achieved only after blacks were removed from the picture. Thus, political prospects for southern blacks were crushed beneath the weight of the consensus reached among whites, a consensus that each figured to benefit from black disenfranchisement. As Woodward described the situation,

> The hopes and prejudices and fears of millions of people were involved in disfranchisement, and the motives behind the movement were undoubtedly many and complex. In general, however, the leaders held up above all others three justifications for disfranchisement: (1) the removal of the Negro vote, they argued, would put an end to the corrupt elections that had long disgraced Southern politics; (2) the removal of the Negro as arbiter between white factions would enable the white men to divide freely again on basic issues and enjoy a vigorous political life; (3) disfranchisement would force the Negro to abandon false hopes, find his "place" and as a consequence race relations would improve.[29]

None of these hopes was actually realized. Southern politics remained "corrupt" if only because such a large percentage of the population was prevented from voting. Although "free" to disagree on "basic issues," white southern politics entered a period of prolonged torpor as a result of the strengthened dominance of the white supremacist Democrats after disenfranchisement. And it is certainly difficult to consider the early decades of the twentieth century as a period of improved race relations.

The procedures for disenfranchisement varied from state to state. However a common mechanism was the constitutional convention, which several states held around the turn of the century. There was nothing surreptitious about the intentions of the majority of whites who participated. They sought to devise strategies that would reduce southern blacks to political impotence. In all cases this involved the imposition of a poll tax, and in most others the passage of property and literacy requirements. Although the class-specific nature of these measures was obvious, they were not necessarily race-specific. Thus, many poor whites also faced the threat of disenfranchisement. Indeed, many convention participants viewed the disenfranchisement of some poor whites as a perfectly tolerable price to pay for the virtually complete disenfranchisement of blacks; for some, it was even a desirable outcome in its own right.

In most cases, however, loopholes were created to minimize the impact of restrictive voting measures on the white franchise. Most states adopted "understanding clauses" or "grandfather clauses" that introduced the potential for greater discretion on the part of polling officials to exempt whites from the restrictive statutes. As long as whites could adequately interpret a section of the state constitution, demonstrate that they could have voted in 1867, or were descendants of men who were voters, then they could circumvent some of the other measures. Clearly, the first two conditions could be applied more rigorously for blacks and the third was virtually inapplicable to most southern African-Americans. Therefore, the loopholes, unlike the restrictive measures themselves, were clearly race-specific (Table 6-1).

In many cases the effect of these measures on black political participation was immediate and dramatic. Before Louisiana's constitutional convention, 130,344 blacks were registered to vote within the state. Within two years, that number had plummeted to only 5,320, a 96 percent reduction.[30] The comparable change for Louisiana whites was a decline of only 24 percent. A similar transformation occurred in Mississippi. At its constitutional convention of 1890, Mississippi imposed a variety of restrictive voting statutes, including a poll tax

Table 6-1. Selected Disenfranchising Legislation among Ten Southern States[a]

State	Poll Tax	Literacy Test	Property Test
Alabama	1901	1901	1901
Arkansas	1892	—	—
Florida	1889	—	—
Georgia	1877	1908	1908
Kentucky	—	—	—
Louisiana	1898	1898	1898
Mississippi	1890	1890	—
North Carolina	1900	1900	1900
South Carolina	1895	1895	—
Tennessee	1890	—	—

a. Adopted from Kousser (1974, 239), Table 9.1.

and a literacy test. The measures had a dramatic effect on black voting. Kousser estimates that 29 percent of black adult males voted in the 1888 presidential election, a number that dropped to 2 percent by 1892.[31] By the 1895 gubernatorial elections, virtually no Mississippi blacks voted. The same story was repeated throughout the South as state after state adopted restrictive voting legislation.

The possible impact of black disenfranchisement on lynchings would seem to be straightforward. To the extent that blacks were lynched because they represented a political threat to some segment of the white community, lynchings should have declined precipitously. This should have occurred irrespective of the exact nature of the black political threat. Political motivations for lynching should have dropped to near zero after disenfranchisement, whether black voters jeopardized the hegemony of conservative Democrats because of the danger of their possible coalition with other whites or whether their exploitation by the dominant Democrats threatened the aspirations of contesting political groups such as the Populists.

The broad trends in black lynchings are generally supportive of this interpretation (chapter 2). During the 1890s, 799 blacks were victims of mob violence, whereas only 604 blacks were lynched during the first decade of this century. Whether this substantial decline was actually the result of disenfranchisement is one of the questions that we will address in the remainder of this chapter.

Assessing the Evidence for the Political Threat Model

Southern politics were extremely complex, and class and race were prominent divisions on the political landscape. Thus, any simple hypothesis about the relationship between black political activity and lynching is guaranteed to be inadequate. And any attempt to discern patterns of relationship between southern voting and lynchings is certain to become entangled in the confusing conflicts, coalitions, and compromises that were southern politics. We intend to tread lightly on this terrain, for it has the potential to turn to quicksand. Nonetheless, it may be possible to glean a set of hypotheses from the preceding overview that is reasonably faithful to the way things were.

The Effect of Disenfranchisement on Lynching

The implementation of restrictive voting measures around the turn of the century allows for a relatively straightforward test of the political threat model of lynchings. Put simply, if African-Americans were lynched because of their political participation, then the number of

lynchings should have declined significantly after disenfranchisement. Moreover, this effect should have occurred regardless of the
specific groups of whites threatened by black political activity before
disenfranchisement. The general trend in black lynchings is consistent with the hypothesized effect of disenfranchisement. Lynchings
experienced a protracted decline after the early years of the twentieth century (Figure 6-1). However, this general trend was not without
reversals, as indicated by the spikes in lynchings around 1909 and
1919. Unfortunately, inference of a significant effect of disenfranchisement requires more than a simple visual examination of the time trend
in lynchings.

In order to assess more systematically the support for an effect of
disenfranchisement on the lynching trend shown in Figure 6-1 we
have conducted an interrupted time-series analysis.[32] Although the
mechanical and mathematical details of this procedure are rather
complex, the underlying principle is appealingly simple. Basically, the
trend in lynchings before disenfranchisement is compared with the
trend after disenfranchisement. If the difference between the two is
greater than we would expect from chance, then a significant effect
of disenfranchisement is inferred; the trend has been interrupted by
an intervention, the disenfranchisement of the African-American
population. Specifically, we would expect to find that the level of

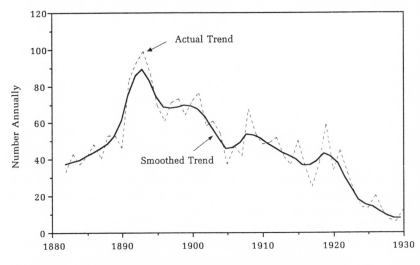

Figure 6-1. Trends in Black Victims of White Lynch Mobs.

lynching declined markedly with the implementation of restrictive voting measures.

In general, the interrupted time-series framework posits that the annual frequency of antiblack mob violence is some function of an intervention—in our case, that means whether disenfranchisement had occurred—and a random disturbance. In order to determine whether this intervention had an effect on lynchings, it is first necessary to specify a function linking the two, and this is somewhat complicated because four alternative specifications can be invoked.

First, disenfranchisement might have an abrupt and permanent effect, so lynchings would have declined sharply after disenfranchisement and then remained at a lower level than in the era before disenfranchisement. A second possibility would be a gradual and permanent change due to disenfranchisement, beginning with a relatively small decline in lynchings that grew larger over the years after disenfranchisement. The third possibility is for an abrupt and temporary change. In this case, after the immediate impact of disenfranchisement, its effect would decay, eventually returning the frequency of mob violence to its level before disenfranchisement. Finally, the effect might be gradual but temporary; in this instance, there would be a gradual short-term reduction in lynching followed by a gradual return to the level of mob violence before disenfranchisement.

The first three of these alternative ways of modeling the effect of disenfranchisement can be represented by a simple set of zero-order and first-order transfer functions.[33] We conducted extensive preliminary research exploring each of these three alternatives, but the only specification that consistently performed without obvious and unacceptable flaws was the model of abrupt and permanent change. Thus we chose that model for estimating the effects of disenfranchisement upon the number of black victims of white lynch mobs:

$$\text{Lynchings}_t = \omega(\text{Disenfranchisement}_{t-1}) + \beta_{\text{blk}}(\text{Population Black}_t)$$
$$+ \beta_{\%\text{blk}}(\text{Percent Black}_t) + \beta_{\text{wht}}(\text{White Lynchings}_t) + \varepsilon_t$$

where Lynchings_t is the number of black victims of white mobs in year t, and ω is the effect of disenfranchisement. Disenfranchisement is a binary variable coded 1 for years 1900 through 1930 and zero otherwise,[34] the β_ks are effect parameters for the other explanatory factors (size of the black population, percent population black, and the number of white lynchings by white mobs), and ε_t is a disturbance term. If ω is negative and statistically significant, we have evidence that disenfranchisement had the anticipated effect of reducing antiblack mob violence. In this model, we assume that there is a one-year lag between disenfranchisement and the onset of decline in the frequency of black lynchings.

The empirical results for the interrupted time-series models are presented in Table 6-2. Looking first at the findings for the analysis that includes all ten states, we find no support for a disenfranchisement effect on lynching, regardless of whether we employ an autoregressive or moving-average specification for the disturbance term[35] and regardless of whether we consider the bivariate effect of disenfranchisement or its effect net of the control variables. Although the disenfranchisement effects for the entire south are negative, the correct direction, none of the coefficients are twice their standard errors.

On the basis of this analysis, we are unable to conclude that political disenfranchisement had an appreciable effect on black lynchings in the South as a whole. This does not mean, of course, that no lynchings were motivated by political concerns. In at least a few cases, we know that African-Americans were lynched for political activity (chapter 3). Rather, our findings indicate that violence against blacks, in a broad sense, was not part of a systematic attempt by southern whites to neutralize black political influence. Surely, if such motivation had been a major force driving white mobs, then our statistical evidence would have shown a marked decline in lynching after the widespread disenfranchisement of African-Americans.

It is possible, however, that the results presented thus far are lim-

Table 6-2. Interrupted Time-Series Regression of Number of Black Lynch Victims on Disenfranchisement for the Entire South[a]

	Total Effect of Disenfranchisement[c]		Net Effect of Disenfranchisement[d]	
Process[b]	Coefficient	t-ratio	Coefficient	t-ratio
Auto-regressive disturbance	−2.036	−1.12	−3.703	−0.69
Moving-average disturbance	−2.048	−1.34	−4.875	−1.26

a. All models assume a one-year delay between disenfranchisement and the onset of the decline in the lynching of blacks by white mobs. All variables except the disenfranchisement variable have been differenced.
b. Both processes are first-order.
c. This is the effect of disenfranchisement before the introduction of control variables.
d. This is the effect of disenfranchisement after controlling on the number of white lynchings, size of the black population, and percent population black.

ited in their ability to describe the true effect of disenfranchisement on lynching because they are based on groups of states rather than individual states. The various states instituted disenfranchising mechanisms at different times. By looking at the experiences of individual states we can be more accurate about the date of disenfranchisement and possibly conduct a better test of the impact of disenfranchisement on lynching.

The same analytic techniques can be applied to Alabama, Georgia, Louisiana, and Mississippi, the four states that claimed the largest numbers of black lynch victims during the period. The most reasonable date for disenfranchisement in Alabama is 1901, when the state introduced a number of restrictive voting statutes, including a poll tax, a literacy test, and a property test. For Georgia, we shall fix the date of disenfranchisement at 1908, when the state introduced the secret ballot, a literacy test, a property test, and an "understanding clause."[36] The best date for disenfranchisement in Louisiana is 1898, when the state passed a poll tax, a literacy test, and a property test. We use 1890 for the date of disenfranchisement in Mississippi because that year the state enacted a poll tax and literacy test as well as other measures to restrict the black vote.

Visual examination of the trend in lynchings for these four states (Figures 6-2a, 6-2b, 6-2c, 6-2d) does not provide unambiguous evidence either for or against an effect of disenfranchisement on black lynchings, indicating a need for the more sophisticated techniques.

When interrupted time-series techniques are applied to the state-level trends, we obtain the results described in Table 6-3. Again, we are assuming a one-year delay in the onset of a depressing effect of disenfranchisement on lynching. Although disenfranchisement had the expected negative relationship with black lynchings in Alabama, this effect was not statistically significant in any of the four models estimated. In Georgia, our estimates of the disenfranchisement effect are negative in the two bivariate models but statistically insignificant. In the more complicated multivariable models, the effect is positive but again insignificant. The patterns for Louisiana and Mississippi are similar. In most specifications, the effect of disenfranchisement is negative, but it is not sufficiently large relative to its standard error.[37]

Our exploration into the effect of disenfranchisement on black lynchings yields virtually no support for the notion that southern blacks were less vulnerable to mob violence after they lost the vote. The temporal patterns of lynching were not altered appreciably with the introduction of restrictive voting statutes. Therefore, the political

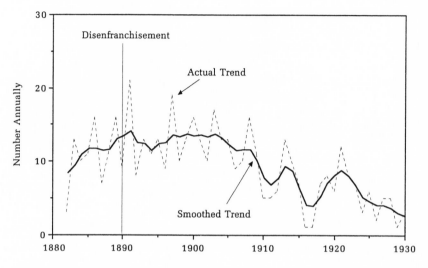

Figure 6-2a. Trends in Black Victims of White Lynch Mobs in Mississippi.

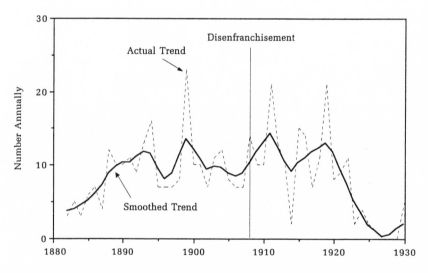

Figure 6-2b. Trends in Black Victims of White Lynch Mobs in Georgia.

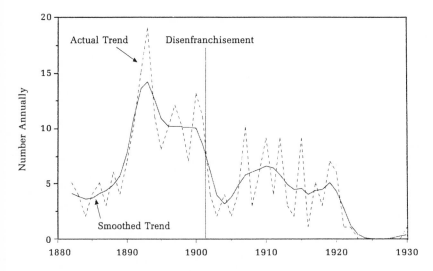

Figure 6-2c. Trends in Black Victims of White Lynch Mobs in Alabama.

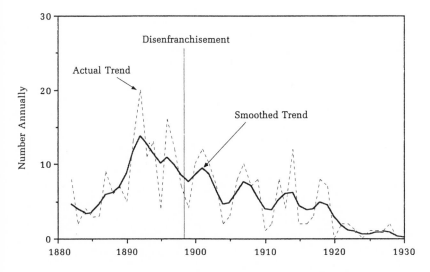

Figure 6-2d. Trends in Black Victims of White Lynch Mobs in Louisiana.

threat model of lynching remains unsubstantiated, at least in its more general formulation.

Table 6-3. Interrupted Time-Series Regression of Number of Black Lynch Victims on Disenfranchisement for Alabama, Georgia, Louisiana, and Mississippi[a]

State	Process[b]	Total Effect of Disenfranchisement[c]		Net Effect of Disenfranchisement[d]	
		Coefficient	t-ratio	Coefficient	t-ratio
Alabama	AR(1)	−0.326	−0.65	−0.001	−0.01
	MA(1)	−0.289	−0.95	−0.303	−0.48
Georgia	AR(1)	−0.380	−0.45	0.645	0.24
	MA(1)	−0.459	−1.52	1.898	1.59
Louisiana	AR(1)	−0.234	−0.40	−0.537	−0.43
	MA(1)	−0.314	−4.16	−0.223	−0.52
Mississippi	AR(1)	−0.279	−0.62	0.113	0.08
	MA(1)	−0.242	−1.06	−0.766	−0.99

a. All models assume a one-year delay between disenfranchisement and the onset of the decline in the lynching of blacks by white mobs. All variables except the disenfranchisement variable have been differenced.
b. AR(1) is a first-order auto-regressive disturbance; MA(1) is a first-order moving-average disturbance.
c. This is the effect of disenfranchisement before the introduction of control variables.
d. This is the effect of disenfranchisement after controlling on the number of white lynchings, size of the black population, and percent population black.

African-American Lynching during Redemption

Shifting from the temporal to the spatial patterns in black lynchings requires a completely different set of questions. Now, we are interested in determining whether areal (or geographic) variation in the intensity of lynching was related to the strength of particular political parties. For example, were lynchings more common in areas dominated by Democrats or by Republicans?

The period of southern history known as "redemption" was so named because the previously dominant southern Democratic party "redeemed" political control from the Republicans, who had increased their influence following the Civil War. To the extent that black voters contributed to the strength of the Republican party, they were threatening to the reestablishment of Democratic hegemony and the white supremacy it represented. Other things being equal, this "threat" to Democratic success would have been greater in areas in which the Republican party was relatively strong. As Republican strength approached majority proportions, the African-American vote could have been instrumental in defeating Democratic candidates. It is precisely in those areas that blacks would have been most vulnerable to mob violence, either as an explicit attempt to intimidate black voters or as a more subtle form of racial terrorism intended to define clearly the appropriate place for African-Americans in southern society. That "place" did not include the voting booth.

Thus, if the political threat model of lynchings is accurate, the level of black lynching during the redemption period would have been higher where the Republican party was stronger. This expectation is based on two simplifying assumptions: (1) that blacks were aligned with Republicans, and (2) that Republican strength threatened efforts by Democrats to regain political control of the South. We refer to these as "simplifying" assumptions because we realize that the political landscape was actually more complex than this. For example, other political parties were active during the period, which may have affected the basic tension between Democrats and Republicans. In addition, the Republican party did not exert monolithic control over black voters, who were often exploited by Democrats in an effort to regain control of the South. Nonetheless, we believe that our assumptions are not serious misrepresentations of the reality of the era and are robust enough to offer a reasonable test of the political threat model for the redemption period.

Our examination of the relationship between party strength and black lynching during the redemption era is based on the presidential election of 1884, roughly at the middle of the era. The election pitted the Democrat Grover Cleveland against the Republican James G. Blaine. Cleveland squeaked out a victory over Blaine by a margin of only thirty-seven electoral votes, garnering less that 50 percent of the popular vote. We have chosen to use the results of the presidential election rather than gubernatorial voting results because the candidates and timing are constant across the states and counties. It is not so much the level of support for these two presidential candidates that we are interested in tapping; rather, it is the relative strength of the Republican and Democratic parties within individual counties.

Considering no other sources of difference across counties the evidence does suggest a relationship between the relative size of the Republican party in the county and the intensity of lynching between 1880 and 1889. The zero-order correlation between the two variables is modestly negative, $r = -0.102$. Contrary to the expectations of the political threat model, however, this negative correlation suggests that there were fewer, not more, lynchings where the Republican party enjoyed greater strength. Yet the counties in the ten states differed in other important ways that may make this bivariate relationship somewhat misleading. For example, we know that the racial composition of counties varied substantially across the South, and it is quite likely that the intensity of lynching and Republican party strength were also related to racial composition. In addition, economic conditions, especially those affecting the farm economy, also differed across counties. These characteristics may also have been related to the frequency of black lynchings and to the level of support for the Republican party within counties. Before concluding that the bivariate correlation provides a reasonably accurate description of the true relationship between lynching and local Republican party strength, we need to consider the simultaneous influence of additional variables.

In order to do this, we have estimated a multiple regression equation that has as its dependent variable the number of black lynchings that occurred within each county between 1880 and 1889. On the righthand side of the equation is the percent of all votes cast in each county that went to the Republican presidential candidate in 1884. Also included are a series of relevant control variables. First, we include a set of demographic variables that describe the racial composition within counties. The absolute size of the African-American population is included to allow for the possibility that more lynchings occurred where there was a greater number of potential lynch victims. Inclusion of this variable is advisable given that the dependent variable is the raw number of lynch victims. Variables reflecting the relative size of the local black population are also included. Both linear and quadratic measures of percent black within the county are included. Second, a set of variables meant to describe the local farm economy and agricultural opportunity is included. Average Farm Size is included to tap the relative dominance of larger landholdings (and therefore wealthier planters) within the county. Percent of Farms Owned describes the dominant form of land tenure (owner versus tenant) within the county. Percent Farmland Improved is introduced to control for cross-county variation in the availability of additional farmland.[38] All of the control variables are measured at the beginning of the decade under consideration. Using these variables, we estimate the following Poisson-Gamma regression equation:

$$\text{Log } \lambda_i = \beta_0 + \beta_{\%rep}(\text{Percent Republican}_i)$$
$$+ \beta_{blk}(\text{Log Size of Black Population}_i)$$
$$+ \beta_{\%blk}(\text{Percent Population Black}_i)$$
$$+ \beta_{\%blk2}(\text{Percent Population Black}_i^2)$$
$$+ \beta_{farm}(\text{Average Farm Size}_i)$$
$$+ \beta_{\%own}(\text{Percent of Farms Owned}_i)$$
$$+ \beta_{\%imp}(\text{Percent Farmland Improved}_i) + \varepsilon_i$$

where λ_i is the ith county's Poisson parameter, β_0 is a constant across counties, the β_ks are effect parameters for the explanatory variables, and ε is a random disturbance assumed to have a Gamma distribution.[37]

The power threat model of lynchings predicts a positive value for $\beta_{\%rep}$ and will represent the key test of the model in these analyses. The other variables are included primarily to reduce the possibility of drawing misleading conclusions about the effect of Republican party strength on lynching due to spurious or suppressed relationships.

The results derived from this Poisson regression reveal that Republican party strength in 1884 had a strong negative effect on black lynchings throughout the decade and that adding the control variables to the equation does not reduce the effect of Republican party strength on lynchings (Table 6-4). Again, the direction of this effect is opposite of that expected by the power threat model, which predicts more lynchings where the Republican party represented a greater threat to the resurgent Democrats. It appears that where the Republican party enjoyed greater strength, African-Americans had less reason to fear the violence of white mobs. Apparently, the net influence of the Republican party was to reduce racial hostility within communities rather than to spawn racial violence as a result of increased political competition, as predicted by the power threat model.

Perhaps, however, the relationship between Republican party strength and black lynchings is not linear. It is possible that Democrats had little reason to fear Republican competition until their numbers approached majority proportions. Furthermore, it is possible that the reduction in lynchings associated with increased Republican influence is restricted to counties in which Republicans represented a clear majority and therefore were able to shape local politics (and race relations) over the objections of Democrats. This alternative scenario proposes a nonlinear relationship between percent Republican and black lynchings that is not represented by the equation reported in Table 6-4. In light of this possibility, we estimated a variety of mod-

Table 6-4. Poisson-Gamma Regression of Number of Black Lynch Victims (1882–89) on Percent Voting Republican in 1884 and Other County Characteristics

Predictor Variable[a]	Model A[b]	Model B
Constant	−0.257	−1.944
	(−1.32)	(−2.96)
Percent voting Republican, 1884	−0.016	−0.019
	(−3.37)	(−3.74)
Percent population black	—	0.027
		(1.33)
Percent population black^2	—	−0.0003
		(−1.55)
Log size of black population (1,000s)	—	0.641
		(4.44)
Average farm size	—	0.0005
		(0.44)
Percent of farms owned	—	0.008
		(1.15)
Percent of farmland improved	—	−0.006
		(−0.93)
Number of counties = 784		

a. Size of the black population, percent black, average farm size, percent farms owned, and percent of land improved measured in 1880.
b. Asymptotic t-ratio in parentheses.

els that did allow for nonlinear effects of percent Republican on lynching. We found no evidence of such nonlinearity. The negative effect of Republican party strength on lynching implied by the results in Table 6-4 appears to be real and offers no support for the power threat model of lynchings.

Our examination of the distribution of black lynchings throughout the South during the redemption period yields no support for the political threat model of lynching during the 1880s. Indeed, the findings provide intriguing contradictory evidence. Areas in which the Republican party was relatively strong also offered blacks greater protection from the horrors of white mobs. It is likely that this resulted from the less hostile racial and political climate in areas where the Republican party exerted greater influence. However, simple measures of party strength, such as that used in our statistical analyses, may not be sophisticated enough to tease out the true extent of political competition that existed within counties.

African-American Lynching during the Populist Era

Southern politics entered a new era in the 1890s as the Populist party grew in size and influence. Having redeemed the South from the dominance of the Republican party during the 1880s, southern Democrats faced a new, and in many ways more disconcerting, challenge during the 1890s. For the most part, the Populists were not "nigger loving" carpetbaggers, abolitionists, or Union sympathizers. They were good, solid white folk with strong ties to the land and enduring pride in Dixie. For many, it was extremely difficult and painful when economic interests and political frustration compelled them to bolt the Democratic party in order to form a third political party. As the Populist message was spread throughout the South, the party gained enough momentum and support to represent a real challenge to the dominant Democrats.

The presidential election of 1892 provides a vehicle for testing the usefulness of the political threat model of lynching during the Populist Era. Although the party remained active throughout the 1890s, it never quite regained the same intensity, nor enjoyed the same enthusiastic level of support, that it did early in the decade. Indeed, as the decade wore on, southern Democrats co-opted many of the central Populist issues. Populists had their own presidential candidate in the 1892 elections, unlike the race in 1896 when William Jennings Bryan ran on both the Populist and Democratic tickets. In 1892, the Populist candidate, James B. Weaver, ran against Grover Cleveland, the Democrat, and Benjamin Harrison, the Republican. Weaver managed to garner more than a million popular votes (about 9 percent of the total) and twenty-two of the 444 electoral votes. Cleveland won the election with 277 electoral votes but only 46 percent of the popular vote.

An initial indication of the cross-county relationship between lynchings during the 1890s and Populist party strength is provided by the bivariate correlation between the two variables. The Pearsonian Correlation of $r = +0.07$ is consistent with the political threat model of lynching, suggesting more lynchings in areas of greater Populist support. The association is quite weak, however, and could possibly reflect the influence of additional county characteristics that are not considered by the bivariate correlation.

To obtain a purer estimate of the relationship between Populist party strength and lynchings, we once again introduce relevant control variables in order to reduce the possibility that the observed relationship between the two variables is really due to spurious or suppressed effects. The same set of demographic variables is included that was used in our analysis of lynchings and Republican party strength during the 1880s. Percent of the county's population that is black, in both its linear and quadratic forms, as well as the absolute size of the county's black population, reflect cross-county differences in racial composition. We also include the same set of variables used to describe county differences in the farm economy and agricultural opportunity: (1) Average Farm Size; (2) Percent of Farms Owned; and (3) Percent of Farmland Improved. Finally, given the strong association between Republican party strength and lynchings inferred for the 1880s, we also include a measure of Republican strength during the Populist Era. Like the measure of Populist party strength, the Republican measure refers to the 1892 presidential election.

To assess support for the political threat model for the Populist Era, we estimate the following Poisson-Gamma regression:

$$
\begin{aligned}
\text{Log } \lambda_i = \beta_0 &+ \beta_{\%pop}(\text{Percent Populist}_i) \\
&+ \beta_{\%rep}(\text{Percent Republican}_i) \\
&+ \beta_{blk}(\text{Log Size of Black Population}_i) \\
&+ \beta_{\%blk}(\text{Percent Population Black}_i) \\
&+ \beta_{\%blk2}(\text{Percent Population Black}_i^2) \\
&+ \beta_{farm}(\text{Average Farm Size}_i) \\
&+ \beta_{\%own}(\text{Percent of Farms Owned}_i) \\
&+ \beta_{\%imp}(\text{Percent Farmland Improved}_i) + \varepsilon_i
\end{aligned}
$$

where again λ_i is the ith county's Poisson parameter, β_0 is a constant across counties, the β_ks are effect parameters for the explanatory variables, and ε is a random disturbance assumed to have a Gamma distribution.

The estimates derived for the analytic model are presented in Table 6-5. In Model A, we include the percent voting Populist and percent voting Republican as the only predictors of the frequency of black lynchings, whereas in Model B we add the control variables to the model. Model A shows that Populist party strength had a small negative effect on lynchings; when the control variables are added, this small effect becomes even more marginal. This suggests that, net of other factors, blacks were actually somewhat insulated from mob violence in counties with a greater Populist influence. Again, however, this negative relationship is too weak to dismiss the possibility that it is simply due to chance.

Table 6-5. Poisson-Gamma Regression of Number of Black Lynch Victims (1890–99) on Percent Voting Populist and Republican in 1892 and Other County Characteristics

Predictor Variable[a]	Model A[b]	Model B
Constant	0.600	−0.690
	(4.51)	(−1.38)
Percent voting Populist, 1892	−0.007	−0.005
	(−1.75)	(−1.19)
Percent voting Republican, 1892	−0.033	−0.023
	(−8.67)	(−5.74)
Percent population black	—	−0.0003
		(−0.06)
Percent population black^2	—	0.0001
		(0.25)
Log size of black population (1,000s)	—	0.469
		(5.21)
Average farm size	—	0.001
		(0.84)
Percent of farms owned	—	0.007
		(1.49)
Percent of farmland improved	—	−0.004
		(−0.95)
Number of counties = 802		

a. Size of the black population, percent black, average farm size, percent farms owned, and percent of land improved measured in 1890.
b. Asymptotic *t*-ratio in parentheses.

Our findings in both Model A and Model B also suggest a continued influence of Republican party strength on lynchings during the 1890s. As was observed for the redemption period, the number of African-American lynch victims was significantly lower in southern counties with more successful Republican parties. Obviously, the negative effects of Populist and Republican strength on black lynchings do not provide support for the political threat model, which would predict positive coefficients for both variables. In recognition of the possibility that the relationship between Populist party strength and lynchings is not linear, we also estimated a variety of models that permitted the relationship to assume a nonlinear form. None of these alternative models showed evidence of nonlinearity.

Once again, our exploration fails to yield evidence supporting the

political threat model. In fact, during the Populist Era, as for the redemption period, it appears that African-Americans faced a relatively smaller threat of mob violence in counties with stronger opposition parties. Although all of the same caveats mentioned earlier in
relation to our examination of spatial patterns of lynching during the
1880s also apply to our examination of lynchings during the 1890s,
we believe that the consistency of findings across decades leads to
an intriguing, and important, conclusion: The social atmosphere of
southern counties was shaped by the political parties that operated
within their boundaries. Part of this social atmosphere was the racial climate that determined the place of blacks in society and set
the tone for the treatment of blacks by co-resident whites. Where the
climate was more hostile, blacks faced greater risks of mob violence.
Where the climate was more benign, the risk of lynching declined.
At the risk of oversimplification, we contend that the racial climate
was harsher where the party of white supremacy exercised greater
control. In contrast, where the rival parties (Republican and Populist) were present in nontrivial proportions, the climate was less lethal for African-Americans.

Exactly what mechanisms accounted for the greater level of racial
tolerance in counties with stronger opposition parties we cannot say.
That such a possibility existed, however, was observed even by the
earliest commentators on lynching. For example, Raper speculated
that overwhelming support for the Democratic party within a county
was suggestive of underlying racial antagonism and thereby may have
contributed to a higher frequency of lynching: "Ardent supporters of
the doctrine of 'white superiority' . . . cling to the Democratic party for
protection from 'nigger-lovin' administrations in Washington and for
a guarantee of 'pure white' rule at home."[40]

Conclusions

Scholars have long suspected that political competition during the
last part of the nineteenth century contributed to the tragedy of lynching during that same era. Indeed, we know from several specific incidents that African-Americans were lynched for explicitly political
reasons (chapter 3). To those victims, the costs of political freedom
were all too real. Surprisingly, however, the statistical evidence mar-
shaled in this chapter offers little support for drawing broader linkages between complex, confusing, and often corrupt southern politics
and black lynchings.

We find no indication that temporal patterns of lynching changed

appreciably after the widespread adoption of restrictive voting statutes throughout the South. Similarly, although there does appear to
have been a relationship between Republican and Populist strength
and the intensity of lynchings within counties, the direction of association is opposite of that predicted by the political threat model.
During the redemption period (1880–89), blacks were actually safer
from white mobs in counties with proportionately larger Republican
parties. During the Populist Era (1890–99), counties with stronger
Republican and Populist parties offered greater protection to African-
Americans. Rather than endangering southern blacks because of the
competition they offered the dominant Democrats, these opposition
political parties somehow offered blacks a less threatening, more hos-
pitable environment. It seems that the political complexion of local
areas was a key factor determining the vulnerability of resident blacks
to illegal execution. However, the political threat model is inadequate
for describing exactly how politics and lynching were related.

NOTES

1. See, for example, Blalock (1967), Olzak (1990, 1992), and Olzak and
Nagel (1986).

2. Phillips (1982, 371–72).

3. See Phillips (1987) and Beck et al. (1989) for more details of these
analyses.

4. Blalock (1967) includes a thorough statement of his threat models
of discriminatory behavior.

5. Reed (1972).

6. Corzine et al. (1983).

7. The mathematical structure of their index included a definitional
dependency on percent black of a nonlinear form. See Tolnay et al. (1989).

8. See Reed (1972), Corzine et al. (1983), and Tolnay et al. (1989) for
more information about these attempts to link black population concentration to southern lynchings.

9. See Inverarity (1976) and Olzak (1990, 1992).

10. Soule (1992).

11. See, for example, Woodward (1951, 1966), Gaither (1977), and
Kousser (1974).

12. For an interesting survey of violence against blacks during Reconstruction, see Vandal's (1991) description of Caddo Parish, Louisiana.

13. See Wright (1990).

14. Shapiro (1988, 24), emphasis added.

15. See Wright (1990) for a notable exception.

16. Redemption was not endorsed in all parts of the South nor in all segments of southern society. See Hyman (1990) for an analysis of the antiredemption movement.

17. Woodward (1951, 50).

18. Woodward (1951, 105–6).

19. Woodward (1951, 220).

20. Farmers were not the only segment of the southern economy that had complaints. Workers in manufacturing and industry watched as the use of convict labor put them out of work or seriously undercut their wages.

21. See Hicks (1931), McMath (1976, 1993), Schwartz (1976), and Holmes (1990).

22. Woodward (1951, 244).

23. Woodward (1951, 254).

24. Gaithers (1977, 61).

25. See Hoffman (1896) for an excellent example of the scientific literature that sought to portray blacks as an inferior race. Also, Newby (1965) describes how this "scientific racism" was used to justify the discriminatory treatment of blacks.

26. Gaither (1977, 101), emphasis in the original.

27. See, for example, Inverarity (1976) and Olzak (1990, 1992).

28. Kousser (1974).

29. Woodward (1951, 347–48).

30. Woodward (1951, 342–43).

31. Kousser (1974, 145).

32. For discussions of interrupted time-series analysis, see McCleary and Hay (1980, 141–203) and McDowall et al. (1980, 64–85).

33. A transfer function is a mathematical relationship specifying how the intervention (disenfranchisement) affects the dependent variable (lynching). There is no easy way of specifying the gradual but temporary model using simple zero-order and first-order transfer functions (McCleary and Hay 1980, 1980, 171; McDowall et al. 1980, 66), so this specification was not explored.

34. This strategy assumes that disenfranchisement occurred in 1900 which, of course, is not true for all ten states. Nonetheless, the year 1900 represents a reasonably good approximation of the timing of the introduction of restrictive voting statutes throughout the South.

35. Preliminary analysis demonstrated that modeling the disturbance as a first-order auto-regressive process yielded better fits than assuming a first-order moving-average disturbance, as we have in previous analyses. For this reason, we report the empirical findings produced by each specification.

36. Kousser (1974) has noted that black political participation in Georgia had been declining long before 1908, and that state had introduced a poll tax in 1877. Therefore, it must be recognized that 1908 is a somewhat arbitrary date for disenfranchisement in Georgia, however, there is no preferable alternative.

37. The case of the Louisiana bivariate model with a moving-average disturbance is an exception. In this model, the estimated effect of disenfranchisement is –0.314 with a t-ratio of –4.16. On the face of these results, it would seem that disenfranchisement had a significant negative effect in Louisiana. However, we also found the estimated moving-average coefficient for this model (–1.075) exceeded the bounds of invertibility, thus bringing into question the reliability of these results. The "bounds of invertibility" refers to the necessary requirement that the moving-average coefficient not exceed unity (see McCleary and Hay 1980, 63–64). Because of this mis-specification we dismiss this finding as artifactual.

38. We are somewhat restricted in the variables that can be included on the righthand side of the equation. The variety of county-level characteristics available for 1880 and 1890 is considerably smaller than for later periods. For example, race-specific farm tenure information is not available for 1880 or 1890, but is for 1900 and 1910.

39. See chapter 4 for the logic of the Poisson specification and justification of the Gamma assumption.

40. Raper (1933, 170).

7

The Great Migration
and the Demise of Lynching

One of the more puzzling aspects of the lynching era is its rapid decline after the mid-1920s. To be sure, African-Americans continued to be lynched well into the middle of this century and beyond—as the very recent lynching of Michael Donald in Alabama makes all too clear.[1] However, mob violence never really regained the intensity of the 1890s, or even the early years of the twentieth century. Although the 1890s claimed 799 black victims of white mob action, only 206 and 88 blacks were lynched by whites in the 1920s and 1930s, respectively.[2] Moreover, there was a marked shift in the public mood toward lynchings as they occurred less and less frequently. Reflective of this shift is a national poll of public opinion conducted by the Gallup organization in 1937, which found that 65 percent of all southerners supported legislation that would have made lynching a federal crime. Although somewhat weaker than support in the northeast and north central regions, southern sentiment concerning antilynching legislation was identical to that in mountain states and even more supportive than public opinion on the West Coast.[3] Of course, we cannot know what a similar Gallup poll would have revealed during the height of the lynching era, but it is probably safe to assume that the average southerner was more tolerant of federal intrusion into southern race relations in 1937 than in 1897.

Even social institutions that had acquiesced to the mob mentality of earlier eras began to show evidence of a willingness to oppose violence. For example, the southern press became less apologetic and more willing to express strong opposition to the outrages of mob violence as the number of lynchings waned. And even some southern politicians mustered the courage to speak openly in opposition to lynchings, to mobilize the state militia to prevent lynchings, and to endorse state-level legislation to discourage them. From southerners themselves, as well as from the institutions through which they expressed their desires and wills, a new message was heard—a message considerably less sympathetic to the radical racism that had prevailed during previous decades.

Although black lynchings did decline sharply after the mid-1920s, the drop in the number of black victims may actually overstate the true extent of the social transformation that was occurring in southern states. A substantial part of the overall decline was an impressive rise in the number of prevented lynchings. The information available on prevented lynchings is of questionable accuracy and must be considered only suggestive of general patterns and trends. Statistics compiled by the Commission on Interracial Cooperation (CIC) indicate that only 39 percent of attempted lynchings were prevented between 1916 and 1920. That percentage rose to 77 percent during the next decade and to 84 percent during the 1930s.[4] It appears that some segments of the southern white community were still willing to get out the rope and faggot when it served their purposes. But other members of the community became increasingly willing to thwart the efforts of would-be lynch mobs to consummate their grisly deeds. The rise in prevented lynchings suggests once again that southern whites were not monolithic in their approach to race relations—at least in their willingness to endorse, or engage in, mob activity.

Explaining the Demise of Lynching

It is much simpler to document the erosion of mob violence than to explain it. Why would southern whites abandon this form of terroristic control over the African-American population? What convinced some within the white community that it was in their own best interest to combat the efforts of friends and neighbors who were still willing to lynch? Several possible explanations have been suggested. According to Jesse Daniel Ames, executive director of the Association of Southern Women for the Prevention of Lynching (ASWPL), the decline of lynchings in the mid-1930s was due to three factors: (1) growing opposition by the southern press; (2) effects of New Deal programs on the economic status of southern rural whites; and (3) an increased reliance on radio-dispatched state patrols.[5] Walter White, executive secretary of the National Association for the Advancement of Colored People (NAACP), agreed with Ames's assessment of the role of the white press but also emphasized a variety of other factors, including (1) the antilynching work of organizations such as the NAACP and the Commission on Interracial Cooperation; (2) increased resistance of the black community to lynch mobs; and (3) the mass migration of southern blacks to northern states during and after World War I.[6] Others have suggested that lynchings declined as southern states assumed the role of the mob by increasing the number of blacks who were legally executed.[7] To this list might be added the increased willingness of southern state legislatures to entertain antilynching measures, as well as the shift in public opinion.

We are skeptical of most of these explanations and suspect that some were symptomatic of larger social transformations. Thus, they were either spuriously related to the decline in black lynchings or they were the mechanisms through which the larger social changes were translated into fewer black lynch victims. Little empirical evidence supports the hypothesized effect of increased legal executions on black lynchings (chapter 4); the other explanations have not been examined critically.

The Southern Press

There is no doubt that the press was a powerful institution, or that its treatment of lynchings shifted dramatically over time. An early apologist for mob violence, the press had been complicit in perpetuating a hostile atmosphere for race relations. Although the press had not become progressive by the 1930s, it had moved toward abandoning its practice of race-baiting and excusing the behavior of white mobs. Nonetheless, just as we do not attribute the peak in lynchings during the "bloody 1890s" to the work of the southern press, we cannot ascribe the relatively benign atmosphere after 1930 to its conversion. Rather, we prefer to view the southern press during both eras as a tool that certain segments of the white community used effectively to construct an image that served their own selfish interests. We must look beyond the machinations of the white press to the underlying social forces that committed some members of the white community to an altered racial climate, at least to the abatement of mob violence against African-Americans.

New Deal Policies

New Deal policies had a profound impact on southern society, especially in rural areas. The Agricultural Adjustment Act of 1933, for example, encouraged many planters to withdraw acreage from cultivation in an effort to restore fertility to soil exhausted after decades of abuse. Although potentially a financial boon to farm owners, the increased amount of land lying fallow worked a serious hardship on tenants and sharecroppers, who were squeezed out of the benefits to which the program rightfully entitled them and forced off the land taken out of cultivation. This was aggravated by later policies that contributed to a dramatic increase in the use of tractors and other machinery. Again, tenants and croppers were displaced as farm owners found it more efficient to rely on wage laborers to prepare fields for planting and to harvest the mature crops with the assistance of farm machinery.

Thus, the effects of New Deal policies in the rural South were probably mixed. While owners were certain to benefit, the large class of landless tenants and croppers were much less inclined to celebrate, not to mention the wage laborers who occupied the bottom rung of the agricultural ladder.[8] We doubt that these were the kinds of social transformations that necessarily would have led to reduced mob activity among the rural dependent classes. More problematic for this explanation of lynching's demise, however, is its timing. By the time the New Deal policies were implemented and had sufficient opportunity to work, the number of lynchings was already on a steep downward course. Indeed, the sharpest drop occurred between 1920 and 1930, before Franklin D. Roosevelt assumed the presidency in 1933.

Improved Efficiency of Southern Law Enforcement

Is it possible that technological innovations in southern policing, including radio-dispatched state patrol cars, played an important role in the demise of lynching, as Ames and others claimed? The rapid rise in the proportion of attempted lynchings that were prevented suggests that more efficient and determined law enforcement did have an effect on the shrinking number of lynchings during the 1920s and 1930s. Gordon suggested that lynching was reduced when states established police forces, when sheriffs could be removed for failure to carry out their legal responsibilities, and when provisions were made to rotate judges.[9]

This explanation is unsatisfactory, however, because it fails to identify the underlying reason for the relatively sudden decision by southern lawmen to intervene when mob activity threatened. Surely, this enthusiasm for law and order had not characterized the behavior of southern sheriffs during earlier eras. Indeed, a large percentage of lynch victims were snatched while in the custody of local police, and in other cases the authorities were actual accomplices in mob violence. In most cases, the mobs' success in abducting victims was due to sher-

Figure 7-1. From *The Crisis*, January 1935, 27.

iffs' refusals to resist rather than an inability to resist. The unwritten code of southern law enforcement seemed to have been that white lives would not be sacrificed in an effort to save black lives, no matter how unlawful the behavior of the whites.[10] The more interesting question then is what accounts for the greater willingness of southern police to use the equipment in their arsenal to frustrate white mobs, not the improving effectiveness of that equipment. Thus, like the shifting editorial policies of southern newspapers, we view the changing behavior of law enforcement to have been a tool that certain groups used to erase mob violence from the southern landscape. But why?

The Role of Antilynching Organizations

A good deal of attention has been devoted to the impact of such organizations as the National Association for the Advancement of Colored People, the Committee on Interracial Cooperation, and the Association of Southern Women for the Prevention of Lynching on the decline in mob violence.[11] Although these organizations varied considerably in tactics and strategies, they all worked vigorously for the end of lynching and were generally successful in carrying their antilynching message to northern states and even to Europe. They were also able to mobilize external pressure against southern states in which lynchings were most common. The CIC and ASWPL were even able to raise the legitimacy of antilynching sentiment within the South.

Despite their considerable success, we doubt that the activity of these groups can be considered the fundamental driving force behind the disappearance of lynching. We base this contention on three primary issues. First, aside from the NAACP, which was established in 1908, the other groups given credit for ending the terror of mob violence arrived relatively late on the scene. The CIC was founded in 1919, and the ASWPL in 1931. Lynchings had begun to decline before either organization became influential. Furthermore, both organizations were most active during the 1930s, after the number of lynchings had already dropped sharply.[12] Second, southern whites had been quite successful at resisting the attacks of previous crusaders. The fate of Ida B. Wells is a good example.

Wells was editor of *The Free Speech,* which was published in Memphis and which she used as a forum for her fight against lynching. She attracted considerable attention and caused great controversy when she suggested that many southern white women voluntarily entered into sexual liaisons with African-American men. Then, when exposed, the same white women often cried rape in order to protect their own reputations. Eventually, after Wells vociferously objected

Figure 7-2. "Woman to the Rescue!" From *The Crisis,* May 1916, 43. The fleeing man in the suit says, "I don't believe in agitating and fighting. My policy is
to pursue the life of least resistance. To h—— with Citizenship Rights! I want
money. I think the white folk will let me stay on my land as long as *I stay in
my place.*—(Shades of Wilmington, N.C.) The good whites ain't responsible for
bad administration of the law and lynching and peonage—let me think awhile;
or—."

to the lynching of three black Memphis businessmen in 1892, whites destroyed the presses of *The Free Speech* and made it clear that Wells would not be safe if she returned from her visit to New York City.[13] It was several years before she again returned to the South. The historical record is replete with other examples of southern whites foiling the efforts of black individuals or groups that attempted to alter the status quo as long as social change was not in their best interest.

Third, it is our suspicion that increasing southern tolerance for antilynching activity by groups such as the NAACP, CIC, and ASW-PL was the product of the same social forces that caused lynchings to decline. That is, when it served the purpose of certain southern whites, a variety of tools were used to bring about the demise of lynching. It is more efficacious to focus on the social transformations that led that group of whites to conclude that lynchings were disruptive than it is to become preoccupied with the tools they used or the byproducts of their profound decision.

African-American Resistance

White believed that an increasing willingness among blacks to resist mob action increased the cost of lynching to whites and thereby reduced its frequency. Shapiro has also noted the relatively frequent occurrence of black resistance, especially during the later phases of the lynching era.[14] Southern mobs sometimes were dissuaded when they encountered resistance. When sheriffs were willing to protect their prisoners—even if it meant shooting into mobs—attempted lynchings often were foiled successfully. And, in some cases, the African-American community was able to discourage mob action by showing fight.

An excellent illustration of successful black resistance is offered by the Darien Insurrection of 1899.[15] Matilda Hope of McIntosh County, Georgia—who was white—gave birth to a black child, claiming that she had been raped by Henry Delegale, a neighbor. Not waiting for the expected lynch mob to form, Delegale turned himself in to the local sheriff. The next day the sheriff decided to move Delegale from jail in Darien to Savannah for "safekeeping." This was not a good sign, because it was common for lynch mobs to intercept transported suspects. The Darien African-American community felt that Delegale was safer in Darien and organized a protest to prevent the sheriff from moving him to Savannah. Faced with staunch opposition from local blacks, the sheriff asked Georgia Governor Allen Candler for troops to quell the black "insurrection." Shortly, the state militia arrived in Darien to escort and protect Henry Delegale on his trip to Savannah.

Figure 7-3. "For the Children!" From *The Crisis,* October 1934, 294.

In his subsequent trial, the jury found Delegale not guilty of the accused rape, and he was set free.

Although African-American resistance may have saved the life of Henry Delegale of Darien, Georgia, resistance often produced less desirable outcomes. During the frenzy of mob violence at the peak of the lynching era, armed resistance by blacks often simply resulted in violence on a larger scale and more black corpses. Indeed, this was also often the case during the twilight of the lynching era. A good example is the series of events that transpired in the black community of Rosewood, Florida, in early January 1923.[16]

Following an all-too-typical claim that a white woman had been assaulted by a black man, a Klan-led posse was formed to hunt down the alleged culprit, Jesse Hunter. Although frustrated in their attempt to locate the accused, the mob did manage—with the help of bloodhounds—to track down an apparent accomplice. According to the newspaper account, Sam Carter admitted to the mob that he had helped Hunter elude the posse. In exchange for his honesty the mob riddled Carter with bullets and left his body lying in the sandy soil. After the incident, indignant members of the African-American community armed themselves and engaged the Klansmen in a furious gunfight. Three whites and two blacks were killed in the initial hostilities. As the fighting continued and intensified, twenty-five armed blacks barricaded themselves in a house and fended off the white mob.

Eventually, the mob exhausted its supply of ammunition, and the surviving blacks fled the house. As a result of the protracted armed resistance, four more black lives were lost, including those of Sylvester Carrier and his mother, Sarah. A symbolic end to the carnage occurred on Saturday, January 6, when another member of the Carrier family was lynched. According to a newspaper account, the white mob dragged James Carrier to the black graveyard in Rosewood and "made him stand on the newly dug graves of his brother and mother . . . while they riddled his body with shots." While the armed conflict was in progress, most of the black community sought refuge in the forests and marshes. They feared reprisals, and they were right. Not yet satisfied by the bloodletting, angry whites burned virtually the entire town of Rosewood to the ground.[17] Thus, armed resistance sometimes exacted a ghastly price. Furthermore, it is questionable whether such cases of black resistance were a driving force in the sharp reduction in black lynchings after the mid-1920s or whether they were relatively isolated examples.

Political Efforts

Some southern political voices became more sympathetic to the antilynching message during the 1920s and 1930s, at about the same time that the southern press changed its posture on lynching.[18] Despite the strong resistance in southern political circles to federal antilynching legislation, some states entertained legislative measures aimed at discouraging mob violence. For example, Kentucky led the way by passing antilynching legislation in 1920. In 1921, West Virginia followed suit when it passed a law that required a $1,000 fine as well as a year's imprisonment for convicted lynchers and a $5,000 fine for officials whose negligence aided in a lynching.

Once again, however, we believe that these measures reflected a new perspective on lynchings within some segments of the southern white population rather than a root cause of that shifting perspective. Southern states had implemented antilynching measures long before the sharp decline in mob activity. For example, in 1893 the Georgia legislature passed a law providing for the imprisonment of from one to twenty years for any person found guilty of "mobbing or lynching any citizen . . . without due process of law, and authorized a sheriff to require service of any citizen to help protect a prisoner threatened with lynching."[19] North Carolina also passed an antilynching law in 1893, and in 1895 South Carolina adopted a provision requiring counties to pay $2,000 to the next of kin of lynch victims.

The historical record shows clearly that these same states found it very convenient to ignore those laws. Potentially severe punishment for mob members was virtually irrelevant when coroners consistently concluded that lynch victims met their fates at the hands of a "party or parties unknown," or when juries refused to convict known members of lynch mobs. Thus, the net effect of such legislation on the frequency of lynching was probably quite limited. If antilynching measures became more "effective" during the 1920s and 1930s, it was only because their enforcement benefited some members of white society.

We do not doubt that some of the measures discussed played a role as the number of southern lynchings dropped strikingly during the 1920s and 1930s. That they did so, however, is an inadequate explanation for what motivated southern whites to endorse, or tolerate, such antilynching messages or activity. Therefore, we believe that these measures were primarily mechanisms through which some larger social transformation operated. Specifically, southern police more effectively thwarted mob activity because some whites benefited from them doing so. Likewise, the southern press, because it reflected the sentiment of an important segment of the southern white population, changed its treatment of black lynchings.

The Role of African-American Migration

A primary theme that has emerged throughout this book is that economic motives played an important role in mob violence against southern blacks. At various times, lynchings served the economic interests of all whites. Although this point has been made in previous chapters, a brief recapitulation is in order here. When the economic fortunes of marginal whites soured (e.g., because of shifts in farm tenure or swings in the price of cotton), violence against blacks increased. Either out of frustration or with more instrumental motives in mind, whites responded to economic stress by terrorizing blacks. For whites in the upper social strata, racial antagonism was an effective means to prevent the dreaded coalition between black and white laborers, and lynchings could also be used to maintain control over African-American workers at critical times during the agricultural cycle. When the interests of whites at both ends of the class spectrum aligned, southern blacks were especially endangered. Indeed, one of the reasons that the gruesome and shameful practice of lynching was so common and so tolerated is probably because it had the potential to benefit all classes of whites. There were also, however, periods when the interests of poor and well-to-do whites diverged.

As developed thus far, the economic model of lynching has emphasized the motivations that led southern whites to lynch blacks. It is possible, however, to turn this model on its head and ask whether there were occasions when economic forces motivated southern whites to resist and oppose racial violence. In other words, were there some circumstances in which reduced racial hostility benefited certain groups within the white community? As White argued, we believe that exactly this situation arose during the 1920s as massive waves of black migrants either left the South entirely or relocated within the South, especially to urban areas.[20] White planters and employers grew concerned as they witnessed the rapid evaporation of the cheap and pliable labor force upon which they had built and maintained their fortunes. In order to preserve the status quo, the white elite somehow had to devise a strategy to stanch the flow of labor. Given the widely held perception that some black migrants were fleeing the threat of mob violence, it would not be surprising to find that the white elite eventually implemented a strategy of reduced racial terror in order to hold onto its black workers.

The Great Migration

African-Americans were not complete strangers to residential mobility even before the Great Migration that began around the time of World War I. Indeed, one of the most noticeable benefits of emancipation was the freedman's ability to relocate. Between 1870 and 1900, many took advantage of this freedom and either moved to growing urban areas in the South or left the South.[21] More common, however, were short-distance moves within the rural South as landless farmers sought better remunerative arrangements with new landlords.[22] Although most locally migratory farmers never ventured far from home, others relocated to southwestern states where cotton cultivation was expanding and opportunities were greater. Arkansas, Texas, and the Oklahoma Territory all experienced considerable in-migration of blacks between 1870 and 1900.[23]

After 1900, especially during the teens, the pace of African-American migration accelerated, and its character was transformed. Even as many blacks continued to circulate within the rural South and gravitate toward southern urban areas, more and more began to make the longer trek north. To illustrate the extent and variation of the post-1900 migration of blacks, the figures in Table 7-1 report intercensal net migration for the first three decades of this century. At least three points emerge. First, some southern states lost huge numbers of their

Table 7-1. Estimated Net Black Migration for Ten Southern States by Decade, 1900–1930[a]

State	1900–1910	1910–20	1920–30
Alabama	−22,100	−70,800	−80,700
Arkansas	22,500	−1,000	−46,300
Florida	40,700	3,200	54,200
Georgia	−16,200	−74,700	−260,000
Kentucky	−22,300	−16,600	−16,600
Louisiana	−16,100	−51,200	−25,500
Mississippi	−30,900	−129,600	−68,800
North Carolina	−28,400	−28,900	−15,700
South Carolina	−72,000	−74,500	−204,300
Tennessee	−34,300	−29,300	−14,000
All ten states	−179,100	−473,400	−677,700

a. Source: U.S. Bureau of the Census (1975).

African-American populations, for instance, both Georgia and South Carolina experienced a net loss of more than two hundred thousand blacks between 1920 and 1930. This represented 22 percent and 24 percent, respectively, of their black populations in 1920.[24] Second, the net loss of black population accelerated substantially across the decades, reaching its peak between 1920 and 1930 when the ten states lost a total of 677,700 blacks. Third, the experiences of these states varied considerably. Some suffered net losses of black population during all decades, yet Florida actually increased its black population through net migration throughout the period. The net migration estimates in Table 7-1 actually understate the total amount of black residential mobility. They include only interstate migration and not the vast numbers of southern blacks who moved across or within counties but not across state borders.

If one looks closer at those states contributing most of the African-American migrants, it becomes clear that rates of black out-migration within the South also were not uniform. Some areas were characterized by extremely high out-migration, whereas others maintained relatively stable black populations or even experienced net in-migration. To illustrate this intraregional variability, we have estimated county-level black net migration rates (per one hundred population) for Georgia and South Carolina, both of which experienced very heavy losses of blacks through migration. Figure 7-4 has been shaded according to the rate of black out-migration experienced between 1920 and 1930.[25]

Clearly, the heaviest African-American out-migration occurred in a swath running roughly through the middle of Georgia and South Carolina, an area that defined the Black Belt and was dominated by a plantation cotton economy.[26] Other counties in the two states experienced much lighter out-migration. Two general conclusions can be gleaned from these patterns: (1) The forces driving the exodus of blacks apparently varied substantially across the southern landscape; and (2) the effects of the out-migration would have been felt more keenly in some areas than in others.

Whatever the causes and effects of this massive population movement, it substantially altered the geographic and residential profile of the black population of the United States. Whereas 90 percent of all blacks resided in southern states in 1900, that percentage had dropped to 79 by 1930. And the percentage of southern blacks living in urban places grew from 17 in 1900 to 33 by 1930, and much of the black urbanization was due to migration. Eventually, what had been an overwhelmingly southern and largely rural population became more northern and urban.[27] The demographic shift had profound effects on

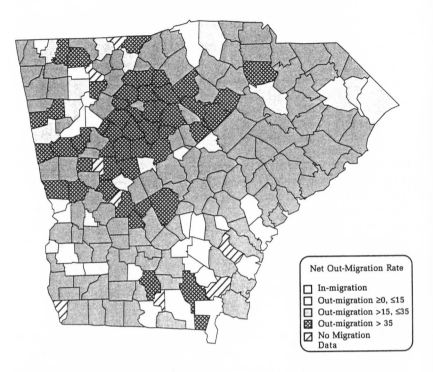

Figure 7-4. Net Black Out-Migration Rate from Counties in Georgia and South Carolina, 1920–30.

the social and political environments of the areas of destination, especially the large urban centers of the northeast and north central states where many black migrants relocated. It also posed substantial new challenges to those southern regions that saw large proportions of their African-American populations heading north or relocating within the South.

Explanations for the Great Migration

Three general types of explanations have been offered for the increased mobility of southern blacks during the Great Migration: (1) those that stress underlying economic forces, including regional wage differentials and expansion of employment opportunities in the North; (2) those that stress underlying social forces, for example, educational opportunities, racial violence, and voter disenfranchisement; and (3) those that focus on more precipitating causes such as floods or boll weevil infestation. The consensus of contemporary observers and modern investigators seems to be that the precipitating causes combined with festering economic dissatisfaction to trigger the exodus, especially as employment opportunities for blacks expanded in the North. Aggravating these economic difficulties, however, were social factors, including racial violence.

Economic Forces

Most contemporary observers of the Great Migration ascribed primary importance to economic factors. For example, one student of the migration argued, "The cause of the migration, like that of practically all great movements of peoples, is fundamentally economic."[28] Another observed, "The economic motive stands among the foremost reasons for the decision of the group [blacks] to leave the South."[29] Many others also expressed the same sentiments.[30]

The economic push factors operating on southern blacks were formidable. Since emancipation, southern rural blacks had languished in a plantation economy that provided little hope of moving up the "agricultural ladder" and offered few employment opportunities outside of farming. At the bottom of a pecking order defined by class and caste, they were also caught in the clash of competing class interests that split the white community. On the one hand, white planters and employers benefited from the availability of cheap black labor as long as it remained docile and servile. On the other hand, poor whites competed with that labor. Further, it was in the interest of planters and employers to restrict alternative opportunities available to the black laboring class as well as to prevent a coalition of black and white labor. The economic advancement of rural blacks was not in the interest of either class of whites, but their subordination served the interests of both.

Although a fortunate few were able to purchase land, most rural blacks remained sharecroppers, tenant farmers, or farm laborers.[31] Subject to the whims of landlords or employers and to the vagaries of cotton prices, most scratched a subsistence living from year to year and could offer no different future for their children. As this dismal economic situation persisted, an environment conducive to out-migration was created. Many perceived greater opportunity in the North or in southern cities. As industries geared up to produce the armaments required for the new war and the previously steady stream of European migrants slowed to a trickle, northern employers looked south for an alternative source of cheap labor. Many southern blacks drifted north to fill this labor vacuum. Even after the war, restrictive immigration legislation further limited the flow of European migrants and opportunities for African-American migrants continued. At the same time, many black migrants circulated within rural areas of the southern region or pursued opportunities in southern cities.

Social Forces

Social causes of African-American migration were as widely acknowledged by contemporary observers as the economic forces but generally considered as secondary in importance. Woofter enumerated many of the primary social factors: "Injustice in the courts, lynching, denial of suffrage, discrimination in public conveyances, and inequalities in educational advantage."[32]

Elaborate arrangements were made to guarantee that blacks occupied, and recognized, their inferior caste position. The passage of various Jim Crow laws provided for separate, and unequal, facilities.[33] Restrictive voting statutes became more and more common after the turn of the century and effectively curtailed the black vote.[34] State legislatures allocated vastly unequal financial support, and county officials still sometimes supported white schools with siphoned off meager resources earmarked for blacks.[35] Such social abuses, as well as chronic economic hopelessness, created an atmosphere conducive to out-migration.

One of the most telling indicators of the inferior social position of African-Americans in southern society was the level of lethal violence to which they were exposed. There has been much speculation that lynchings may have been instrumental in contributing to the willingness of southern blacks to leave their homes, either for the North or for more peaceful locations in the South.

By many accounts, the fear of violence terrorized southern blacks. As a report prepared by the U.S. Department of Labor concluded, "Another of the more effective causes of the exodus, a cause that appeals to every Negro whether high or low, industrious or idle, respected or condemned, is the Negroes' insecurity from mob violence and lynchings."[36] Several specific cases of heavy black out-migration have been linked to particular lynching incidents. For example, one section of Georgia experienced such an exodus following a series of horrible lynchings in 1915 and 1916. According to Woofter, "The planters in the immediate vicinity of these lynchings attributed the movement from their places to the fact that the lynching parties had terrorized their Negroes."[37] Another notorious lynching in South Carolina was followed by increased out-migration of blacks from the area around Abbeville.[38]

A particularly vivid example of the terrorizing effect of lynching was that of Jim McIlherron in Estill Springs, Tennessee.[39] McIlherron had been accused of killing two white men. On February 12, 1918, he was taken to the scene of the murders by a mob of twenty masked men. In their effort to extract a confession, the mob tortured him with hot irons as black residents of the community were forced to watch. Finally, McIlherron was chained to a tree and burned alive in front of 1,500 spectators. After the incident the black population of Estill Springs quickly disappeared.

A second specific example can be drawn from the lynching record in the state of Georgia. Ernest Cox, who was black, was suspected of raping and murdering a young white girl in Forsyth County in 1912. It was widely suspected in the county that Cox had been assisted in his attempt to conceal the body by his friend, Edward Collins. Soon after the incident, Cox fled from the area. Collins remained but was arrested and placed in the county jail in the small town of Cumming. On September 10, 1912, a large and angry mob of whites entered the jail and shot Collins to death.[40]

In the wake of the Cox-Collins affair, white vigilantes blanketed the area with broadsides demanding that all blacks leave Forsyth County or suffer the consequences. The black community took these threats seriously, and many families fled. Census figures confirm the exodus. In the decades before the lynching, Forsyth County had a stable black population of about 1,100; only thirty remained by 1920, and, by 1930, Forsyth County had only seventeen black residents. Clearly, the black families that left Forsyth County in the aftermath of the Collins lynching and the circumstances surrounding it were refugees from racial violence.

Finally, African-American migrants themselves mentioned the fear of violence as a reason for leaving their homes. As one migrant wrote eloquently to the *Chicago Defender,* "After twenty years of seeing my people lynched for any offense from spitting on a sidewalk to stealing a mule, I made up my mind that I would turn the prow of my ship toward the part of the country where the people at least made a pretense at being civilized."[41]

Consequences of the Great Migration

As with any episode of population redistribution of this magnitude, there were important consequences for those areas that experienced heavy out-migration. As the Great Migration accelerated, many locations in the South were reeling from the massive exodus, a concern that was primarily economic in nature.

By the turn of the twentieth century, the southern economy had become extremely dependent upon cheap African-American labor. As the black exodus intensified, the economic impact of the loss of such labor began to be felt. "As the trains and boats pulled out week after week and month after month," Henri noted, "the South began to hurt from a loss of the black labor force, especially the Deep South."[42] In response, planters and employers mounted a desperate attempt to restrict the labor hemorrhage. At first, their effort consisted of coercive measures. Migrants were intimidated, threatened, and abused. The spike in black lynchings that occurred shortly before 1920 (Figure 2-3b) was likely a partial reflection of this effort.

When it became clear that coercive tactics were ineffective, some southern communities turned to enticement. If African-Americans were migrating because they were unhappy or mistreated, then they should be made to feel more comfortable. In some areas, wages rose in response to the black exodus.[43] In other areas, local elites saw an increasing need to improve the plight of blacks. As a report by the U.S. Department of Labor observed, "They see in the growing need for Negro labor so powerful an appeal to the Self-interest of the white employer and the white planter as to make it possible to get an influential white group to exert itself actively to provide better schools; to insure full settlements between landlord and tenant on all plantations by the end of the year; to bring about abolition of the abuses in the courts of justice of the peace."[44] It appears that in some cases local white elites were even willing to appeal for a reduction in the level of violent persecution of the subordinate caste. White commented on this important consequence of the migration,

> The more intelligent South . . . began to show signs of awakening to the gravity of the situation. They realized that, now that Negroes had a place to which they could go for freedom from lynching and insult, for decent wages, living conditions, and school facilities, they would require more decent treatment in the South or they would leave. This realization led to the strengthening of the work of the Interracial Commission, to plans for better schools for Negroes in states like North Carolina and Louisiana, to much more outspoken condemnation of lynching by the press and the better element of the public.[45]

Historically, southern blacks have used their labor value to extract concessions from the white majority, even if unintentionally. After the

Civil War, blacks "took advantage" of a labor-starved southern economy to prevent the perpetuation of a slavelike "gang labor" agricultural system.[46] It was through compromise that the tenancy and sharecropping system emerged. We are suggesting that blacks again "exploited" their increased labor value during the era of heavy migration. Faced with the loss of their cheap labor force, and with no feasible substitutes, white planters and employers began to perceive the benefits of a less hostile and exploitative environment.

This is not to argue, however, that well-to-do whites wished to scuttle the southern caste system altogether or to make blacks social equals. Rather, we suggest that the Great Migration and the shrinking black labor force made the white elite realize that mob violence was a luxury that southern society could no longer afford. Other forces may also have led to this conclusion. First, increasing farm mechanization reduced the need for violence as a means of control. Second, the virtually complete disenfranchisement of black voters by 1910 reduced the political threat of a coalition between white and black workers. Thus, given the relatively successful alternatives to lynching that were available for maintaining control over southern blacks (e.g., disenfranchisement and Jim Crow legislation), the moderation of racial violence was a small price for white planters and employers to pay. Naturally, these sentiments were more likely to emerge in areas that were suffering greater losses of their African-American population.

It would be naive, however, to believe that the South was monolithic in its response to black migration and the loss of African-American labor. In fact, there is good reason to suspect that reactions to the black exodus were split along class lines. Bonacich's Split Labor Market theory of antagonistic ethnic relations is useful for developing this important point.[47] According to Bonacich, blacks were one of three class groups represented in the southern economy, the other two being white planters and employers and white laborers. Planters and employers were dependent upon cheap black labor, and the higher-priced white laborers were in competition with black labor. White laborers had everything to gain from the exodus of blacks, but planters and employers had much to lose.[48]

Competition between white and black southern labor intensified considerably during the late nineteenth and early twentieth centuries. The growing rural population put extreme pressure on southern land, and more and more white farmers were reduced to tenancy.[49] As a result, despite membership in the dominant caste, more rural whites began to share the same disadvantaged economic position with African-Americans and to be in direct economic competition with southern black farmers. To the extent that the migration of blacks from southern counties removed economic competitors, poorer whites would have improved their position with regard to planters and employers.[50]

Holmes presents clear evidence of this effect in the case of Mississippi, where many borderline white farmers organized to terrorize black farmers and tenants. Because of the crop-lien system, it was common for merchants to become landed gentry through foreclosure and then hire black tenants and sharecroppers to work the cotton fields. This had two immediate effects: It reduced the number of small landholding white farmers and replaced white tenants with more easily controlled black tenants. These actions were detrimental to the economic interests of borderline landholding whites and those whites who were landless, and, as Holmes has demonstrated, did not go unchallenged. Much violence was directed at offending blacks.[51]

Thus, it is unlikely that planters and employers responded equally to the loss of black laborers. While planters and employers may have reacted to African-American migration with efforts to moderate the grievances blacks held against their white oppressors, poor whites had little motivation to do so. This divergence of white class interests may partially account for the rapid rise in prevented lynchings in the second and third decades of this century. While one segment of white society continued to perceive certain benefits accruing to racial violence, another segment began to view things much differently.[52] The social and economic composition of the white community is a critical factor in understanding that community's responses to the Great Migration and its siphoning-off of local populations of African-Americans.

Linking the Great Migration and Racial Violence

Central to our examination of the empirical evidence bearing on the linkages we have proposed are the questions of whether it can be demonstrated that heavier out-migration of African-Americans led to reduced racial violence, and whether evidence exists that the reactions of the white community to black migration were split along class lines.

The temporal patterns of the two phenomena are certainly consistent with the hypothesis that the levels of black migration and black lynchings were associated. The decade-by-decade totals of migration and lynching reveal quite clearly that the number of black lynch victims declined steadily as the intensity of black out-migration accelerated. For instance, the number of black lynchings by white mobs

Figure 7-5. "The Reason." From *The Crisis,* 1920, 264.

dropped from 604 between 1900 and 1909, to 444 between 1910 and 1919, and continued falling to 206 between 1920 and 1929. The net loss of black population rose from 179,100 between 1900 and 1910, to 474,400 between 1910 and 1920, then increased further to 677,700 during the 1920s.

Unfortunately, it is virtually impossible to offer more rigorous temporal evidence. For example, relatively sophisticated time-series analyses like those conducted in earlier chapters are not suitable in this situation because annual estimates of black migration are not available and the interval under consideration is relatively brief, spanning only two decades. For these reasons, we must approach the questions from a cross-sectional perspective. Did local areas within the South that lost larger proportions of their black populations through out-migration also experience reductions in the level of racial violence, and did the white class structure of local areas play a role in determining whether black out-migration was translated into declining racial violence?

The general conceptual framework that guides the following investigation is shown in Figure 7-6. Consistent with our earlier discussion, the model proposes a negative effect of African-American out-migration on the level of black lynching. Furthermore, there is good reason to suspect that class structure among the local white population may have influenced this relationship. The effect of migration on racial violence may have been stronger in areas where more white planters and employers suffered from the exodus of the local black population. However, in areas where fewer whites were directly affected by the

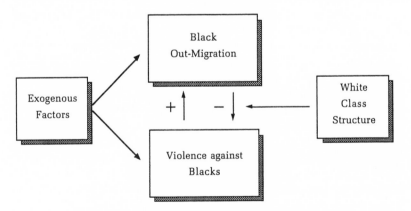

Figure 7-6. Conceptual Model Describing Relationship between Black Migration and Lynching.

migration (or possibly even benefited from the shrinking black population), its negative impact on black lynchings was likely more muted, if present at all.

The relationship proposed in Figure 7-6 is made more complex by the possibility that the level of racial violence simultaneously affected the rate at which the local black population was leaving the county. It has long been suspected that some blacks migrated to the North or relocated within the South because they felt threatened by the possibility of lynching. Consequently, as we attempt to estimate the impact of black out-migration on lynching within geographic areas, it is important to also consider the possibility of a simultaneous effect of lynching on out-migration. Failure to take the reciprocal nature of this relationship into account could result in misleading conclusions, most likely in an underestimation of the influence that migration had on the decline of southern lynchings. Finally, our conceptual model allows for the influence of social, economic, and demographic exogenous forces in empirical models.

Consistent with the timing of the Great Migration, data for the decades 1910–20 and 1920–30 are used in our analyses. Although the level of African-American migration did accelerate after the turn of the century, the second decade is generally considered the beginning of the truly massive relocation of southern blacks.[53]

The conceptual model proposed in Figure 7-6 describes two reciprocally linked endogenous variables: the net migration rate for blacks and the frequency of black lynchings. Little description of the source of the lynching variable is required because our inventory has been cited repeatedly in previous chapters. For the following analyses, the number of black victims of lynching within each county simply has been summed within each of the two decades.

Our measure of county-level black out-migration requires somewhat more description. County-level net migration rates for blacks are estimated using a forward census survival rate method.[54] Although computationally tedious, this method is conceptually simple. An observed population at some point in time is compared with the expected population for the same period. The expected population is estimated by surviving the population at some earlier point in time forward. The difference between the two represents net migration. If the observed population is larger, then the county has experienced net in-migration; if the expected population is larger, then net out-migration has occurred.[55]

To facilitate the presentation and discussion of findings, we have multiplied the net migration rates by [−1] so that a larger value indicates greater out-migration (or smaller in-migration). Although we will generally refer to this dependent variable as a measure of black out-migration, it should be recognized that many counties in our analyses actually experienced net in-migration. Counties with net out-migration of blacks will have positive values on this variable, whereas those that experienced net in-migration will have negative values.

Although our primary interest is in the impact of African-American out-migration on racial violence and the role the white class structure played in shaping that impact, it is necessary to include relevant exogenous variables in the model to avoid conclusions based on spurious or suppressed relationships.[56] The exogenous variables have been selected in recognition of their potential association with either of the endogenous variables—black lynchings and migration. Some have the potential to influence violence and migration. However, because they are of only incidental relevance, we devote comparatively little space to the description and interpretation of the predetermining variables.

Consistent with much of the discussion in earlier chapters, we believe that lynchings were more common where whites perceived a greater threat (economically, politically, or socially) from coresident blacks. In this analysis, we are less concerned with the specific dimensions of that perceived threat than with simply controlling for their existence. Therefore, we use a more generic measure of perceived threat: the percent of the adult male population that was black. The African-American population would have been seen as more "threatening" to coresident whites where the black adult male population was relatively larger. Therefore, percent black is expected to have a positive impact on lynching.[57]

The absolute size of the county's black population is included because the dependent variable is based on the raw number of black lynch victims during each decade. This accounts for the likelihood that the number of lynchings was greater where the black population was larger in absolute terms. By including the size of the black population in our analysis, we also take into consideration the possibility that greater out-migration reduced the number of potential black lynch victims, a possible alternative explanation for any observed effect of black migration on lynching. Finally, population density is also included in the equation in recognition that lynching was primarily a phenomenon of less densely settled areas, although not unheard of in towns and cities.

We now turn to a description of the exogenous variables used as predictors of black out-migration. The percent of black farm operators who were tenants is expected to have a positive effect on out-migration. Rural blacks were more likely motivated to escape plantation counties where opportunities for black farm ownership were more severely restricted. It is possible, however, that blacks in plantation counties may have been less mobile due to the more repressive influence of debt peonage in such counties.[58]

In a similar vein, we anticipate greater out-migration from counties in which additional farmland was relatively limited. Thus, out-migration should be positively related to the percentage of improved farmland. In essence, both the prevalence of black farm tenancy and the availability of undeveloped farmland are included in recognition of the migration of blacks in search of better agricultural opportunities.

Not all migratory forces were rural in character, however. A substantial component of the Great Migration was to urban areas. The percent of the county's urban population is included to tap this dimension of black migration. We expect to find a negative effect of percent urban on out-migration, because urban areas probably attracted more migrants than they sent to other areas. If Marks is correct, however, in asserting that southern urban areas contributed disproportionately to the northward flow during the Great Migration, then the negative relationship between percent urban and black out-migration may be somewhat attenuated.[59] We also anticipate heavier out-migration from areas in which African-Americans were denied access to education. Therefore, out-migration should be positively related to the percent of black population that was illiterate. Finally, the rate of white out-migration is included as a predictor of black out-migration to capture those forces that contributed similarly to the migratory behavior of the two races but are not included in our model. We expect the two migration rates to be positively related.[60] With the exception of the rate of white out-migration, all exogenous variables are measured as of the beginning of the respective decade: 1910 for our analysis of 1910 to 1920 and 1920 for our analysis of 1920 to 1930.

It is somewhat more difficult to derive a suitable measure of the white class structure within southern counties during this period. Conceptually, we would like to tap the relative dominance of well-to-do whites within each county. The greatest determinant of class position among southern whites was land ownership. Although not all farm owners were financially comfortable, it was generally true that they enjoyed somewhat greater security than either tenants or wage laborers. In light of this importance of land tenure, we shall use as our measure of white class structure the percent of white farm operators who were tenants. As implied by Figure 7-6 and the earlier discussion of our conceptual framework, we expect this measure of the local white class structure to interact with black migration to influence lynchings. Specifically, we believe that the hypothesized negative influence of out-migration on racial violence will be stronger where the concentration of farm owners was greater.

These data and variables have been used to assess empirically the adequacy of the conceptual framework presented in Figure 7-6. Two equations are required to estimate the hypothesized reciprocal relationship—one with black out-migration as the dependent variable and the other with black lynchings as the dependent variable.[61] Ordinary least squares techniques are inappropriate for estimating the two equations because the reciprocal association implies correlation between the disturbance terms for the two equations. Therefore, three-stage least squares (3SLS) procedures have been used to estimate the simultaneous equations for migration and lynching.[62] Separate sets of equations have been estimated for each period, 1910–20 and 1920–30. The general form of these equations is as follows (lumping all exogenous variables together):

$$\text{Lynchings}_i = \beta_{0l} + \beta_{\text{mig}}(\text{Migration}_i) + \Sigma(\beta_k X_{ik})$$
$$+ \beta_{\text{int}}(\text{Migration}_i \times \text{WCS}_i) + v_i \qquad \text{Eq. [1]}$$

$$\text{Migration}_i = \beta_{0m} + \beta_{\text{lyn}}(\text{Lynchings}_i) + \Sigma(\beta_k X_{ik}) + \varepsilon_i \qquad \text{Eq. [2]}$$

where Migration_i is the black out-migration rate for the ith county, Lynchings_i is the number of blacks lynched by white mobs within the ith county, X_{ik} is the kth exogenous factor predicting lynching or migration, WCS_i is the measure of white class structure for the ith county, β_{0l} and β_{0m} are constants, β_ks are coefficients representing the effects of variables in the equation on the endogenous variables, and ε_i and v_i are potentially correlated disturbance terms.[63]

To simplify our discussion of the findings from this relatively complex statistical analysis, attention is focused on the coefficients that are key to answering the primary research questions. First, from Equation 1, the coefficient β_{mig} will reveal whether black migration had the anticipated impact on lynching. We expect this coefficient to have a negative value, indicating, other things begin equal, fewer lynchings where black out-migration was heavier. Second, also from Equation 1, β_{int} is expected to have a positive sign, indicating that the depressing effect of black out-migration on lynching was weaker in settings dominated by tenancy, rather than ownership, among white farmers.

Table 7-2 presents the 3SLS solutions to the simultaneous equations for black lynching and migration for each decade. Panel A reports the

Table 7-2. Three-Stage Least-Squares Regression Results for Analysis of Black Lynching Victims of White Mobs and Black Out-Migration, 1910–20 and 1920–30[a]

Predetermining Variable	1910–20		1920–30	
	Coefficient	t-ratio	Coefficient	t-ratio
Panel A: Eq. [1][b]				
Constant	0.177	1.69	0.415	7.28
Black out-migration rate	−0.109	−2.60	−0.163	−8.14
Percent white farm tenancy	−0.002	0.93	−0.012	−7.65
Black migration x white tenancy	0.003	2.80	0.004	9.07
Population density	−0.001	−3.20	−0.001	−2.36
Size of black population (1,000s)	0.013	4.11	0.007	3.44
Percent black among adult males	0.007	5.12	0.004	4.32
Panel B: Eq. [2][c]				
Constant	−0.627	−1.36	−2.710	−5.02
Number of black lynch victims	0.870	1.66	3.976	4.14
Percent black farm tenancy	−0.004	−0.66	−0.001	−0.25
Percent black males illiterate	0.036	3.37	0.058	4.96
Percent population urban	0.004	0.57	−0.014	−2.29
Percent farmland improved	0.009	1.49	0.031	4.65
White out-migration rate	0.693	19.16	0.683	18.11

a. In both equations, the black out-migration rate and the number of black lynch victims have been square-root transformed.
b. Number of black lynch victims is dependent variable.
c. Black out-migration rate is dependent variable.

results from the equation predicting black lynching, and Panel B contains the results from the equation predicting black out-migration. The first two columns present the findings for 1910–20; the last two columns contain the results for 1920–30.

Focusing first on the results for the earlier decade, we find support for the hypothesized reciprocal linkage between black migration and racial violence. Panel B reveals a significant positive effect of black lynchings on out-migration, net of other variables in the equation.

Blacks were more likely to abandon counties in which they had greater reason to feel threatened by the activity of white lynch mobs. Simultaneously, the results in Panel A indicate that a heavier rate of black out-migration had an ameliorative effect on racial violence.

The significant negative effect of black out-migration on lynching supports our hypothesis that counties experiencing greater losses of their black populations were somehow able to reduce the number of black lynch victims. However, the significant coefficient for the interaction term also indicates that the effect of black migration on lynching was not consistent across settings with varying white class structures. Specifically, as expected, black out-migration had a stronger negative influence on lynchings in counties that had especially low concentrations of white farm tenants. We can illustrate this variation by describing the impact of black migration on lynching for counties with different levels of white tenancy (Figure 7-7).[64] The curve for 1910–20 shows clearly that the inhibiting influence of migration was restricted to counties with levels of white tenancy below 40 percent. For counties with higher levels of white tenancy, the projected effect of black migration on lynchings is actually positive. This pattern is consistent with our hypothesis that African-American out-migration was more likely to be translated into reduced levels of violence in settings more dominated by well-to-do whites.

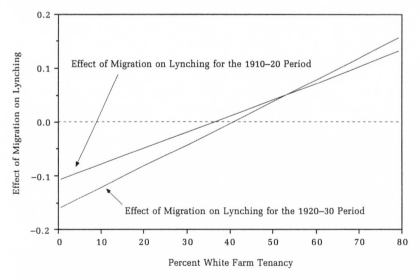

Figure 7-7. Effect of Black Migration on Black Lynching by Level of White Farm Tenancy.

Turning to the evidence from the later decade, we find additional support for the hypothesized mutual dependence between black out-migration and mob violence. Panel B shows that the number of black lynchings continued to have a strong positive impact on out-migration between 1920 and 1930. This finding supports the conclusion that blacks were leaving areas where the threat of lynching was more intense. Panel A offers further evidence that out-migration had a simultaneous negative influence on the level of black lynchings. Once again, however, the effect of migration on lynching varied significantly across areas with different white class structures. As was the case for the earlier period, the strongest negative impact of migration on lynching occurred in counties with relatively low concentrations of white farm tenants. Indeed, as was the case for the earlier decade, Figure 7-7 reveals that the negative influence of migration on lynching between 1910 and 1920 was restricted to those counties with levels of farm tenancy below about 40 percent. Again, the effect of migration actually turned positive in counties with higher levels of white tenancy.

Turning to the exogenous predictors of lynching in Panel B, we find considerable support for our expectations. During both decades, population density was negatively related to lynching, as anticipated. Also consistent with our hypotheses, both the absolute and relative sizes of the black population were positively related to lynching in both periods.

The performance of the exogenous predictors of black migration is somewhat more mixed. Illiteracy was positively related to migration during both decades, suggesting that blacks were more likely to abandon counties in which they had been denied educational opportunities. The level of white migration also had a significant effect during both decades. The strong and positive relationship between white and black migration suggests that the mobility of both races responded to similar social forces not included in our model. For the 1920–30 period, the proportion of improved land and percent of urban population had the expected effects on black migration. During the earlier decade these two items had no significant impact. The level of black farm tenancy was unrelated to migration in both decades, perhaps reflecting the operation of counterbalancing forces. On the one hand, blacks could have been more strongly motivated to leave counties in which their opportunities for farm ownership were minimal. On the other hand, in areas of high tenancy, the mobility of black farmers may have been inhibited by the crop-lien system and the debt peonage it fostered.[65]

Thus, our empirical findings offer strong support for the most important aspects of the conceptual framework we proposed earlier in this chapter: (1) black migration did have an important impact on the level of racial violence; (2) the effect of black migration on lynching was variable across areas that differed in white class structure; and (3) blacks were more likely to leave areas in which lynchings were more common.

Conclusions

Fortunately, by the middle of the century, the appalling sight of black men hanging from shade trees like so much "strange fruit" had grown much less common.[66] The virtual eradication of mob violence represents a significant transformation in southern culture. We believe that in order to understand fully the reasons for that relatively dramatic social change we must go beyond such obvious explanations as improved police practices or equipment and growing enlightenment among the southern press. Rather, we view these largely as mechanisms through which more fundamental social forces operated. One such social force was the massive surge in African-American migration during the second and third decades of the century.

According to our argument, black migration played a critical role in transforming southern culture because it threatened economically the most influential segments of the white community. We are not naive enough to believe the white elite experienced a revelation that exposed the "evil" of prejudice, discrimination, and racial violence. Rather, their transformation was much more pragmatic and self-interested. They witnessed the exodus of the very population that provided their supply of cheap and pliant labor.

After failing to halt the exodus through intimidation and force, they abandoned the stick for the carrot. Using the impressive means at their disposal, they set out to reduce the level of violence directed at the black community. They also made other attempts to improve living conditions by improving black schools and reforming landlord-tenant relations.[67] As the woeful condition of African-Americans in the South at the beginning of the civil rights movement in the 1950s attests, progress on these latter changes was slow and incomplete. Moreover, well-to-do whites never really intended to move southern society toward full social equality. Rather, they sought to reduce the terrifying threat of physical violence, a relatively small price to pay in their desperate attempt to maintain the economic status quo.

If the Great Migration was such an influential force in the demise of southern lynchings, why was there not a major resurgence of lynching during the Great Depression, when black migration to the North declined? We have two potential answers to this question. First, those mechanisms that the white elite employed to reduce racial violence were not so easily disengaged. Southern police practices had changed for the better, and the southern press did alter its treatment of racial violence. And, as suggested by the 1937 Gallup poll, southern public opinion regarding lynching had changed. To return to the practices of the bloody 1890s would have meant running counter to these powerful transformations. Second, influential southern whites were becoming increasingly sensitive to the opinions of outsiders. The image of the South as a region where African-Americans were routinely burned at the stake worked against their desires for economic investment and integration into external markets. Lynching had become something of which to be embarrassed rather than a convenient means for exercising control over blacks. It had become an anachronism from an earlier era, confined to fringe elements of southern white society who were themselves anachronistic.

NOTES

1. See chapter 1 for a full discussion of the Michael Donald lynching.

2. These figures are for the ten southern states dealt with throughout this book. The data for the 1930s have been adapted uncritically from the inventory published by the Commission on Interracial Cooperation in Ames (1942). Although this source is certain to contain errors, our own confirmed inventory of lynch victims ends in 1930.

3. Gallup (1972, 48).

4. Ames (1942, 11).

5. Ames (1942).

6. White (1929 [1969]).

7. See, for example, Wright (1990).

8. Of course, there were other New Deal programs that would have benefited the displaced tenants and croppers, such as assistance for the unemployed and the employment opportunities created by the Works Progress Administration. But in many instances those who benefited from these programs required assistance because of other rural-oriented New Deal policies.

9. Gordon (1937, 327–33).

10. Apparently, Virginia was an interesting exception to the rule. Strong opposition to lynching by Governor Charles O'Ferrall and other prominent conservatives led to early attempts to thwart mob violence, including a willingness to deploy the state militia (Brundage 1993, 169–78).

11. See, for example, Ames (1942), Grant (1975), Miller (1978), White (1929 [1969]), and Zangrando (1980).

12. John Shelton Reed (1968) concludes, however, that the ASWPL had a significant effect on the number of lynchings in rural counties between 1931 and 1936. Again, the number of lynchings had fallen substantially before 1931.

13. See Tucker (1971) for an account of Ida Wells and the Memphis lynchings.

14. See Shapiro (1988) and White (1929 [1969]).

15. Our discussion of this incident is based on the scholarship of Brundage. See Brundage (1990) for further details on the Darien incident and its aftermath.

16. Details of this incident have been drawn from issues of the Savannah *Morning News*, January 1–7, 1923.

17. See "Massacre in a Small Town," Atlanta *Constitution*, January 17, 1993, M1, M4.

18. See Grant (1975), Ferrell (1986), and Zangrando (1980) for thorough discussions of state and federal efforts to pass antilynching legislation during this period.

19. White (1929 [1969], 201).

20. White (1929 [1969]).

21. See, for example, Donald (1921) and Gottlieb (1987).

22. See Daniel (1985), Jaynes (1986), Mandle (1978, 1992), Novak (1978), and Ransom and Sutch (1977).

23. U.S. Bureau of the Census (1975, 95).

24. These figures for southern states simply report the net loss (or gain) of black population in absolute numbers. They do not indicate where the migrants were going. Some left the South entirely, whereas others relocated to other southern states.

25. The net migration estimates represented on this map were generated using a forward census survival rate method (Shryock and Siegel 1980, 630–34). It is the same method used by Fligstein (1981). Figure 7-4 simply describes the rate of net-migration but reveals nothing about the destinations of migrants.

26. Mandle (1978, 1992).

27. U.S. Bureau of the Census (1975, 22–23).

28. Scroggs (1917, 1040).

29. Scott (1920, 13).

30. See, for example, Donald (1921), Kennedy (1930), Lewis (1931), U.S. Department of Labor (1919), Woodson (1918 [1969]), and Woofter (1920).

31. Daniel (1985), Flynn (1983), Higgs (1977), Mandle (1978, 1992), Novak (1978), and Ransom and Smith (1977).

32. Woofter (1920, 121).

33. Flynn (1983), Newby (1965), Novak (1978), and Woodward (1966).

34. Kousser (1974).

35. Kennedy (1930), Kousser (1980), Margo (1990), Myrdal (1972), and Woodson (1930).

36. U.S. Department of Labor (1919, 107).

37. See Woofter's chapter in the report prepared by the U.S. Department of Labor (1919, 79).

38. Ballard (1984) and Scott (1920).

39. Nashville *Banner,* February 13, 1918, 1.

40. Atlanta *Constitution,* September 11, 1912, 2; see also Dittmer (1980, 26).

41. Quoted in Henri (1975, 130).

42. Henri (1975, 70).

43. For example, see Scott (1920, 86) and Scroggs (1917, 103).

44. U.S. Department of Labor (1919, 32).

45. White (1929 [1969], 190–91).

46. Ransom and Sutch (1977).

47. Bonacich (1972, 1975).

48. See also Holmes (1969).

49. See, for example, Ayers (1992), Myrdal (1972), and Wilson (1978).

50. Bloom (1987) disagrees with Bonacich's (1972) assumption that black and white laborers were in direct competition. He adopts a more traditional Marxist interpretation of the sources of racial antagonism by locating primary responsibility within the white elite.

51. Holmes (1969).

52. Brundage (1993, 24–28) also refers to differential class interests in lynchings, especially those lynchings that he terms "terroristic."

53. Because estimates of net migration are relatively unreliable when the population base is small, we have also restricted our analyses to those southern counties that had black populations of at least one hundred at the beginning of each decade period. Because some counties were created or abolished during the period, and due to missing data for certain variables that are included in our analyses, the number of cases in our analyses varies over time, from a total of 756 counties for 1910–20 to 804 for 1920–30.

54. Refer to Fligstein (1981, Appendix C) and Shryock and Siegel (1980, 630–34).

55. If we take the period from 1920 to 1930 as an example, then,

$$M_{1920-30} = P_{1930} - (S)(P_{1920})$$

where $M_{1920-30}$ is the net migration between 1920 and 1930; P_{1930} is the observed population size in 1930; S is the survival probability between 1920 and 1930; and P_{1920} is the observed population size in 1920. The net migration rate ($NM_{1920-30}$) is derived as follows:

$$NM_{1920-30} = (M_{1920-30}/P_{1920}) \times 100.$$

The actual computational procedure is made more complex by an effort to be as precise as possible by allowing for separate survival probabilities for different age groups, for males and females, and for urban and rural residents. For each state, separate survival probabilities were estimated using age distributions by sex and urban-rural residence. It is necessary to use state-level age distributions because county-level distributions are not available for this period (U.S. Bureau of the Census (1913, 1943).

These age distributions were then exposed to forward census survival ratios, by age and sex, for the southern black population between 1920 and 1930 (Lee et al. 1957, 21–22). The result of this procedure is an estimate of the surviving population in 1930 by age, sex, and residence. These figures were then used to derive estimated survival probabilities between 1920 and 1930 for each sex and residence group for all ages combined. Finally, the estimated survival probabilities were applied to county-level populations, by sex and residence, for 1920 to produce the expected total population in 1930. Actually, only the county population ten years and older for the later point in time is used because the youngest surviving person from the earlier year would then be ten. The difference between the actual observed population in 1930 and the expected population represents estimated net migration. The same procedure was used to estimate net migration between 1910 and 1920.

These procedures are identical to those used by Fligstein (1981). Although Fligstein graciously made his estimates available to us, we have replicated his procedures to derive our own complete set of migration estimates for the ten states. Our analysis includes three states not examined by Fligstein, Florida, Kentucky, and Tennessee, which required original migration estimates. As a check on our estimation procedure we compared our migration rates with Fligstein's for those states in common between the two analyses. Although the two sets were correlated across states at least at $r = 0.999$ in both decades with a slope virtually equal to 1.0, the intercept was significantly different from zero. Because of this admittedly mild discrepancy, we decided against combining our original estimates for Florida, Kentucky, and Tennessee with Fligstein's estimates for the other states.

56. With the exception of black lynchings, data for all variables in the analyses have been drawn from the decennial censuses of 1910, 1920, and

1930. These include information from the agricultural, population, and manufacturing censuses, most of which has been drawn from the archives of the Inter-University Consortium for Political and Social Research (ICPSR). Specifically, the data are from the ICPSR file Historical, Demographic, Economic, and Social Data: The United States, 1790–1970 (ICPSR 1989, MRDF no. 0003).

57. We also considered the effect of a quadratic term for percent black as a predictor of black lynchings. In analyses conducted in previous chapters the relative size of the black population has exhibited a nonlinear relationship with lynchings. In this case, however, the quadratic term had a non-significant effect for both decades.

58. See, for example, Mandle (1978).

59. Marks (1989).

60. We considered other predetermining variables for black lynching and black migration, including direct measures of racial competition such as racial differences in tenancy and literacy. However, we have chosen to report the findings from a more parsimonious model because (1) our primary focus is the effect of black migration on lynching and variation in that effect by differences in white class structure, and (2) the inclusion of additional predetermining variables did not alter the inferred effect of migration on lynching. Elsewhere, we have used a more complex system of equations to model the relationship between black migration and lynching during these two decades (Tolnay and Beck 1992). In that analysis the white migration rate was treated as a third endogenous variable in the system. Whether the two-equation system or the three-equation system is used, the same basic results are obtained regarding the effect of black migration on lynching and the role of the white class structure in modifying that effect.

61. It is not obvious whether the number of lynching victims or the number of lynching incidents is the more appropriate dependent variable for our analyses. Therefore, we replicated all analyses using incidents rather than victims and found only trivial differences that had no bearing on our substantive conclusions.

62. For identified structural equations with jointly dependent endogenous variables, the most common least squares estimation is two-stage least squares (2SLS). Although the 2SLS estimators are consistent, they are not asymptotically efficient when applied to overidentified models because they cannot exploit all of the information in the model. Because three-stage least squares (3SLS), on the other hand, uses all of the information in the structural equations, they are, as a consequence, asymptotically more efficient than the 2SLS estimators. See Judge et al. (1982, 378–84) or Kmenta (1971, 573–78) for further discussion of 3SLS.

63. Proper identification is an important issue in the use of simultaneous equations such as these. Equations 1 and 2 are formally identified, so the parameters for the reciprocal effects of lynching and migration can be estimated. Other model specifications are, of course, possible. We have specified these equations based on relevant theory and literature. Substantially different findings are obtained when ordinary least squares techniques are used rather than 3SLS.

Because the number of black lynchings is a positively skewed count variable, we have used a square root transformation. Although Poisson regression is the preferable statistical specification when using count variables, it is difficult to incorporate the Poisson technique into a system of simultaneous linear equations like that involved here. We have also used a square root transformation of the black and white migration variables in order to reduce the impact of a small number of influential counties.

64. In 1910, the level of white tenancy ranged from 1 to 82 percent; in 1920, the observed range was 1 to 85 percent.

65. See Mandle (1978).

66. Smith refers to lynch victims this way in the title of her 1944 novel.

67. See for example, Grossman (1991) and McMillen (1991) for excellent discussions of the response of the southern white community to the loss of black labor.

8

The Tragedy of Lynching:
An Overview

Social Change, Development, and Lynching, 1930–60

Lynchings did not disappear completely from southern culture with the exodus of black labor to northern urban areas during the
Great Migration. Records compiled by the National Association for the
Advancement of Colored People show that mob violence continued
throughout the 1930s, 1940s, and 1950s. Indeed, some of the most
well-documented lynching incidents occurred during these decades.
It was during the 1930s that the mob from south Alabama orchestrat-
ed the lynching of Claude Neal in the swampy marshes of the Florida
panhandle.[1] It was during the 1940s that a gang of white Georgians
murdered Roger Malcolm, George Dorsey, and their wives on the banks
of the Apalachee River.[2] It was during the 1950s that Emmett Till, a
young boy from Chicago, was killed for whistling at a white woman
in a country store in rural Mississippi.[3] During the 1960s, lynchings
occasionally were used in an attempt to blunt the progress of the southern civil rights movement. Perhaps the most notorious incident involved the lynching of three civil rights volunteers—James Chaney,
Andrew Goodman, and Michael Schwerner—near Philadelphia, Mississippi, in 1964.[4] Racial violence even continues into the present, as
indicated by the killing of Michael Donald in Alabama in 1981.[5]

In many ways, however, this trail of violence is much less revealing than it first appears. Although descendants of the same traditions
that gave rise to the bloody 1890s, later lynchings could no longer be
considered an essential part of the fabric that held southern society
together. Whereas lynchings had once been an implicit part of the
social contract that governed black-white interaction, later they increasingly became grim reminders of an earlier era. Whereas they

previously had enjoyed widespread support among southern people and institutions, they gradually fell into disfavor. Popular support for lynchings eroded substantially during the 1930s, as indicated by the strong majority of southerners who supported the effort to persuade Congress to enact legislation making lynching a federal crime.[6] Media support also waned, as newspapers increasingly abandoned their role as apologists for mob violence and became cheerleaders for economic development in the "New South." Strong voices opposing mob violence were also heard from students of southern society, as well as from social activists. It is probably indicative of the increasing social disapproval and reduced tolerance for mob violence that Jesse Daniel Ames, Arthur Raper, and Walter White rose to prominence during the twilight era of lynching.[7] Although others, for example, Ida B. Wells, had condemned lynching during its heyday, their receptive audiences were much smaller and largely not southern.[8]

The specter of mob violence continued to rear its ugly head long after the Great Migration, but it did so within an evolving social and economic milieu. We believe that this is the primary reason that lynchings did not rebound significantly during the 1930s, despite the crushing economic hardship and reduced out-migration of blacks during the Great Depression (chapter 7). The South changed substantially during the first half of the twentieth century, and these changes carried important implications for the need and usefulness of mob violence.

After losing well over a million blacks through out-migration between 1900 and 1930, the South began a profound transformation of its agricultural economy. Spurred by incentives created by Franklin D. Roosevelt's Agricultural Adjustment Act (AAA) of 1933, southern farmers made fundamental changes in the way they did business, including planting fewer acres of cotton and increasing the mechanization of their operations. As part of its larger strategy to restructure southern agriculture, the AAA introduced a program to pay farm owners for letting their fields lie fallow. Although the manifest reason for the program was to give the exhausted southern soil a chance to regain some of its fertility, its latent effect was to displace sharecroppers and cash tenants who had worked the fields for decades. Although the AAA also included provisions for compensating tenants, landowners (with the help of county agents) generally were successful at circumventing those provisions.

It was also part of the AAA's overall strategy to help encourage and assist farmers to modernize their productive efforts. While southern agriculture had lagged seriously behind other regions in its progress toward farm mechanization, the number of tractors on southern farms rose sharply during the 1930s. For instance, the number of tractors per thousand acres of farmland harvested rose by 65 percent between 1930 and 1940. Plantation counties experienced an even sharper increase, 113 percent.[9] The modernization of farming operations further displaced croppers and tenants and moved the southern farm economy away from its historical dependence on tenant families and toward increasing reliance on wage laborers.

The ultimate effect of these programs was to alter the organization of production in southern agriculture fundamentally and shift the class structure that had persisted since Reconstruction. For example, between 1930 and 1950 the number of white tenants fell by 50 percent, while the number of black tenants dropped by 48 percent. During the same period, the number of farm owners actually increased somewhat for both races.[10] In addition, these programs led to an unprecedented redistribution of the southern population.

During the 1920s, the South lost roughly 10 percent of its black population to out-migration.[11] The exodus weakened somewhat during the Great Depression, although it continued to siphon off about 5 percent of the black population during the 1930s. In the following two decades, however, the out-migration again rose to new heights; roughly 15 percent of all blacks left the South during the 1940s and another 15 percent exited during the 1950s. In absolute terms, the southern states experienced a net loss of more than a million African-Americans during each of these decades.

Comparable trends in net migration for whites are complicated by the deviant pattern for Florida, especially after 1940. During the 1940s, but particularly during the 1950s, Florida experienced massive in-migration. Because the migration history of Florida was dramatically different from that of the other nine states and has such a disproportionate impact on the overall regional migration picture, we will concentrate on patterns with Florida omitted. However, two migration trends are reported for whites in Figures 8-1 and 8-2, one with and the other without Florida.

Whites also left the South in large numbers following the Great Depression, with a net loss of around nine hundred thousand during the 1940s and more than a million during the 1950s. Of course, given the larger size of the white populations, these figures represented a smaller proportionate loss for whites than was experienced for blacks. At no time did the southern white population shrink by significantly more than 5 percent due to net migration during the first five decades of the century.

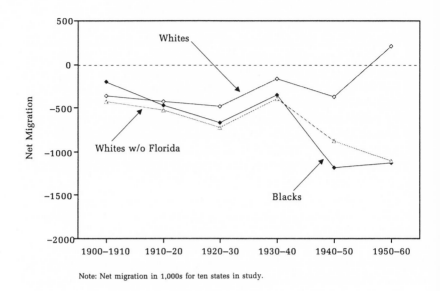

Note: Net migration in 1,000s for ten states in study.

Figure 8-1. Net Migration by Decades for Southern Blacks and Whites.

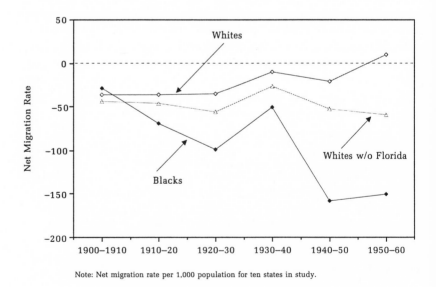

Note: Net migration rate per 1,000 population for ten states in study.

Figure 8-2. Net Migration Rate by Decades for Southern Blacks and Whites.

At the same time that huge numbers of southern blacks and whites were heading toward northern urban areas and the promise of industrial employment, still others were abandoning the countryside for southern cities. At the beginning of the Great Depression fewer than one-third of all southerners were located in urban areas. However, by the time of the U.S. Census in 1960, a majority of the southern population resided in cities (Table 8-1). The combined causes of urbanization had transformed an overwhelmingly rural society into a predominantly urban one within the span of a few decades.

Added to the profound transformation in agricultural production and the population redistribution that it spawned, the South continued to expand its industrial base during the first half of the century. For example, between 1929 and 1958 the percentage of all personal income derived from manufacturing rose from 16 to 23 percent. During this same period, the South was also able to reduce the gap between its manufacturing base and the North's. The South's share of all manufacturing employment rose from 16 to 19 percent, while its share of all manufacturing payrolls increased from 11 to 15 percent.[12]

The South has an image of a region that lay sleeping until it was awakened by the civil rights movement during the 1950s and 1960s. The characterization of the South as a "backward" region that, with the vibrant growth of the sunbelt during the seventies and eighties, joined mainstream American society only recently is somewhat misleading because it overlooks the substantial social, economic, and demographic changes of the first half of the century. Those changes radically altered the class structure of rural society and led to population displacement and redistribution that had not been seen since

Table 8-1. Percent Urban,
by Census Year in the South[a]

Year	Percent
1900	14.9
1910	19.1
1920	23.3
1930	29.5
1940	31.8
1950	38.5
1960	52.5

a. For ten states in study.

emancipation. It is little wonder that the logic of mob violence also changed.

Throughout this book we have portrayed lynching as an integral part of the southern economy and class structure that emerged during the 1870s and 1880s to replace slavery.[13] That new system remained more or less intact until the early decades of the twentieth century. During this era, blacks were lynched when it served the economic interests of well-to-do or poor whites. They were particularly vulnerable when violence benefited more than one class of southern whites. When the interests of white society diverged, however, blacks were offered some degree of protection. At all times, racial violence and the terroristic control of the black population were an integral part of the southern society and economy, which was built upon an uninhibited pursuit of King Cotton. The success of that pursuit was heavily dependent upon the availability of sedentary, docile, and subordinate tenant farmers, who were not always in great supply.

Although the pursuit of King Cotton persisted after the Great Depression, rural class relations were altered substantially, and the structural arrangements that had given rise to the lynching phenomenon began to fade. In addition, increasing farm mechanization created a superfluous rural work force, black and white, which fled the countryside and the South in search of better opportunities. The cotton economy changed irrevocably. The use of wage laborers gave landlords greater control over the work force, who could be hired when needed and let go when the work was done. While they worked, their productivity was easily monitored. Tenant families were a year-long responsibility, however, even though their contribution to crop production was seasonal. Clearly, the potential for tension and conflict was greater in the landlord-tenant relationship than it was between planters and wage workers. As the social and economic foundation that had supported the use of mob violence began to crumble, lynchings continued to decline in frequency and became increasingly uncoupled from the southern rural economy.

During this period of incipient social and economic change, southern states also grew more concerned about the image they projected. The newfound sensitivity was due largely to the effort to attract northern investments and promote growth in the southern economy. It was during the 1920s that politicians and policy makers first became seriously committed to "selling the South." Several states created agencies responsible for promoting investment and tourism in the region. For example, in 1923 Alabama established the Department of Commerce and Industries to promote the advancement of agriculture and manufacturing; Florida created a Bureau of Immigration in 1925 to attract tourists, new residents, and investors; and South Carolina, Virginia, and North Carolina all created similar promotional agencies during the decade.[14] Although the depression deflected many southern states from the effort to attract external investment, regional boosterism resumed with great enthusiasm following World War II.

Pictures of a black corpse, charred and chained to a tree, or of mobs of grinning white men and boys surrounding the body of a black man hanging by a rope, were not the best images with which to promote investment in economic development. Many whites realized that lynchings could hurt their effort to attract northern companies to the region. Once again, when it was in their own best economic interest, some whites could be mobilized to act on behalf of humanity and appeal for the eradication of mob violence.

Zangrando has summed up well how the social and economic changes occurring within the South during the first half of the twentieth century combined to reduce the frequency with which white mobs got out guns and gasoline in order to punish blacks.

> For two consecutive generations, from World War I to 1960, the effects were cumulative. Various modernizing trends, including the mechanization of agriculture, industrial expansion, and the migration of blacks and whites from rural to urban areas within and beyond the region produced considerable change and mandated techniques of social control other than lynching. Northern investors and southern merchants preferred steady economic performance to the unsettling emotions of open race conflict. . . . advocates of industrialism—journalists, business managers, and public officials—rallied to suppress violence or the evidence of violence that might damage the region's image and retard its growth.[15]

We want to be careful not to overstate this transformation in race relations. It was entirely possible for influential southern whites to call for the end of lynching while still insisting on a clear separation of the races. Indeed, segregation remained the norm in all aspects of southern society and was not threatened seriously until long after lynchings had been reduced to a rare event. There was no enthusiasm within any sizable segment of the white South to move the society toward full racial equality. Rather, for some there was a gradual realization that lynchings were no longer necessary under the new social order and might be sacrificed for the greater good.

When segregation eventually came under full assault, whites initially reacted defensively, as they had in response to early criticisms of mob violence a half-century before. Outside "agitators" were advised to leave the South's problems to southerners. They were told that special social arrangements were required to deal with special problems (to be read as "a large minority population"), and they were referred to the North's own peculiar social blemishes. Eventually, however, legal segregation of the races succumbed to the same pressures that previously had eroded social support for lynching. That is, economic interests dictated its disposal, at least in its most rigid forms. In language very similar to Zangrando's account of the forces contributing to the earlier demise of lynching, Cobb described the economic motive for the decline of segregation: "As civil rights concerns mounted, it seemed reasonable to conclude that most image-conscious, nationally known firms would shy away from an area whose racial policies were becoming so offensive to mass society values. Thus, in the interest of continued growth, many of those responsible for recruiting new industry became reluctant advocates of a peaceful transition to token desegregation."[16] Although certainly not the only catalyst for social change, the prospect of economic growth and development proved to be a powerful inducement for whites to forsake what had been fundamental aspects of southern culture—first mob lynchings and later legal segregation of the races.

Taking Stock

This book has been more about how and why lynchings occurred between 1880 and 1930 than about the process through which southern society largely abandoned the practice. What progress have we made toward filling the gaps in our knowledge about lynching that prompted Ayers to write as recently as 1984 that "the triggers of lynching, for all the attention devoted to it by contemporaries, sociologists, and historians, are still not known"?[17] To do this, it is necessary to examine the origins of lynching as a critical ingredient in southern racial life.

The key to the beginning of the lynching era rests with the collapse of slavery. Lethal punishment was hardly a rational behavior; slave owners would have been unwise to destroy systematically the very capital that generated their profits, and poor whites certainly were reluctant to incur the wrath of plantation owners by hunting down their property like animals and hanging them from trees. Ironically, the social and economic arrangements of the slavery system—as brutal and indefensible as it was—afforded blacks some protection from the atrocities that would become all too common after the war.

There was something about freedom that endangered the southern black man. A fundamental paradox of freedom was that it thrust blacks into the impossible position of trying to straddle two worlds. On the one hand, they inherited their inferior social status from the slavery era. This was an immutable position for southern blacks as long as their skin color marked them as members of the subordinate caste. On the other hand, in order to survive and progress in the new political and economic regime of the South, blacks sought to do all the same things that whites did in order to succeed: work hard, buy land, educate their children, and pursue their own interests at the voting booth. The contradiction is obvious. As blacks strove toward their own betterment, they increased concern among whites that they would no longer accept their inferior station as the natural order of things. Free blacks threatened southern whites and their caste system in a way that slaves never could, and lynching was one of the mechanisms used to neutralize that threat.

The Commission on Interracial Cooperation recognized this in 1936 when it reported, "Formerly an instrument of popular justice in frontier communities, and still retaining something of its frontier character, lynching and the threat of it are now primarily a technique of enforcing racial exploitation—economic, political, and cultural."[18] There can be no question that southern whites perceived a variety of threats from their black neighbors.[19] They were convinced that blacks were criminally inclined and intellectually inferior and therefore incapable of fitting into a society based largely on voluntary cooperation and adherence to the written law.[20] The tenets of scientific racism supported these beliefs and legitimized the notion of the "black brute criminal" as a menace to civilized white society.

Whites also believed that black voters could never constitute an informed electorate, were vulnerable to corruption, and therefore would jeopardize the integrity of southern politics. Consequently, despite the willingness of virtually every southern political party to exploit black voters, there was general relief among whites when blacks were nearly totally disenfranchised by the early twentieth century. Whites viewed economic success in the New South as a zero-sum game. Progress by blacks came at the expense of whites, whether it meant success in the competition between poor blacks and poor whites or greater power for blacks in their relationship with white employers. Whites also feared that any type of progress by blacks—political, economic, or social—threatened to weaken the caste line that separated the races and guaranteed at least some measure of superiority to even the lowliest poor white dirt farmer.

It is possible to select specific examples of lynching incidents consistent with each of these dimensions of racial threat. Many blacks were lynched by mobs concerned that southern justice was too slow and lenient to punish adequately what they believed was an inherently criminal black population. Some blacks were lynched for trying to vote or for playing a too active and visible role in politics. Others were lynched because they were "too successful," or because they occupied land or held jobs that whites felt rightly belonged to the dominant caste. Lynchings also occurred for petty offenses that broke no laws yet violated some caste-defined boundary of behavior.

We have used the details of specific lynching incidents for illustrative purposes or to provide a flavor for the types of mob violence. Generally, however, we have shied away from using the purported reasons for specific incidents, or the circumstances surrounding events, to draw broader inferences about the underlying social forces that drove the lynching phenomenon. There are good reasons for this. First, it is not entirely clear that the reasons mobs reported for lynchings were accurate reflections of their true motivations. Second, even if we accept the reported circumstances at face value, it would still be possible to cite such evidence in support of virtually any explanation of mob violence. For example, how many blacks had to be lynched for political reasons in order to make the political threat model viable?

Instead, we have chosen to scrutinize the general contours of mob lynchings—especially their distribution over time and across space— to determine whether interpretable patterns emerge. Those patterns may suggest the most useful explanations for lynchings. In this sense, our approach represents a marriage of theory and numbers. Theory tells us what patterns we should expect to find, and the numbers either confirm or contradict those expectations. The evidence in earlier chapters is quite revealing about the nature of southern lynchings during the late nineteenth and early twentieth centuries. It is possible to extract some primary themes that tell the story of southern lynchings during the period.

Our findings are not kind to the popular justice explanation for lynchings, despite its popularity among whites during the lynching era. Time after time, mobs expressed frustration with cases in which expected guilty verdicts were not rendered or in which sentences were more lenient than anticipated. In article after article, the media attempted to justify the lynching outrage by bemoaning the inadequacy of the southern justice system for dealing with black criminality. In fact, however, we could find no systematic evidence of a linkage between the level of mob activity and the actions of the formal criminal justice system. In both the temporal and spatial senses there was little relationship between lynchings and the frequency with which blacks were marched off to the gallows. This suggests that informal lethal sanctioning was not a substitute for active and efficient formal sanctioning, as maintained by the popular justice model. Furthermore, if an inefficient formal justice system did account for mob violence, then why were lynchings used so disproportionately against blacks before 1900 and almost exclusively after? Surely there was no shortage of white criminals who were processed too slowly, and punished too lightly, by southern courts. We conclude that the southern justice system was more than adequately prepared and willing to handle black criminality in a discriminatory fashion if necessary. Thus, we must sift the historical evidence more carefully to identify the real underlying reasons for the willingness of whites to flaunt the very law they professed to revere in order to punish blacks.

Perhaps the most common explanation given for lynching in prior work assigns primary responsibility to political motivations. Put simply, it has been argued that whites felt politically threatened by the newly franchised black population and their proportionately large numbers and turned to terrorism to neutralize the competition. Unfortunately, our inventory of lynchings does not extend back into the Reconstruction period.[21] It is not possible to assess the adequacy of the political model in the immediate postwar period when blacks were assuming prominent positions in the southern political system. Some have concluded that lynchings during Reconstruction were largely political in nature. For the post-Reconstruction era, however, our findings offer little support for that conclusion.

Southern politics during the redemption and Populist periods involved a large cast of characters as well as a large number of subplots. It is a challenge to ferret out the relationship between political machinations and mob violence during those eras. Nonetheless, it seems a rather straightforward proposition that if lynchings were primarily motivated by whites' political fears of black political participation— no matter what the root cause of the concern—then lynchings should have declined precipitously after blacks were nearly completely disenfranchised by the early 1900s. In fact, however, we can infer no significant effect of political disenfranchisement on the intensity of black lynchings.

The activity of white mobs was impervious to the introduction of

restrictive voting statutes and the subsequent plunge in black political participation. This was true for black lynchings in the South as a
whole as well as in individual states. It might be possible to argue that
whites after disenfranchisement needed to continue lynching when
blacks threatened to challenge their subordinate political status. However, such sporadic mob violence should have paled in comparison
with the intensity of the purportedly politically motivated lynchings
that would have been required before disenfranchisement. In fact, the
evidence provides no support that disenfranchisement altered long-
term trends in the frequency of lynching.

Similarly, our findings do not indicate that lynchings rose in response to the activity of opposition political parties. Some scholars
have suggested that members of the white supremacist southern
Democratic party resorted to violence when their political hegemony was threatened by insurgent political movements, for example the
Populist party during the 1890s.[22] We examined the relationship
between opposition party strength and lynching across the counties
of ten southern states during two key periods of southern political
history, redemption and the Populist Era. No evidence emerged that
lynchings were positively related to the strength of the Republican
party during either era or to the strength of the Populist party during the latter period. Indeed, it appears that the viability of political
opposition to the dominant Democratic party actually provided a
measure of protection from lynching. During the 1880s and 1890s,
significantly fewer blacks were lynched in counties with strong Republican parties. Fewer lynchings also occurred in counties with
strong Populist parties, although the relationship was considerably
weaker. Rather than creating an atmosphere of terror for blacks, significant political opposition to the Democratic party appears to have
buffered local blacks somewhat.

The post-Civil War economy in much of the South can be summarized with a single word: cotton. Within the cotton economy, poorer
whites looked for a small piece of land to buy or a tenant farm with
good soil. Well-to-do whites looked for reliable tenants to occupy their
fragmented landholdings and tried to replace the slave labor lost
through emancipation. Blacks struggled to find a niche that would
represent at least some improvement over slavery. The issue of race
aggravated an already volatile situation. Wealthier whites resented the
need to treat former slaves as free labor and the resultant loss of control over their workers. Poorer whites resented having to compete with
the "inferior" caste for economic survival.

The intersection of race and economics created the potential for violence, and our analysis yields strong support for the conclusion that economic factors were important in motivating lynchings. Pursuing a line of inquiry that extends back to at least the 1930s, our findings show that lynchings did respond to the economic cycles of King Cotton, at least before the early twentieth century. Increases in the real price of cotton paid to farmers resulted in fewer black lynch victims. Increases in inflation led to more black lynchings. Blacks were safer from mob violence when the profits from cotton were high and purchasing power was strong. Although Hovland and Sears would have concluded that this relationship reflects the operation of a frustration-aggression process whereby blacks were victimized by economically disappointed whites,[23] others have suggested that more sinister forces were also at work. For example, Raper argued that during economic hard times, struggling whites used violence to displace black farmers from the best land and replace them with whites.[24]

We suspect that Raper's interpretation was correct but doubt that poorer whites were the only ones to react to economic distress by terrorizing blacks. Rather, well-to-do whites also had something to gain by heightened racial tensions during periods of economic stagnation. The risk of a coalition between black and white labor was probably highest during economic downturns. By contributing to an environment of racial antagonism, employers could reduce the likelihood of successful cooperation. Of course, such interpretations for the linkage between cotton prices and lynching must remain largely speculation. The existence of the linkage, however, is now quite clear.

The seasonal cycle of mob violence revealed further evidence of an economic dimension to lynching. After adjusting for seasonal variation in the level of violent crime (i.e., white lynchings), we observed that lynchings in cotton-producing regions were concentrated when the need for labor was greatest. These periods were critical for landlords because profits depended heavily on the successful planting, chopping, and harvesting of the cotton crop. Landlords and merchants benefited from increased control over labor then because they stood to gain from the diligent efforts of a compliant labor force. Lynchings were capable of contributing toward such control by demonstrating the consequences for those who would cause trouble and disrupt the production process. Through increased terrorism, lynching could also heighten the general level of fear among black workers.

The economic environment in the South was not stagnant throughout the five decades we considered. By the second decade of the twentieth century, it appears that terroristic control over black workers was no longer the most efficient way to guarantee the continued production of cash crops. A fundamental change had occurred. Blacks had the choice of migrating to northern states to pursue the economic opportunities that the industrial war effort and the constricted flow of immigrant laborers from southern and eastern Europe created. Many families chose to relocate, and an exodus from the South flowed into a growing labor vacuum in the North. Racial violence was one important reason behind the northbound stream.

Black migration resulted in a huge loss of laborers for landlords and employers and threatened their ability to continue generating profits. Our findings suggest that employers reacted quite rationally to the threat of a shrinking labor supply. That is, they took steps to reduce the level of violence directed at local blacks. As a result, areas that had experienced the greatest losses of black population during the 1910s and 1920s subsequently had fewer lynchings than areas with more modest levels of out-migration. As we would expect, the ameliorative effect of black out-migration on lynching was strongest in those areas dominated by higher-status whites who had the most to lose from the migration. Although economic circumstances could endanger blacks by increasing the risk of mob violence (e.g., declining cotton prices and competition with poor whites), they could also protect blacks from violence as long as such protection served the interests of the most powerful members of society.

It is much more difficult to grapple directly with threats to status that may have motivated violence. Certainly, we know that southern whites were preoccupied—obsessed might be a better description—with the integrity of the caste line that split the South by skin color. The concern with keeping blacks in their "place" was capable of extending to the use of violence, as indicated by those cases of lynching that were prompted by such relatively minor behavioral transgressions as failing to yield the sidewalk to a white person, being rude or imprudent, being obnoxious, or "acting like a white man." Such incidents were a relatively small minority of all lynchings, however (chapter 2). The primary difficulty with estimating the role of status threats in the overall tragedy of lynching is that "status" for whites was connected so intimately to other sources of friction and competition, especially economics and politics.

Virtually any progress or achievement by blacks could be interpreted as an assault on the southern caste line, and therefore on the privileged social station of whites. Undoubtedly, this is an important reason for the strong reaction by whites to black political progress during Reconstruction. It was simply not consistent with a worldview of white supremacy and black subordination to have blacks holding positions of political power and influence. It can also help explain the lynching of prominent or successful blacks such as Frazier Baker in South Carolina or Dennis Cobb in Louisiana (chapter 3). As more and more blacks approached or surpassed the economic positions of southern whites (especially those on the bottom rungs of the economic ladder), the caste line became more salient. For marginalized and struggling whites, it was, in many instances, their only claim to social supremacy.

Although it is virtually impossible to disentangle the status motives for lynching from the political or economic motives, the evidence in chapter 5 suggests at least some viability for the status threat model. Our findings indicate that lynchings were more frequent in areas with larger concentrations of white tenants. For white farmers, tenancy was the bottom rung on the agricultural ladder. It was supposed to be a status reserved for poor black farmers. Whites were supposed to be owners of land rather than tillers of someone else's soil. However, white tenancy grew sharply during the late nineteenth and early twentieth centuries, forcing more and more farmers to the margins of southern agriculture. They were clinging desperately to that marginal position along with their black neighbors, who were also tenant farmers. With virtually no legitimate claim to economic superiority, poor whites resorted to mob violence in order to shore up the caste line that represented a claim to superiority based on the color of their skin.

Revisiting Raper and Friends

The story of southern lynchings that we have told complements the important work of those who have preceded us. But how do our conclusions differ from, or agree with, theirs? A brief survey of a few of the better-known commentators may help to better place our work within the broader literature on lynching.

Raper expressed the outrage of southerners over mob violence when he wrote *The Tragedy of Lynching*. All subsequent work on lynching owes a heavy intellectual debt to this pioneering book. Raper tended to view mob violence as the product of the deprived and backward culture shared by many poorer whites and also to the unwillingness of more respectable citizens to intervene. For example, he claimed that "mobs and lynchings eventually can be eliminated if the irresponsive and irresponsible population elements can be raised into a more abundant economic and cultural life."[25] He also believed that African-Americans had a part to play in erasing the disgrace of mob violence from southern society. Raper argued, for instance, that blacks should take better advantage of the limited opportunities available to them and refuse to become engaged in crime or to shelter criminals from the legal authorities.

Williamson has described, in compelling fashion, the rise of radical racism in the South during the late nineteenth and early twentieth centuries. During this era the southern psyche regarding African-Americans and race relations was transformed fundamentally. No longer were blacks viewed as the shuffling, obsequious, and harmless "darkies" who deserved paternalistic protection. Suddenly, they became threatening, atavistic animals who posed a threat to the security of white society, especially to white womanhood. According to Williamson, this psychological transformation was instrumental in the epidemic of mob violence that spread throughout the 1890s and after: "There were an infinite number of ways in which Radicalism manifested its presence among the white masses, but easily the most visible was the syndrome of violence."[26] Not only did radicalism justify the selection of blacks as legitimate targets for lynching, but it also vindicated the behavior of white mobs, no matter how brutal. It was necessary for society to experience another psychological transformation before the extremes of radical racism, including the terror of the lynch mob, became obsolete.

Ayers has written extensively and eloquently on the character of the New South, including the shame of mob violence. He concluded in 1984 that prior studies had been unsuccessful in identifying the triggers of lynching. More recently, he has tried his hand at characterizing lynching and its role in society. Ayers believes that many black victims of lynching were transients or labor migrants.[27] With fears of black criminality running rife, and with no local advocates to turn to for support, these strangers to the white community were especially vulnerable to mob "justice."

> Lynchings tended to flourish where whites were surrounded by what they called 'strange niggers', blacks with no white to vouch for them, blacks with no reputation in the neighborhood, blacks without even other blacks to aid them. Lynching seemed both more necessary and more feasible in places such as the Gulf Plain, the cotton uplands, and the mountains. In those places most blacks and whites did not know one another, much less share ties of several generations. The black population often moved from one year to the next in search of jobs at lumber camps and large plantations.[28]

Ayers suggests a fatal combination of a paranoid white population, a rootless black population, and a racist ideology as the best explanation for the brutal activities of the mob. In some respects, Ayers's framework combines the basic elements of Raper's and Williamson's perspectives.

There are many lenses through which to view the phenomenon of lynching, and we do not wish to claim that the conclusions reached by Raper, Williamson, and Ayers are wrong. However, based on our own work, we are willing to say that they are incomplete because they do not do justice to the fundamental role that mob violence played in the maintenance of southern society and economy. Our evidence suggests that lynching was an integral element of an agricultural economy that required a large, cheap, and docile labor force. Compromises following the Civil War led to an organization of agricultural production that was built more around the tenant farmer than upon yeoman farmers working their own land. At least at first, this niche was filled primarily by newly freed African-Americans. Any shocks or threats to the arrangement carried the potential for conflict and violence. Southern blacks were vulnerable from more than one direction. The white elite was willing to see the black community terrorized when it served the elite's purposes, for example, to exert control over workers or to drive a wedge between struggling blacks and whites. And poor white dirt farmers were equally willing to resort to violence when their meager claim to social superiority was at risk when their economic fortunes waned.

Thus, the story of lynching is much more than uncultured white peckerwoods engaging in drunken carnage, or a shift in the southern psyche that changed the popular image of African-Americans, or vulnerable transient workers who may or may not have broken the law. Rather, these were all manifestations of a much grander, more complex, set of social arrangements that saw African-Americans at the bottom of a status hierarchy defined by race and class. Only when the status quo was threatened by forces that could not be blunted through the use of violence and terrorism would lynchings begin to disappear. And that is exactly what occurred when African-Americans finally had the option to go north.

Although we have arrived at our respective destinations by traversing very different terrain, our conclusions overlap significantly with those reached much earlier by White and those described only recently by Brundage. Both investigators describe lynchings, and the terror they created in the African-American community, as crucial mechanisms for assuring perpetuation of the southern status quo, especially the continuation of an exploitative plantation economy. As White argues,

Poverty, the ravages of the boll-weevil, disastrous rainy seasons, unintelligent farming resulting in exhaustion of the soil, combined with the great demand for cotton, led to the stultifying one-crop system and to the wasteful and often viciously abused share-cropping and tenant-farming systems out of which peonage developed. Negroes were lynched, or intimidated and cowed when not killed, for daring to question this exploitation or seeking to elude the clutches of rapacious landlords, merchants, and bankers.[29]

Although the actual historical record of lynching suggests that events were usually more subtle than White portrays, he clearly appreciated the deepseated utility of racial terror in the southern economy that rose from the ashes of the Civil War.

Writing more than sixty-years after White, and using a more rigorous approach, Brundage describes a "geography of lynching" that shares much in common with White's. For example, Brundage concludes,

Lynch mobs seem to have flourished within the boundaries of the plantation South, where sharecropping, monoculture agriculture, and a stark line separating white landowners and black tenants existed. In such areas, mob violence became part of the very rhythm of life: deeply rooted traditions of violent labor control, unhindered by any meaningful resistance from either institutions or individuals opposed unconditionally to racial violence, sustained a tradition of mob violence that persisted for decades.[30]

Our statistical evidence lends strong empirical support to these generalizations.

Conclusion

Where does this story about black lynchings end? What sound bite most accurately portrays the contents of the previous pages? We suggest that southern whites did not resort to mob violence to compensate for a weak and inefficient criminal justice system. Rather, they used lynchings as a tool for maintaining dominance in a society that was forced to accept a revolutionary change in the status of blacks—from slaves to freedmen. Although a free black population threatened southern whites in many different ways, our findings suggest that economic forces were clearly the most important undercurrent that carried southern society to such outrageous extremes of brutality. Economic forces also turned the tide against mob violence during the 1920s and 1930s, as employers agonized over the exodus of their cheap black workers. This leads to a final observation: Blacks were most vulnerable to the rope and faggot when lynching had the potential to benefit most of white society, for example, during periods of economic distress. They were least vulnerable where cleavages developed in white society, as where strong opposition political groups existed or where well-to-do whites suffered from the loss of cheap labor. However, at no time between 1880 and 1930 could southern blacks assume that they were totally immune from mob violence.

As with all sound bites, the previous paragraph does not do the full story justice. Perhaps readers have gained a much fuller understanding of the tragedy of lynching than is contained in those few sentences of generalization. This was an extraordinary period of American history, during which ordinary folks did unspeakable things. They were not monsters who temporarily assumed the persona of southern whites. They were the town barber, the local blacksmith, and even the county sheriff. Clearly, they must have been swept along by very strong social forces to feel justified in committing more than two thousand atrocities against their black neighbors. We hope that this book has moved us further along the road toward understanding what those social forces were—and were not.

NOTES

1. McGovern (1982).

2. Ginzburg (1988, 238–40).

3. Whitfield (1988).

4. See Williams (1987, 230–35) for a description of the Chaney-Goodman-Schwerner lynching and reactions to it in the South and North.

5. Even more recently, New York experienced the lynching of Yusef Hawkins in Bensonhurst. Hawkins was beaten and shot by a mob of young white boys for no reason other than being in the "wrong" part of town.

6. As indicated by the Gallup poll of 1937 (Gallup 1972), which asked, "Should Congress pass a law that would make lynching a federal crime?"

7. Ames (1942) and White (1929 [1969]).

8. Wells (1892 [1969]).

9. Wright (1986, 234).

10. Wright (1986, 245)

11. We continue to refer only to the ten southern states dealt with in our analysis: Alabama, Arkansas, Florida, Georgia, Kentucky, Louisiana, Mississippi, North Carolina, South Carolina, and Tennessee.

12. Hanna (1964).

13. Brundage (1993) also stresses the importance of economic organization, class relations, and lynching.

14. See Cobb (1982) for a detailed description of the effort to "sell the South," especially following World War II.

15. Zangrando (1980, 11).

16. Cobb (1982, 122).

17. Ayers (1984, 238).

18. Commission on Interracial Cooperation (1936, 23).

19. These alternative sources of perceived threats to the southern white population were described in some detail in chapter 3 and are only summarized here to help us take stock of the evidence.

20. We use "they" in this context as though it refers to all southern whites. Of course, we realize that southern society was not monolithic. Some whites did not feel threatened by blacks and opposed the brutal treatment of freedmen from the day of emancipation. This discussion is meant to be an overview and therefore does not deal with these issues in the same depth as previous chapters.

21. None of the known general inventories of lynchings predates 1882, although Wright's (1990, 307–23) inventory for the state of Kentucky extends back to 1866.

22. For example, Inverarity (1976), Olzak (1990), and Soule (1992).

23. Hovland and Sears (1940).

24. Raper (1933).

25. Raper (1933, 38).

26. Williamson (1984, 180).

27. The basis for Ayers's conclusion is unclear. He offers no data on the residential status of lynch victims. Although certainly there are examples of transients being lynched, there are counterexamples of lynch victims being permanent residents of their communities. The residential status of lynch victims remains an open question until systematic data can be brought to bear. Unfortunately, our lynching inventory does not contain the appropriate residential data to test Ayers's hypothesis.

28. Ayers (1992, 157).

29. White (1929 [1969], 103).

30. Brundage (1993, 159).

Appendix A

The Creation of a New Inventory of Southern Lynchings

Public inventories of southern lynchings have been available for a long while. Three of these inventories are especially well-known and have served as the bases for previous investigations of southern lynchings.[1] First, in 1919 the NAACP published *Thirty Years of Lynching in the United States, 1889–1918*, which included a list of all lynch victims known from 1889 through 1919. Later, the NAACP included lists of lynch victims in subsequent annual reports. Second, from 1882 to 1918 the Chicago *Tribune* published an annual inventory of lynch victims in one of the first issues of the paper each year. Finally, the Department of Records and Archives at Tuskegee University, initially under the direction of Monroe Work and later under the direction of Jesse Guzman and Daniel Williams, collected information about lynchings that occurred throughout the United States. In 1968, Daniel T. Williams compiled the Tuskegee information in an unpublished volume, *Amid the Gathering Multitude: The Story of Lynching in America. A Classified Listing.* Although these three sources of information provide a useful departure for the creation of a high-quality inventory of lynchings, several types of errors and inaccuracies prevent their uncritical use.[2] In fact, these sources are so flawed that sole reliance on them could possibly lead to misleading conclusions about the era. Thus, we created a new inventory that uses contemporary newspaper reports to confirm and supplement the accounts of lynchings in these three sources.

Beginning with the NAACP, Chicago *Tribune,* and Tuskegee inventories, we constructed an "unconfirmed master list" of all known lynchings between 1882 and 1930. We then attempted to confirm each of the lynchings in the unconfirmed master list by locating a contemporary newspaper account of the event. Newspaper stories were used to determine whether the event truly was a lynching and to correct factual errors that may have been included in the original inventories. Although there is naturally some ambiguity in the definition of a lynching, we adhered as closely as possible to the NAACP's definition, which requires that (1) there must be evidence that a person was killed; (2) the person must have met death illegally; (3) a group of three or more persons must have participated in the killing; and (4) the group must have acted under the pretext of service to justice or tradition. During this confirmation process some events were dropped because they could not be confirmed or because there was insufficient evidence to classify them as lynchings. In addition, some new cases were discovered and added to the inventory. The final product was a confirmed inventory of southern lynchings.

Table A-1 reports by state the number of confirmed lynching victims and the number of victims we have not been able to confirm as of March 1994.

Our inventory includes all known lynchings that occurred in the South between 1882 and 1930. We restricted the inventory to this time period because (1) there were no reasonable data on lynchings in the

Table A-1. Disposition of Entries in Master Lynching Inventory[a]

State	Confirmed Lynch Victims[b]	Remaining Unreconciled Entries
Alabama	300	17
Arkansas	241	27
Florida	250	22
Georgia	458	31
Kentucky	191	21
Louisiana	360	16
Mississippi	538	45
North Carolina	97	7
South Carolina	156	5
Tennessee	214	34
Total	2,805	225

a. As of March 1994.
b. Regardless of race.

entire South prior to 1882, and (2) 1930 marked the end of widespread lynching in the South. Lynchings in the following ten states are included in our inventory: Alabama, Arkansas, Florida, Georgia, Kentucky, Louisiana, Mississippi, North Carolina, South Carolina, and Tennessee.[3] For most lynching events included in our inventory we have been able to determine (1) state and county of occurrence, (2) date of occurrence, (3) race of the victim or victims, (4) sex of the victim or victims, and (5) the reported reason for the lynching.[4]

Although these data are not beyond reproach and are subject to revision when new information is uncovered, we believe that they are the most accurate data on southern lynchings that now exist. All lynch data, however, are subject to criticism that inventories based on newspaper reports undercount lethal mob violence.[5] This undercount could be created by any one of three situations: (1) if the lynching was unknown to the news media; (2) if the lynching was known but went unreported, either because the event was not considered newsworthy or because of the fear that publicizing mob violence would reflect negatively on the local community; or (3) if the lynching was reported locally in a small community but the story was not picked up by a news service or a larger regional newspaper.

We suspect that the first situation occurred only infrequently. To be an effective mechanism for social control, lynchings had to be visible, with the killing being publicly known, especially to the target population. On the other hand, a murder (even a racially motivated one) was more likely hidden from public scrutiny. As for the second argument, it does not appear, through reading numerous newspaper accounts describing mob violence, that editors were at all inhibited in reporting morbid and gory details. They often used sympathetic language in describing lynch mobs while reserving callous damnation for lynch victims.[6] The southern press was extremely creative when it came to providing moral, if not legal, justification for the action of lynch mobs, as was clear in the treatment of the lynching of Frazier Baker, the black postmaster of Lake City, South Carolina.[7] Turning to the third issue, that of obscure lynchings, it is possible that a lynching occurred in some isolated, rural area and was never noticed by one of the larger newspapers, in which case it may not have been recorded by the Chicago *Tribune,* the NAACP, Tuskegee University, or our confirmation process. However, given the frequency with which lynchings were reported, we doubt if the number of obscure lynchings (again, in contrast to murders) is large. Again, we must reiterate that we do not claim that our inventory includes every lynching that occurred in the South between 1882 and 1930. However, we have no reason to believe that the undercount is large, or that it threatens the representativeness of the inventory.

Rather than a problem of undercount, we believe that a possibly more serious problem with the previous public inventories is one of reporting error, including the reporting of events that were not really lynchings. The term *lynching* was used in prior inventories to describe a variety of phenomena, some of which were simple murders and other nonlynchings. In other instances, there were reports of expected or supposed lynchings without sufficient evidence that a killing actually took place. Based on our confirmation process it appears that roughly one of every six previously reported lynchings failed to meet our definition of a lynching and therefore were excluded from our inventory. This leads us to believe that the problem of overcounting in previous lynching inventories is as potentially serious as that of undercounting.

Any inventory of southern lynch victims is certain to include errors and omissions, especially an inventory that covers a broad geographic area over an extended period. If the historical decennial enumeration of the population by the Census Bureau was incapable of perfection (as it was), it would certainly be unreasonable to expect perfection from a lynching inventory. It is not unreasonable, however, to expect an intensive effort to minimize the flaws of such an inventory. We believe that our revised, confirmed lynching inventory reflects such an effort. Moreover, comparisons between our inventory and independently constructed inventories for individual states are extremely reassuring. For instance, our records for the state of Kentucky, for the years 1882 to 1930, agree very closely with the one prepared by George Wright for *Racial Violence in Kentucky, 1865–1940: Lynchings, Mob Rule, and "Legal Lynchings."*

NOTES

1. Another listing appears in Ginzburg (1962), but Ginzburg's inventory appears to be identical to the one compiled by the NAACP, including the errors of that inventory.

2. See Appendix B for examples of the errors and inaccuracies in these three inventories.

3. Other southern states also had sizable numbers of lynchings, especially Texas, Virginia, and Oklahoma. However, we were unable to locate convenient newspaper sources to confirm lynchings in those states. For an analysis of lynchings in Virginia, see Brundage (1993).

4. Determining the location of the lynching was generally a simple mat-

ter of identifying the site of the killing, but in a few instances we deviated from this practice. For example, Dick Wofford was lynched near Landrum, South Carolina, in November 1894. However, Wofford was a citizen of Polk County, North Carolina, and he was killed by a mob from Polk County, North Carolina. Although the actual site of the murder was in South Carolina, we allocated the Wofford lynching to Polk County, North Carolina.

5. For a general discussion of the methodological problems of using newspapers as a source of data for social research, see Franzosi (1987).

6. It could be argued, however, that there was a shift in this position after World War I as national antilynching campaigns became more vocal and the business community began to view mob violence as a hindrance to commercial growth.

7. See Charleston *News and Courier,* February 23, 1898, 1.

Appendix B

Types of Errors and Other Problems in Existing Inventories

I. Locational Errors
   A. Mistaking a newspaper's story dateline for location of lynching. Example: All three existing inventories list Ray Rolston as being lynched in Anniston in Calhoun County, Alabama, in November 1909. According to the Atlanta *Constitution* of November 25, Anniston was the story's dateline; the actual lynching took place near Edwardsville in Cleburne County, Alabama.
   B. Misallocating location to wrong state. Example: The NAACP and Tuskegee inventories state that Coat Williams was lynched for murder in Pine Grove, Louisiana, on May 15, 1894. The Chicago *Tribune*, on the other hand, lists Williams as being lynched in Pine Grove, Florida. The Jacksonville *Times-Union* of May 15 confirms that a black male named Coot Williams was lynched in Pine Grove, Florida, on May 13, 1894, for allegedly murdering two women.
   C. Misallocating location to county because of changes in county boundaries between the date of lynching and the date of allocation. Example: The NAACP and Tuskegee report the lynching of Robert Chambers (Charmers) in Cranberry, North Carolina, for arson on April 22, 1896. Both sources place Cranberry in Avery County, but Avery County was not formed until 1911. At the time of the lynching, Cranberry was in Mitchell County, North Carolina.
   D. Correctly locating lynching in appropriate county, but failing to recognize that the lynch mob was from another county or state. Example: On November 22, 1894, Dick Wofford, a citizen of Polk

County, North Carolina, was lynched near Landrum, South Carolina, by a mob from Polk County, North Carolina, for an alleged assault on a girl in Polk County. All three existing inventories place this lynching in South Carolina, but we believe that it should be considered a North Carolina lynching and have designated it as such.

E. Typographical and clerical errors in reporting location. Example: The three inventories give Solomon Jones as being lynched in Forrest, Georgia, on August 1, 1899, yet the Atlanta *Constitution* of August 2 places the lynching in Forest, Alabama, on July 30, 1899.

F. Situations where location is indeterminant. Example: The NAACP and Tuskegee inventories list the lynching of an unnamed Negro man in Dublin in Laurens County, Georgia, on October 5, 1911, for attempted rape. Yet according to the Atlanta *Constitution* of October 6, the man was lynched midway between Eastman in Dodge County, Georgia, and Dublin. In this case, the county location of the lynching is indeterminant.

II. Other Kinds of Errors

A. Double listing of victims.

1. One victim listed by proper name, the other listed by "Unnamed Negro." Example: The NAACP and Tuskegee cite two lynchings in Lancaster, South Carolina, on June 3, 1894: Hardy Gill and an unnamed Negro. According to the Charleston *News and Courier* of June 4, only one lynching occurred, that of Hardy Gill. It appears that the NAACP and Tuskegee's second victim is a double listing.

2. Listing of same victim in two different states. Example: The Chicago *Tribune* and Tuskegee inventories state that George Roose (Rouse) was lynched in Vienna, Alabama, on April 4, 1885, but they also list a George Rouse as being lynched in Vienna, Georgia, on March 30, 1885. We could find no evidence of the lynching in Alabama, but the Atlanta *Constitution* of March 31 states that a George Rouse was lynched in Vienna, Georgia.

3. Double listing because of aliases. Example: All three inventories list John Walker and William Barnes as being lynched in Macon County, Georgia, on the same date in 1910 for the same crime, yet the Atlanta *Constitution* of November 8 indicates that "William Barnes" was an alias of John Walker.

B. Factual errors in basic information: date, name, race, sex, and reported offense. Example: All three inventories have Douglas Bolte lynched on October 15, 1897, in Quarantine in Plaquemines Parish, Louisiana, for "running." In reality, Douglas Boutte was lynched on that date at Barataria Bayou in Jefferson Parish, Louisiana, for "running" a quarantine, as reported by the New Orleans *Daily Picayune* of October 16.

C. Reporting of a rumored lynching that never happened. Example: The Chicago *Tribune* gives Wm. Simmes as being lynched in Morgan County, Alabama, on December 21, 1898, but the Macon *Telegraph* of December 22, 1898, states that the rumored lynching was false, and Wm. Simmes was in the custody of the police and had been transferred safely to Moulton, Alabama.

D. Reporting of a "lynching" that should not have been classified as a lynching.

1. The victim did not die. Example: The three inventories list George Murray as being lynched in Florida on May 11, 1896, yet the Savannah *Morning News* of May 10 notes that George Murray of Madison County, Florida, was whipped by regulators on May 8, 1896. We could find no evidence that Murray died from his beating.

2. The victim was murdered. Example: The NAACP and Tuskegee inventories list Grant Cole as being lynched in Montgomery, Alabama, in December 1925 for insulting a white woman, yet the Montgomery *Advertiser* of December 17, 1925, indicates that Cole was murdered by two men posing as sheriff's deputies. Also, two men wearing women's clothing broke into the Keo, Arkansas, jail on February 7, 1892, and assassinated Hamp Biscoe, his wife, and his son in their cells. All three inventories list the Biscoes as having been lynched, but the murders do not qualify as lynchings by our definition.

3. The victim was legally executed. Example: All three inventories list Bud Beard as being lynched in Carrollton in Pickens County, Alabama, on December 17, 1897, for the alleged rape of a young girl. According to the Atlanta *Constitution* of December 18, 1897, Beard (a.k.a. Bud Brooks) was legally executed at Carrollton, Georgia, at noon on December 17, 1897.

4. Other nonlynching killings. Example: All three inventories report the lynching of Nicholas Hector in New Iberia, Louisiana, on October 12, 1908, for being a "desperado." Yet the New Orleans *Daily Picayune* of October 13, says that the chief of police and his deputies killed Hector after trying to induce him to surrender.

E. Missing lynching altogether. Example: None of the existing inventories recorded the lynching of an unnamed Negro man in Bulloch County, Georgia, on April 21, 1911.

Appendix C

Miscellaneous Tables

Table C-1. Lynching Victims by Race, Gender, and Mob Composition for Ten States in the South, 1882-1930[a]

Race	Male	Female	Gender Unknown	Total
Victims of All Lynch Mobs				
Black	2,364	74	24	2,462
White	283	5	0	288
Other	5	0	0	5
Unknown	49	0	1	50
Total	2,701	79	25	2,805
Victims of Presumed White Lynch Mobs				
Black	2,217	73	24	2,314
White	279	5	0	284
Other	5	0	0	5
Unknown	46	0	1	47
Total	2,547	78	25	2,650
Victims of Presumed Black or Integrated Lynch Mobs				
Black	147	1	0	148
White	4	0	0	4
Other	0	0	0	0
Unknown	3	0	0	3
Total	154	1	0	155

a. Alabama, Arkansas, Florida, Georgia, Kentucky, Louisiana, Mississippi, North Carolina, South Carolina, and Tennessee.

Table C-2. State Summary of Lynching Incidents, 1882–1930

State	Any Victims	Any Black Victims	Only Black Victims	Only White Victims	Black and White Victims	Other Victims[a]
Deep South						
Alabama	243	223	223	18	0	2
Georgia	381	362	360	17	2	2
Louisiana	274	242	239	30	2	3
Mississippi	452	425	425	20	0	7
South Carolina	123	116	116	5	0	2
Subtotal	1,473	1,368	1,363	90	4	16
Border South						
Arkansas	199	157	155	35	2	7
Florida	196	177	175	15	2	4
Kentucky	156	107	105	31	2	18
North Carolina	81	67	66	14	1	0
Tennessee	173	142	140	29	2	2
Subtotal	805	650	641	124	9	31
Total	2,278	2,018	2,004	214	13	47

a. Includes victims whose race is unknown.

Table C-3. Time Series of Victims of Lynchings in Ten States in the
South, 1882–1930[a]

Year	All Victims	Black Victims	Black Victims of Black Mobs	Black Victims of White Mobs	White Victims of White Mobs
1882	44	34	1	33	9
1883	55	47	4	43	7
1884	59	43	6	37	14
1885	62	47	5	42	15
1886	71	56	8	48	9
1887	62	49	9	40	9
1888	67	58	5	53	7
1889	81	58	5	53	20
1890	64	53	7	46	10
1891	121	89	6	83	28
1892	129	106	14	92	16
1893	116	103	4	99	11
1894	117	94	8	86	11
1895	89	74	5	69	14
1896	80	63	2	61	15
1897	79	72	1	71	2
1898	81	77	4	73	4
1899	82	70	6	64	12
1900	76	74	2	72	2
1901	94	86	10	76	8
1902	62	59	1	58	3
1903	73	68	7	61	5
1904	61	58	4	54	3
1905	42	40	3	37	2
1906	49	47	0	47	2
1907	48	45	3	42	3
1908	77	73	6	67	4
1909	55	54	0	54	1
1910	55	50	2	48	4
1911	52	50	1	49	2
1912	54	53	1	52	1
1913	43	43	2	41	0
1914	38	37	0	37	0
1915	58	50	0	50	6
1916	40	39	2	37	1
1917	26	26	1	25	0

Table C-3, continued

Year	All Victims	Black Victims	Black Victims of Black Mobs	Black Victims of White Mobs	White Victims of White Mobs
1918	39	38	0	38	0
1919	63	60	1	59	2
1920	36	35	1	34	1
1921	51	45	0	45	6
1922	37	32	0	32	5
1923	25	23	1	22	2
1924	14	14	0	14	0
1925	13	13	0	13	0
1926	24	20	0	20	4
1927	12	12	0	12	0
1928	7	7	0	7	0
1929	9	6	0	6	3
1930	13	12	0	12	1
Total	2,805	2,462	148	2,314	284

a. Alabama, Arkansas, Florida, Georgia, Kentucky, Louisiana, Mississippi, North Carolina, South Carolina, and Tennessee.

Table C-4. State Summary of Lynching Victims, 1882–1930

State	Total Victims	Black Victims	Black Victims of White Mobs[a]	White Victims of White Mobs[a]	Other Victims[b]
Deep South					
Alabama	300	273	262	24	3
Georgia	458	435	423	21	2
Louisiana	360	304	283	52	3
Mississippi	538	509	462	21	7
South Carolina	156	148	143	5	2
Subtotal	1,812	1,669	1,573	123	17
Border South					
Arkansas	241	184	162	48	9
Florida	250	224	212	19	7
Kentucky	191	128	118	43	20
North Carolina	97	82	75	15	0
Tennessee	214	175	174	36	2
Subtotal	993	793	741	161	38
Total	2,805	2,462	2,314	284	55

a. Mobs presumed to be white.
b. Includes victims whose race is unknown.

Table C-5. Distribution of Number of Victims by Incident of Lynching
in Ten States in the South, 1882–1930[a]

Number of Victims per Incident	All Lynchings	Any Black Victims	Only Black Victims	Black Victims of White Mobs
1	1,938	1,732	1,723	1,617
2	229	190	186	181
3	68	57	57	52
4	27	26	26	26
5	10	8	8	8
More than 5	6	5	4	5
Total incidents	2,278	2,018	2,004	1,889
Total victims	2,805	2,462	2,438	2,314
Mean victims per incident	1.23	1.22	1.22	1.23
Percent of incidents with 1 victim	85.1	85.8	86.0	85.6

a. Alabama, Arkansas, Florida, Georgia, Kentucky, Louisiana, Mississippi, North Carolina, South Carolina, and Tennessee.

Table C-6. Distribution of Counties with Black Lynch Victims of White Mobs, 1882–1930

Number of Black Victims in County	Ten State South (%)	Deep South[a] (%)	Border South[b] (%)
0	34.31	19.39	48.04
1	19.93	18.68	21.09
2	12.68	14.66	10.87
3	6.68	7.33	6.09
4	4.76	6.86	2.83
5	5.55	7.57	3.70
6	4.53	6.38	2.83
7	2.72	4.96	0.65
8	1.93	2.60	1.30
9	1.02	1.89	0.22
10	1.47	2.84	0.22
11	1.13	1.89	0.43
12	0.68	1.18	0.22
13	0.57	1.18	0.00
14	0.57	0.95	0.22
15	0.23	0.24	0.22
More than 15	1.24	1.43	0.87
Total	100.00	100.03	100.02
Mean victims per county	2.595	3.681	1.596
Standard deviation	3.508	3.888	2.767

a. Counties in Alabama, Georgia, Louisiana, Mississippi, and South Carolina.
b. Counties in Arkansas, Florida, Kentucky, North Carolina, and Tennessee.

References

Aitkin, Murray, Dorothy Anderson, Brian Francis, and John Hinde. 1990. *Statistical modelling in GLIM.* Oxford: Clarendon Press.

Ames, Jesse Daniel. 1942. *The changing character of lynching: Review of lynching, 1931–1941, with a discussion of recent developments in this field.* Atlanta: Commission on Interracial Cooperation.

Aptheker, Herbert. 1943. *American Negro slave revolts.* New York: Columbia University Press.

Ayers, Edward L. 1992. *The promise of the new south: Life after reconstruction.* New York: Oxford University Press.

————. 1984. *Vengeance and justice: Crime and punishment in the nineteenth-century American south.* New York: Oxford University Press.

Bagozzi, Richard P. 1977. Populism and lynching in Louisiana: Comment on Inverarity. *American Sociological Review* 42:355–58.

Bailey, Thomas P. 1914. *Race orthodoxy in the south, and other aspects of the Negro question.* New York: Neale Publishing Co.

Balkwell, James W. 1990. Ethnic inequality and the rate of homicide. *Social Forces* 69:53–70.

Ballard, Allen. 1984. *One more day's journey: The story of a family and a people.* New York: McGraw-Hill.

Beck, E. M., James L. Massey, and Stewart E. Tolnay. 1989. The gallows, the mob, and the vote: Lethal sanctioning of blacks in North Carolina and Georgia, 1882–1930. *Law and Society Review* 23:317–31.

Beck, E. M., and Stewart E. Tolnay. 1990. The killing fields of the deep south: The market for cotton and the lynching of blacks, 1882–1930. *American Sociological Review* 55:526–39.

————. 1992. A season for violence: The lynching of blacks and labor demand in the agricultural production cycle in the American south. *International Review of Social History* 36:1–24.

———. 1994. Violence toward African-Americans in the era of the white lynch mob. In *Ethnicity, race, and crime,* ed. Darnell F. Hawkins. Albany: State University of New York Press.

Bennett, Steve. 1988. An extension of Williams' method for overdispersion models. *GLIM Newsletter* 17:12–18.

Black, Donald J. 1976. *The behavior of law.* New York: Academic Press.

Blalock, Hubert M. 1967. *Toward a theory of minority group relations.* New York: John Wiley.

Bloom, Jack M. 1987. *Class, race, and the civil rights movement.* Bloomington: Indiana University Press.

Bonacich, Edna. 1975. Abolition, the extension of slavery, and the position of free blacks: A study of split labor markets in the United States, 1830–1863. *American Journal of Sociology* 81:601–28.

———. 1972. A theory of ethnic antagonism: The split labor market. *American Sociological Review* 37:547–59.

Bowers, William. 1984. *Legal homicide: Death as punishment in America, 1864–1982.* Boston: Northeastern University Press.

Brown, Richard Maxwell. 1969. The American vigilante tradition. In *Violence in America: Historical and comparative perspectives,* ed. Hugh Davis Graham and Ted Robert Gurr. 1:121–80. Washington, D.C.: Government Printing Office.

Bruce, Philip Alexander. 1889. *The plantation Negro as a freeman.* New York: Putnam.

Brundage, W. Fitzhugh. 1990. The Darien "Insurrection" of 1899: Black protest during the nadir of race relations. *Georgia Historical Quarterly* 74:234–53.

———. 1993. *Lynching in the new south: Georgia and Virginia, 1880–1930.* Urbana: University of Illinois Press.

Burton, Vernon. 1978. Race and reconstruction: Edgefield County, South Carolina. *Journal of Social History* 12:31–56.

Cameron, A. Colin, and Pravin K. Trivedi. 1986. Econometric models based on count data: Comparisons and applications of some estimators and tests. *Journal of Applied Econometrics* 1:29–53.

Carpenter, John A. 1962. Atrocities in the reconstruction period. *Journal of Negro History* 47:234–47.

Cash, W. J. 1969. *The mind of the south.* New York: Random House.

Cheatwood, Derral. 1988. Is there a season for homicide? *Criminology* 26:287–306.

Cobb, James. 1982. *The selling of the south: The southern crusade for industrial development, 1936–1980.* Baton Rouge: Louisiana State University Press.

Cohen, William. *At freedom's edge: Black mobility and the southern white quest for racial control, 1861–1915.* Baton Rouge: Louisiana State University Press.

———. 1976. Negro involuntary servitude in the south, 1865–1940: A preliminary analysis. *Journal of Southern History* 42:31–60.

Commager, Henry Steele, ed. 1963. *Documents of American history.* New York: Appleton Century-Crofts.

Commission on Interracial Cooperation. 1936. *The mob still rides: A review of the lynching record, 1931–1935.* Atlanta, Ga.

Corzine, Jay, James Creech, and Lin Corzine. 1983. Black concentration and lynchings in the south: Testing Blalock's power-threat hypothesis. *Social Forces* 61:774–96.

Corzine, Jay, Lin Huff-Corzine, and James Creech. 1988. The tenant labor market and lynching in the South: A test of the split labor market theory. *Sociological Quarterly* 58:261–78.

Crouch, Barry A. 1984. A spirit of lawlessness: White violence; Texas blacks, 1865–1868. *Journal of Social History* 18:217–32.

Culberson, William C. 1990. *Vigilantism: Political history of private power in America.* New York: Greenwood Press.

Cutler, James E. 1907. Capital punishment and lynching. *Annals of the American Academy of Political and Social Science* 29:622–25.

———. 1905. *Lynch-law: An investigation into the history of lynching in the United States.* New York: Longmans, Green, and Co.

Daniel, Pete. 1985. *Breaking the land: The transformation of cotton, tobacco, and rice cultures since 1880.* Urbana: University of Illinois Press.

DeCanio, Stephen. 1974. *Agriculture in the postbellum south: The economics of production and supply.* Cambridge: MIT Press.

Dinnerstein, Leonard. 1968. *The Leo Frank case.* New York: Columbia University Press.

Dittmer, John. 1980. *Black Georgia in the progressive era, 1900–1920.* Urbana: University of Illinois Press.

Dixon, Thomas. 1907. *The clansman: An historical romance of the Ku Klux Klan.* New York: A. Wessels Co.

Donald, Henderson. 1921. The Negro migration of 1916–1918. *Journal of Negro History* 6:383–498.

Doob, Leonard W. 1937. Poor whites: A frustrated class. In *Caste and class in a southern town,* ed. John Dollard. 445–84. New Haven: Yale University Press.

Downey, Dennis B., and Raymond M. Hyser. 1991. *No crooked death: Coatesville, Pennsylvania, and the lynching of Zachariah Walker.* Urbana: University of Illinois Press.

Doyle, Bertram W. 1937. *The etiquette of race relations in the south: A study in social control.* Chicago: University of Chicago Press.

Du Bois, W. E. B. 1903 [1969]. *The souls of black folk.* New York: New American Library.

Eaton, Clement. 1942. Mob violence in the Old South. *Mississippi Valley Historical Review* 29:351–70.

Ferrell, Claudine L. 1986. *Nightmare and dream: Anti-lynching in Congress, 1917–1922.* New York: Garland Publishing.

Fitzgerald, Michael W. 1989. *The Union League movement in the deep south: Politics and agricultural change during reconstruction.* Baton Rouge: Louisiana State University Press.

Fligstein, Neil. 1981. *Going north: Migration of blacks and whites from the south, 1900–1950.* New York: Academic Press.

Flynn, Charles L. 1983. *White land, black labor: Caste and class in late nineteenth century Georgia.* Baton Rouge: Louisiana State University Press.

Foner, Eric. 1988. *Reconstruction: America's unfinished revolution, 1863–1877.* New York: Harper and Row.

Franzosi, Roberto. 1987. The press as a source of socio-historical data: Issues in the methodology of data collection from newspapers. *Historical Methods* 20:5–16.

Fredrickson, George M. 1988. *The arrogance of race: Historical perspectives on slavery, racism, and social inequality.* Middletown: Wesleyan University Press.

Frey, Robert S., and Nancy Thompson-Frey. 1988. *The silent and the damned: The murder of Mary Phagan and the lynching of Leo Frank.* Lanham: Madison Books.

Fry, Gladys-Marie. 1975. *Night riders in black folk history.* Knoxville: University of Tennessee Press.

Gaither, Gerald H. 1977. *Blacks and the populist revolt: Ballots and bigotry in the "new south."* University: University of Alabama Press.

Gallup, George H. 1972. *The Gallop opinion poll.* Vol. 1: *1935–1971.* American Institute of Public Opinion. New York: Random House.

Gambino, Richard. 1977. *Vendetta: A true story of the worst lynching in America: The mass murder of Italian-Americans in New Orleans in 1891.* Garden City: Doubleday Press.

Ginzburg, Ralph. 1988. *100 years of lynchings.* Baltimore: Black Classic Press.

Gordon, Asa H. 1937. *The Georgia Negro: A history.* Ann Arbor, Mich.: Edwards Brothers, Inc.

Gottlieb, Peter. 1987. *Making their own way: Southern blacks' migration to Pittsburgh, 1916–30.* Urbana: University of Illinois Press.

Gottman, John M. 1981. *Time-series analysis: A comprehensive introduction for social scientists.* Cambridge: Cambridge University Press.

Gould, Stephen Jay. 1981. *The mismeasure of man.* New York: W. W. Norton.

Grant, Donald L. 1975. *The anti-lynching movement, 1883–1932.* San Francisco: R and E Research Associates.

Grossman, James. 1991. Black labor is the best labor: Southern white reactions to the great migration. In *Black exodus: The great migration from the American south,* ed. A. Harrison. 51–71. Jackson: University Press of Mississippi.

Hahn, Steven. 1983. *The roots of southern populism: Yeoman farmers and the transformation of the Georgia upcountry, 1850–1890.* New York: Oxford University Press.

Hall, Jacquelyn Dowd. 1979. *Revolt against chivalry: Jessie Daniel Ames and the women's campaign against lynching.* New York: Columbia University Press.

Hanna, Frank A. 1964. Income in the south since 1929. In *Essays in southern economic development,* ed. Melvin L. Greenhut and W. Tate Whitman. 239–319. Chapel Hill: University of North Carolina Press.

Harris, William H. 1982. *The harder we run: Black workers since the Civil War.* New York: Oxford University.

Henri, Florette. 1975. *Black migration: Movement north, 1900–1920.* Garden City: Anchor Press.

Hicks, John D. 1931. *The populist revolt: A history of the Farmer's Alliance and the people's party.* Minneapolis: University of Minnesota Press.

Higgs, Robert. 1977. *Competition and coercion: Blacks in the American economy, 1865–1914.* Cambridge: Cambridge University Press.

Hinde, John. 1982. Compound poisson models. In *GLIM82: Proceedings of the international conference on generalised linear models,* ed. Robert Gilchrist. 109–21. New York: Springer-Verlag.

Hoffman, Frederick L. 1896. *Race traits and tendencies of the American Negro.* New York: Macmillan Co.

Holmes, William F. 1990. Populism: In search of context. *Agricultural History* 64:26–58.

———. 1969. Whitecapping: Agrarian violence in Mississippi, 1902–1906. *Journal of Southern History* 35:165–85.

———. 1973a. The Arkansas cotton pickers strike of 1891 and the demise of the Colored Farmers' Alliance. *Arkansas Historical Quarterly* 32:107–19.

———. 1973b. Whitecapping in Mississippi: Agrarian violence in the populist era. *Mid-America* 55:134–48.

Hovland, Carl I., and Robert R. Sears. 1940. Minor studies of aggression: Correlations of economic indices with lynchings. *Journal of Psychology* 9:301–10.

Hyman, Michael R. 1990. *The anti-redeemers: Hill country political dissenters in the lower south from redemption to populism.* Baton Rouge: Louisiana State University Press.

Inter-university Consortium for Political and Social Research. 1989. *Guide to resources and services, 1988–1989.* Ann Arbor: ICPSR.

Inverarity, James. 1976. Populism and lynching in Louisiana, 1889–1896: A Test of Erikson's theory of the relationship between boundary crises and repressive justice. *American Sociological Review* 41:262–80.

Isaac, Larry, and Larry Griffin. 1989. Ahistoricism in time-series analyses of historical process: Critique, redirection, and illustrations from U.S. labor history. *American Sociological Review* 54:873–90.

Jaynes, Gerald David. 1986. *Branches without roots: Genesis of the black working class in the American south, 1862–1882.* New York: Oxford University Press.

Johnson, Charles S. 1941. *Statistical atlas of southern counties: Listing and analysis of socio-economic indices of 1,104 southern counties.* Chapel Hill: University of North Carolina Press.

Jordan, Winthrop D. 1974. *The white man's burden: Historical origins of racism in the United States.* New York: Oxford University Press.

Judge, Frank. 1987. Slaying the dragon. *American Lawyer* (September):83–89.

Judge, G. G., R. C. Hill, W. E. Griffiths, H. Lutketohl, and T. Lee. 1982. *Introduction to the theory and practice of econometrics.* New York: John Wiley and Sons.

Kennedy, Louise Venable. 1930. *The Negro peasant turns cityward: Effects of recent migration to northern centers.* New York: Columbia University Press.

Kmenta, J. 1971. *Elements of econometrics.* New York: Macmillan.

Kornbluth, Jesse. 1987. The woman who beat the Klan. *New York Times Magazine* (November 1, sec. 6).

Kousser, J. Morgan. 1980. Separate but *not* equal: The Supreme Court's first decision on racial discrimination in schools. *Journal of Southern History* 46:17–44.

———. 1974. *The shaping of southern politics: Suffrage restriction and the establishment of the one-party south.* New Haven: Yale University Press.

Lawless, Jerald F. 1987. Negative binomial and mixed poisson regression. *Canadian Journal of Statistics* 15:209–25.

Lee, Everett S., Ann R. Miller, Carol P. Brainerd, and Richard A. Easterlin. 1957. *Population redistribution and economic growth, United States, 1870–1950.* Vol. 1. Philadelphia: American Philosophical Society.

Lewis, Edward E. 1931. *The mobility of the Negro: A study in the American labor supply.* New York: Columbia University Press.

Liska, Allen E., ed. 1992. *Social threat and social control.* Albany: State University of New York Press.

Maddala, G. S. 1983. *Limited-dependent and qualitative variables in econometrics.* Cambridge: Cambridge University Press.

Mandle, Jay R. 1992. *Not slave, not free: The African-American economic experience since the Civil War.* Durham: Duke University Press.

———. 1978. *The roots of black poverty: The southern planation economy after the Civil War.* Durham: Duke University Press.

Margo, Robert. 1990. *Race and schooling in the South, 1880–1950.* Chicago: University of Chicago Press.

Marks, Carole. 1989. *Farewell—we're good and gone: The great black migration.* Bloomington: Indiana University Press.

Massey, James L., and Martha A. Myers. 1989. Patterns of repressive social control in post-reconstruction Georgia, 1882–1935. *Social Forces* 68:458–88.

McCleary, Richard, and Richard A. Hay, Jr. 1980. *Applied time series analysis for the social sciences.* Beverly Hills: Sage Publications.

McCullagh, P., and J. A. Nelder. 1983. *Generalized linear models.* London: Chapman and Hall.

McDowall, David, Richard McCleary, Errol E. Meidinger, and Richard A. Hay, Jr. 1980. *Interrupted time series analysis.* Beverly Hills: Sage Publications.

McGovern, James R. 1982. *Anatomy of a lynching: The killing of Claude Neal.* Baton Rouge: Louisiana State University Press.

McKenzie, Robert Tracy. 1993. Freedmen and the soil in the upper south: The reorganization of Tennessee agriculture, 1865–1880. *Journal of Southern History* 59:63–84.

McMath, Robert C. 1993. *American populism: A social history, 1877–1898.* New York: Hill and Wang.

———. 1976. *Populist vanguard: A history of the Southern Farmers' Alliance.* Chapel Hill: University of North Carolina Press.

McMillen, Neil R. 1989. *Dark journey: Black Mississippians in the age of Jim Crow.* Urbana: University of Illinois Press.

———. 1991. The migration and black protest in Jim Crow Mississippi. In *Black exodus: The great migration from the American south,* ed. A. Harrison. 83–99. Jackson: University Press of Mississippi.

McPhail, Clark. 1991. *The myth of the madding crowd.* New York: Aldine de Gruyter.

Mellon, James, ed. 1988. *Bullwhip days: The slaves remember: An oral history.* New York: Avon Books.

Miller, Kathleen Atkinson. 1978. The ladies and the lynchers: A look at the Association of Southern Women for the Prevention of Lynching. *Southern Studies* 17:221–40.

Mintz, Alexander. 1946. A re-examination of correlations between lynchings and economic indices. *Journal of Abnormal Social Psychology* 41:154–60.

Mohr, Clarence L. 1986. *On the threshold of freedom: Masters and slaves in Civil War Georgia.* Athens: University of Georgia Press.

Myrdal, Gunnar. 1972. *An American dilemma: The Negro problem and modern democracy.* New York: Pantheon Books.

National Association for the Advancement of Colored People. 1919 [1969]. *Thirty years of lynching in the United States, 1889–1918.* New York: Arno Press.

Newby, I. A. 1965. *Jim Crow's defense: Anti-Negro thought in America, 1900–1930.* Baton Rouge: Louisiana State University Press.

Nolen, Claude H. 1967. *The Negro's image in the South: The anatomy of white supremacy.* Lexington: University Press of Ketucky.

Novak, Daniel A. 1978. *The wheel of servitude: Black forced labor after slavery.* Lexington: University Press of Kentucky.

Olzak, Susan. 1992. *The dynamics of ethnic competition and conflict.* Stanford: Stanford University Press.

————. 1990. The political context of competition: Lynching and urban racial violence, 1882–1914. *Social Forces* 69:395–421.

Olzak, Susan, and Joane Nagel, eds. 1986. *Competitive ethnic relations.* Orlando: Academic Press.

Phillips, Charles D. 1987. Exploring relations among forms of social control: The lynching and execution of blacks in North Carolina, 1889–1918. *Law and Society Review* 21:361–74.

————. 1986. Social structure and social control: Modeling the discrminatory execution of blacks in Georgia and North Carolina, 1925–35. *Social Forces* 65:458–75.

Phillips, Ulrich Bonnell. 1929. *Life and labor in the old south.* Boston: Little, Brown and Co.

Pope, Whitney, and Charles Ragin. 1977. Mechanical solidarity, repressive justice, and lynchings in Lousiana: Comment on Inverarity. *American Sociological Review* 42:363–69.

Principal Keeper of the Penitentiary. 1876. *Reports to the governor of the state of Georgia.* Atlanta: Department of Archives and History.

Quinney, Richard. 1977. *Class, state and crime.* New York: McKay.

Rable, George C. 1984. *But there was no peace: The role of violence in the politics of reconstruction.* Athens: University of Georgia Press.

Ransom, Roger L., and Richard Sutch. 1977. *One kind of freedom: The economic consequences of emancipation.* London: Cambridge University Press.

Raper, Arthur. 1933. *The tragedy of lynching.* Chapel Hill: University of North Carolina Press.

Reed, John Shelton. 1968. An evaluation of an anti-lynching organization. *Social Problems* 16:172–82.

————. 1972. Percent black and lynching: A test of Blalock's theory. *Social Forces* 50:356–60.

Reed, John Shelton, Gail E. Doss, and Jeanne S. Hulbert. 1987. Too good to be false: An essay in the folklore of social science. *Sociological Inquiry* 57:1–11.

Reid, Joseph D. 1981. White land, black labor, and agricultural stagnation: The causes and effects of sharecropping in the postbellum south. In *Market institutions and economic progress in the new south, 1865–1900,* ed. Gary M. Walton and James F. Shepherd. 33–55. New York: Academic Press.

Reynolds, Donald E. 1964. The New Orleans riot of 1866, reconsidered. *Louisiana History* 5:5–27.

Schwartz, Michael. 1976. *Radical protest and social structure: The Southern Farmers' Alliance and cotton tenancy, 1880–1890.* New York: Academic Press.

Scott, Emmett J. 1920. *Negro migration during the war.* New York: Oxford University Press.

Scroggs, W. O. 1917. Interstate migration of Negro population. *Journal of Political Economy* 25:1034–43.

Shaler, Nathaniel S. 1890. Science and the African problem. *Atlantic Monthly* 66:36–45.

Shapiro, Herbert. 1988. *White violence and black response: From reconstruction to Montgomery.* Amherst: University of Massachusetts Press.

Shlomowitz, Ralph. 1979. The origins of southern sharecropping. *Agricultural History* 53:557–75.

Shryock, Henry, and Jacob Siegel. 1980. *The methods and materials of demography.* Washington, D.C.: Government Printing Office.

Skaggs, William H. 1924 [1969]. *The southern oligarchy: An appeal in behalf of the silent masses of our country against the despotic rule of the few.* New York: Negro University Press.

Slaughter, Thomas P. 1991. *Bloody dawn: The Christiana riot and racial violence in the antebellum north.* New York: Oxford University Press.

Smead, Howard. 1986. *Blood justice: The lynching of Charles Mack Parker.* New York: Oxford University Press.

Smith, Lillian. 1944. *Strange fruit: A novel.* New York: Reynal and Hitchcock.

Smith, William B. 1905. *The color line: A brief in behalf of the unborn.* New York: McClure, Phillips and Co..

Soule, Sarah A. 1992. Populism and black lynching in Georgia, 1890–1900. *Social Forces* 71:431–49.

Southern Commission on the Study of Lynching. 1932. *Lynchings and what they mean.* Atlanta: Commission on Interracial Cooperation.

Stagg, J. C. A. 1974. The problem of Klan violence in the South Carolina upcountry, 1868–1871. *Journal of American Studies* 8:303–18.

Takaki, Ronald T. 1979. *Iron cages: Race and culture in nineteenth-century America.* New York: Alfred A. Knopf.

Tolnay, Stewart, and E. M. Beck. 1990. Black flight: Lethal violence and the great migration, 1900 to 1930. *Social Science History* 14:347–70.

———. 1992a. Racial violence and black migration in the south, 1910 to 1930. *American Sociological Review* 57:103–16.

———. 1992b. Lethal social control in the south: Lynchings and executions between 1880 and 1930. Paper presented at the State-of-the-Art Conference on Inequality, Crime, and Social Control, University of Georgia, Athens, April 10–11, 1992.

Tolnay, Stewart E., E. M. Beck, and James L. Massey. 1992. Black competition and white vengeance: Legal execution of blacks as social control in the American south, 1890 to 1929. *Social Science Quarterly* 73:627–44.

———. 1989a. Black lynchings: The power threat hypothesis revisited. *Social Forces* 67:605–23.

———. 1989b. The power threat hypothesis and black lynchings: "Wither" the evidence? *Social Forces* 67:634–40.

Trelease, Allen W. 1971. *White terror: The Ku Klux Klan conspiracy and southern reconstruction.* New York: Harper and Row.

Tucker, David M. 1971. Miss Ida B. Wells and the Memphis lynching. *Phylon* 32:112–22.

Turk, Austin. 1969. *Criminality and legal order.* Chicago: Rand-McNally.

U.S. Bureau of the Census. 1913. *Thirteenth census, 1910.* Vol. 5. *Agriculture 1909 and 1910: General report and analysis.* Washington, D.C.: Government Printing Office.

———. 1922. *Fourteenth census, 1920.* Vol. 5. *Agriculture general report and analytical tables.* Washington, D.C.: Government Printing Office.

———. 1931. *Fifteenth census, 1930, agriculture.* Vol. 1. *Farm acreage and farm values by townships or other minor civil divisions.* Washington, D.C.: Government Printing Office.

———. 1932. *Fifteenth census, 1930, agriculture.* Vol. 3, Part 2. *The southern states, reports by state with statistics for counties and a summary for the United States.* Washington, D.C.: Government Printing Office.

———. 1943. *Sixteenth census of the United States, 1940: Population.* Vol. 2. *Characteristics of the population, reports by states.* Washington, D.C.: Government Printing Office.

———. 1975. *Historical statistics of the United States, colonial times to 1970.* Part 1. Washington, D.C.: Government Printing Office.

U.S. Bureau of Justice Statistics, Department of Justice. 1980. *Crime and seasonality.* National Crime Survey Report SD-NCS-N-15, NCJ-64818. Washington, D.C.: Government Printing Office.

U.S. Census Office. 1883. *Tenth census, 1880: Report on the production of agriculture, general statistics.* Washington, D.C.: Government Printing Office.

———. 1895. *Eleventh census, 1890: Report on the statistics of agriculture in the United States.* Washington, D.C.: Government Printing Office.

———. 1902. *Twelfth Census, 1900: Agriculture.* Part 1. *Farms, livestock, and animal products.* Washington, D.C.: Government Printing Office.

U.S. Congress Joint Select Committee. 1872a. *Ku Klux conspiracy: Report of the joint select committee to inquire into the condition of affairs in the late insurrectionary states.* Vol. 1. *Report of the committee.* Washington, D.C.: Government Printing Office.

———. 1872b. *Ku Klux conspiracy: Report of the joint select committee to inquire into the condition of affairs in the late insurrectionary states.* Vol. 5. *South Carolina.* Part 3. Washington, D.C.: Government Printing Office.

———. 1872c. *Ku Klux conspiracy: Report of the joint select committee to inquire into the condition of affairs in the late insurrectionary states.* Vol. 8. *Alabama.* Part 1. Washington, D.C.: Government Printing Office.

U.S. Department of Agriculture. 1951–52. *Statistics on cotton and related data.* Bureau of Agricultural Economics, Statistical Bulletin No. 99. Washington, D.C.: Government Printing Office.

U.S. Department of Labor. 1919. *Negro migration in 1916–17*. Division of Negro Economics, Washington, D.C.: Government Printing Office.

Vance, Rupert B. 1929. *Human factors in cotton culture: A study of the social geography of the American south*. Chapel Hill: University of North Carolina Press.

Vandal, Gilles. 1991. "Bloody Caddo": White violence against blacks in a Louisiana parish, 1865–1876. *Journal of Social History* 25:373–88.

Wade, Wyn Craig. 1987. *The fiery cross: The Ku Klux Klan in America*. New York: Simon and Schuster.

Walker, Samuel. 1980. *Popular justice: A history of American criminal justice*. New York: Oxford University Press.

Waller, Altina L. 1984. Community, class and race in the Memphis riot of 1866. *Journal of Social History* 18:233–46.

Wasserman, Ira M. 1977. Southern violence and the political process: Comment on Inverarity. *American Sociological Review* 42:359–62.

Wells-Barnett, Ida B. 1892 [1969]. *Southern horrors: Lynch law in all its phases*. New York: Arno Press.

White, Walter. 1929 [1969]. *Rope and faggot: A biography of judge lynch*. New York: Arno Press.

Whitfield, Stephen J. 1988. *A death in the delta: The story of Emmett Till*. New York: Free Press.

Williams, Daniel T. 1968. Amid the gathering multitude: The story of lynching in America: A classified listing. Unpublished manuscript. Tuskegee University.

Williams, Juan. 1987. *Eyes on the prize: American's civil rights years, 1954–1965*. New York: Viking Press.

Williamson, Joel. 1984. *The crucible of race: Black-white relations in the American south since emancipation*. New York: Oxford University Press.

Wilson, William J. 1978. *The declining significance of race: Blacks and changing American institutions*. Chicago: University of Chicago Press.

Winn, Bill. 1987. Lynching on Wynn's Hill. *Southern Exposure* 15:17–24.

Woodman, Harold D. 1968. *King cotton and his retainers: Financing and marketing the cotton crop of the south, 1800–1925*. Lexington: University Press of Kentucky.

Woodson, Carter. 1918 [1969]. *A century of Negro migration*. New York: Russell and Russell.

———. 1930. *The rural Negro*. Washington, D.C.: Association for the Study of Negro Life and History.

Woodward, C. Vann. 1951. *Origins of the new south, 1877–1913*. Baton Rouge: Louisiana State University Press.

———. 1966. *The strange career of Jim Crow*. New York: Oxford University Press.

———. 1963. *Tom Watson: Agrarian rebel*. New York: Oxford University Press.

Woofter, Thomas Jackson. 1920. *Negro migration: Changes in rural organization and population of the cotton belt*. New York: W. D. Gray.

Wright, Gavin. 1986. *Old south, new south: Revolutions in the southern economy since the Civil War.* New York: Basic Books.

————. 1978. *The political economy of the cotton south.* New York: Norton.

Wright, George C. 1990. *Racial violence in Kentucky, 1865–1940: Lynchings, mob rule, and "legal lynchings."* Baton Rouge: Louisiana State University Press.

Wyatt-Brown, Bertram. 1986. *Honor and violence in the old south.* New York: Oxford University Press.

Zangrando, Robert L. 1980. *The NAACP crusade against lynching, 1909–1950.* Philadelphia: Temple University Press.

Index

STEWART E. TOLNAY is a professor of sociology and the director of the Center for Social and Demographic Analysis at the University at Albany, State University of New York.

E. M. BECK is a professor of sociology, head of the Department of Sociology, and fellow in the Institute for Behavioral Research at the University of Georgia.